AN INTRODUCTION
TO COMMUNICATION
NETWORK ANALYSIS

THE WILEY BICENTENNIAL—KNOWLEDGE FOR GENERATIONS

*E*ach generation has its unique needs and aspirations. When Charles Wiley first opened his small printing shop in lower Manhattan in 1807, it was a generation of boundless potential searching for an identity. And we were there, helping to define a new American literary tradition. Over half a century later, in the midst of the Second Industrial Revolution, it was a generation focused on building the future. Once again, we were there, supplying the critical scientific, technical, and engineering knowledge that helped frame the world. Throughout the 20th Century, and into the new millennium, nations began to reach out beyond their own borders and a new international community was born. Wiley was there, expanding its operations around the world to enable a global exchange of ideas, opinions, and know-how.

For 200 years, Wiley has been an integral part of each generation's journey, enabling the flow of information and understanding necessary to meet their needs and fulfill their aspirations. Today, bold new technologies are changing the way we live and learn. Wiley will be there, providing you the must-have knowledge you need to imagine new worlds, new possibilities, and new opportunities.

Generations come and go, but you can always count on Wiley to provide you the knowledge you need, when and where you need it!

WILLIAM J. PESCE
PRESIDENT AND CHIEF EXECUTIVE OFFICER

PETER BOOTH WILEY
CHAIRMAN OF THE BOARD

AN INTRODUCTION TO COMMUNICATION NETWORK ANALYSIS

George Kesidis

Pennsylvania State University

WILEY-INTERSCIENCE
A John Wiley & Sons, Inc., Publication

Library of Congress Cataloging-in-Publication Data:

Kesidis, George.
    An introduction to communication network analysis / George Kesidis.
      p. cm.
    ISBN 978-0-471-37141-0 (cloth)
    1. Telecommunication—Traffic—Textbooks.   2. Network performance
(Telecommunication)—Textbooks.   3. Switching theory—Textbooks.   I. Title.
    TK5102.985.K47 2007
    621.382'1—dc22   2007002535

Printed in the United States of America.

10 9 8 7 6 5 4 3 2 1

For Selena, Emma and Cleo

CONTENTS

PREFACE

This book was the basis of a single graduate course on the general subject of "performance" of communication networks for students from a broad set of backgrounds in electrical engineering, computer science, or computer engineering. The student was assumed to have basic familiarity with networking concepts as discussed in introductory texts on the subject, e.g., [139, 172, 220]. Also the student was assumed to have undergraduate courses in probability theory and linear (matrix) algebra.

Background material on probability and statistics is reviewed in Chapter 1. Graduate courses on probability and stochastic processes in electrical and computer engineering tend to focus on wide-sense stationary processes, typically in order to study the effects of noise in communication and control systems. In two successive chapters this book covers Markov chains and introduces the topic of queueing. Though the continuous-time context is stressed (to facilitate the queueing material), the discrete-time context is covered at the end of each chapter.

The remaining chapters pertain more directly to networking. Chapter 4 is on the subject of traffic shaping and multiplexing using a localized bandwidth resource. The next chapter describes queueing networks with static routing in the rather classical contexts of loss networks and open Jackson networks. Chapter 6 is on dynamic routing and routing with incentives including a game-theoretic model. The final chapter is a discussion of peer-to-peer networking systems, specifically those for the purposes of file sharing.

In general, problems at the end of each chapter review the described concepts and cover more specialized related material that may be of interest to the networking researcher. Worked solutions or references for certain problems are given in an appendix.

The length of the book allows time for about two weeks of lectures on material of specific interest to the instructor. The amount of instructor discretionary time can be increased by, for example, omitting coverage of the concluding sections of Chapters 4, 6, and 7 that are largely drawn from the author's own publications.

I thank my wife Diane, the editing staff at Wiley, and several of my colleagues and students for their time spent reading draft manuscripts and for their sage though often conflicting advice. In particular, I thank my students Y. Jin and B. Mortazavi. All flaws in this book are the sole responsibility of the author. Please contact me to report errors found in the book as an errata sheet will be made available on the Web.

George Kesidis

State College, Pennsylvania
kesidis@gmail.com
April 2007

CHAPTER 1

REVIEW OF ELEMENTARY PROBABILITY THEORY

This book assumes some familiarity with elementary probability theory. Good introductory texts are [63, 192]. We will begin by briefly reviewing some of these concepts in order to introduce notation and for future reference. We will also introduce basic notions of statistics that are particularly useful. See [106] for additional discussion of related material in a computer systems context.

1.1 SAMPLE SPACE, EVENTS, AND PROBABILITIES

Consider a random experiment resulting in an *outcome* (or "sample") represented by ω. For example, the experiment could be a pair of dice thrown onto a table and the outcome could be the exact orientation of the dice and their position on the table when they stop moving. The abstract space of all outcomes (called the *sample space*) is normally denoted by Ω, i.e., $\omega \in \Omega$.

An *event* is merely a subset of Ω. For example, in a dice throwing experiment, an event is "both dice land in a specific region of the table" or "the sum of the dots on the upward facing surfaces of the dice is 7." Clearly, many different individual outcomes ω belong to these events. We say that an event A has *occurred* if the outcome ω of the random experiment belongs to A, i.e., $w \in A$, where $A \subset \Omega$. Now consider two events A and B. We therefore say that A *and* B occur if the outcome $\omega \in A \cap B$. Also, we say that A *or* B occur if the outcome $\omega \in A \cup B$.

1

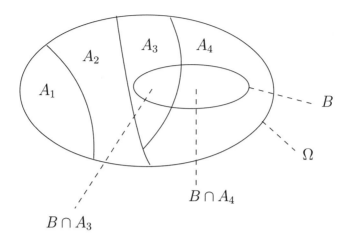

Figure 1.1   A partition of Ω.

A *probability measure* P maps each event $A \subset \Omega$ to a real number between zero and one inclusive, i.e., $P(A) \in [0,1]$. A probability measure has certain properties such as $P(\Omega) = 1$ and

$$P(A) \;=\; 1 - P(\bar{A}),$$

where $\bar{A} = \{\omega \in \Omega \mid \omega \notin A\}$ is the complement of A. Also, if the events $\{A_i\}_{i=1}^n$ are disjoint (i.e., $A_i \cap A_j = \emptyset$ for all $i \neq j$), then

$$P\left(\bigcup_{i=1}^n A_i\right) \;=\; \sum_{i=1}^n P(A_i),$$

i.e., P is finitely additive. Formally, a probability measure is defined to be countably additive. Also, $P(A)$ is defined only for events $A \subset \Omega$ that belong to a σ-*field* (sigma-field) or σ-*algebra* of events. These details are beyond the scope of this book.

The probability of an event A *conditioned on* (or "given that") another event B has occurred is

$$P(A|B) \;\equiv\; \frac{P(A \cap B)}{P(B)},$$

where $P(B) > 0$ is assumed. Now suppose the events $A_1, A_2, ..., A_n$ form a *partition* of Ω, i.e.,

$$\bigcup_{i=1}^n A_i = \Omega \quad \text{and} \quad A_i \cap A_j = \emptyset \text{ for all } i \neq j.$$

Assuming that $P(A_i) > 0$ for all i, the *law of total probability* states that, for any event B,

$$P(B) \;=\; \sum_{i=1}^n P(B|A_i)P(A_i). \qquad (1.1)$$

Note that the events $A_i \cap B$ form a partition of $B \subset \Omega$. See Figure 1.1, where $B = (B \cap A_4) \cup (B \cap A_3)$ and $B \cap A_i = \emptyset$ for $i = 1, 2$.

A group of events $A_1, A_2, ..., A_n$ are said to be *mutually independent* (or just "independent") if

$$P\left(\bigcap_{i \in \mathcal{I}} A_i\right) = \prod_{i \in \mathcal{I}} P(A_i)$$

for all subsets $\mathcal{I} \subset \{1, 2, ..., n\}$. Note that if events A and B are independent and $P(B) > 0$, then $P(A|B) = P(A)$; therefore, knowledge that the event B has occurred has no bearing on the probability that the event A has occurred as well.

In the following, a comma between events will represent an intersection symbol, for example, the probability that A *and* B occur is

$$P(A, B) \equiv P(A \cap B).$$

1.2 RANDOM VARIABLES

A *random variable* X is a real-valued function with domain Ω. That is, for each outcome ω, $X(\omega)$ is a real number representing some feature of the outcome. For example, in a dice-throwing experiment, $X(\omega)$ could be defined as the sum of the dots on the upward-facing surfaces of outcome ω. Formally, random variables are defined to be *measurable* in the sense that the event $X^{-1}(B) = \{\omega \in \Omega \mid X(\omega) \in B\}$ is an event (a member of the σ-field on Ω) for all events $B \subset \mathbb{R}$ (belonging to the *Borel* σ-field of subsets of $\mathbb{R}$). In this way, the quantity $P(X \in B)$ is well defined for any set B that is of interest. Again, the details of this measurability condition are beyond the scope of this book. In the following, all functions are implicitly assumed to be measurable.

The strict range of X is defined to be the *smallest* subset R_X of $\mathbb{R}$ such that

$$P(X \in R_X) = 1,$$

where $P(X \in R_X)$ is short for $P(\{\omega \in \Omega \mid X(\omega) \in R_X\})$.

Note that a (Borel-measurable) function g of a random variable X, $g(X)$, is also a random variable.

A group of random variables $X_1, X_2, ..., X_n$ are said to be mutually independent (or just "independent") if, for any collection $\{B_i\}_{i=1}^n$ of subsets of $\mathbb{R}$, the events $\{X_i \in B_i\}_{i=1}^n$ are independent; see Section 1.9.

1.3 CUMULATIVE DISTRIBUTION FUNCTIONS, EXPECTATION, AND MOMENT GENERATING FUNCTIONS

The probability *distribution* of a random variable X connotes the information $P(X \in B)$ for all events $B \in \mathbb{R}$. We need only stipulate

$$P(X \leq x) \equiv P(X \in (-\infty, x])$$

for all $x \in \mathbb{R}$ to completely specify the distribution of X; see Equation (1.4). This leads us to define the *cumulative distribution function* (CDF) F_X of a random variable X as

$$F_X(x) = \mathsf{P}(X \leq x) \tag{1.2}$$

for $x \in \mathbb{R}$, where $\mathsf{P}(X \leq x)$ is, again, short for $\mathsf{P}(\{\omega \in \Omega \mid X(\omega) \leq x\})$. Clearly, a CDF F_X takes values in $[0, 1]$, is nondecreasing on $\mathbb{R}$, $F_X(x) \to 1$ as $x \to \infty$, and $F_X(x) \to 0$ as $x \to -\infty$.

The *expectation* of a random variable is simply its average (or "mean") value. We can define the expectation of a function g of a random variable X as

$$\mathsf{E}(g(X)) \quad = \quad \int_{-\infty}^{\infty} g(x) \, dF_X(x), \tag{1.3}$$

where we have used a Stieltjes integral [133] that will be explained via explicit examples in the following. Note here that the expectation (when it exists) is simply a real number or $\pm\infty$. Also note that expectation is a linear operation over random variables. That is, for any two random variables X and Y and any two real constants a and b,

$$\mathsf{E}(aX + bY) \quad = \quad a\mathsf{E}X + b\mathsf{E}Y.$$

■ **EXAMPLE 1.1**

Suppose g is an *indicator function*, i.e., for some event $B \subset \mathbb{R}$

$$
\begin{aligned}
g(X(\omega)) &\equiv \mathbf{1}\{X(\omega) \in B\} \\
&\equiv \begin{cases} 1 & \text{if } X(\omega) \in B, \\ 0 & \text{else.} \end{cases}
\end{aligned}
$$

In this case,

$$\mathsf{E}g(X) \quad = \quad \mathsf{P}(X \in B) \quad = \quad \int_B dF_X(x), \tag{1.4}$$

where the notation refers to integration over the set B.

The nth *moment* of X is $\mathsf{E}(X^n)$ and the *variance* of X is

$$\sigma_X^2 \quad \equiv \quad \mathrm{var}(X) \equiv \mathsf{E}(X - \mathsf{E}X)^2,$$

i.e., the variance is the second *centered* moment. The *standard deviation* of X is the square root of the variance, $\sigma_X \geq 0$. The *moment generating function* (MGF) of X is

$$m_X(\theta) \quad = \quad \mathsf{E}e^{\theta X},$$

where θ is a real number. The moment generating function can also be used to completely describe the distribution of a random variable.

1.4 DISCRETELY DISTRIBUTED RANDOM VARIABLES

For a *discretely distributed* (or just "discrete") random variable X, there is a set of countably many real numbers $\{a_i\}_{i=1}^{\infty}$ such that

$$\sum_{i=1}^{\infty} P(X = a_i) = 1.$$

Assuming $P(X = a_i) > 0$ for all i, the countable set $\{a_i\}_{i=1}^{\infty}$ is the strict range of X, i.e., $R_X = \{a_i\}_{i=1}^{\infty}$. So, a discrete random variable has a piecewise constant CDF with a countable number of jump discontinuities occurring at the a_i's. That is, if the a_i are defined so as to be an increasing sequence, F is constant on each open interval (a_i, a_{i+1}), $F(x) = 0$ for $x < a_1$, and

$$F(a_i) = \sum_{j=1}^{i} P(X = a_j) = \sum_{j=1}^{i} p(a_j),$$

where p is the probability mass function (PMF) of the discrete random variable X, i.e.,

$$p(a_i) \;\equiv\; P(X = a_i).$$

Note that we have dropped the subscript "X" on the PMF and CDF for notational convenience. Moreover, for any $B \subset \mathbb{R}$ and any real-valued function g over $\mathbb{R}$,

$$P(X \in B) \;=\; \sum_{a_j \in B} p(a_j)$$

and

$$Eg(X) \;=\; \sum_{j=1}^{\infty} g(a_j) p(a_j) = \sum_{a \in R_X} g(a) p(a).$$

To see the connection between this expression and (1.3), note that

$$
\begin{aligned}
dF(x) \;&=\; F'(x)\, dx \\
&=\; \sum_{i=1}^{\infty} p(a_i) \delta(x - a_i)\, dx,
\end{aligned}
$$

where δ is the Dirac delta function [164]. That is, δ is the unit impulse satisfying $\delta(t) = 0$ for all $t \neq 0$ and

$$\int_{-\infty}^{\infty} \delta(t)\, dt \;=\; 1.$$

1.4.1 The Bernoulli distribution

A random variable X that is *Bernoulli* distributed has strict range consisting of two elements, typically $R_X = \{0, 1\}$. So, there is a real parameter $q \in (0, 1)$ such that $q = P(X = 1) = 1 - P(X = 0)$. Also,

$$Eg(X) \;=\; (1 - q) \cdot g(0) + q \cdot g(1)$$

with $\mathsf{E}X = q$ in particular.

1.4.2 The geometric distribution

A random variable X that is *geometrically* distributed has a single parameter $\lambda > 0$ and its strict range is the nonnegative integers, i.e.,

$$R_X \;=\; \mathbb{Z}^+ \;\equiv\; \{0, 1, 2, ...\}.$$

The parameter λ satisfies $0 < \lambda < 1$. The CDF of X is piecewise constant with

$$F(i) \;=\; 1 - \lambda^{i+1}$$

for all $i \in \mathbb{Z}^+$. The PMF of X is $p(i) = (1 - \lambda)\lambda^i$ for $i \in \mathbb{Z}^+$. To compute $\mathsf{E}X$, we rely on a little trick involving a derivative:

$$
\begin{aligned}
\mathsf{E}X \;&=\; \sum_{i=0}^{\infty} i\, p(i) \\[2mm]
&=\; (1 - \lambda)\lambda \sum_{i=1}^{\infty} i\, \lambda^{i-1} \\[2mm]
&=\; (1 - \lambda)\lambda \frac{\mathrm{d}}{\mathrm{d}\lambda}\left(\sum_{i=1}^{\infty} \lambda^i \right) \\[2mm]
&=\; (1 - \lambda)\lambda \frac{\mathrm{d}}{\mathrm{d}\lambda}\left(\frac{1}{1 - \lambda} - 1 \right) \\[2mm]
&=\; (1 - \lambda)\lambda \frac{1}{(1 - \lambda)^2} \\[2mm]
&=\; \frac{\lambda}{1 - \lambda}.
\end{aligned}
$$

Similarly, the moment generating function is

$$
\begin{aligned}
m(\theta) \;&=\; (1 - \lambda) \sum_{i=0}^{\infty} (e^\theta \lambda)^i \\[2mm]
&=\; \frac{1 - \lambda}{1 - \lambda e^\theta}
\end{aligned}
$$

for $e^\theta \lambda < 1$, i.e., $\theta < -\log \lambda$.

1.4.3 The binomial distribution

A random variable Y is *binomially distributed* with parameters n and q if $R_Y = \{0, 1, ..., n\}$ and, for $k \in R_Y$,

$$\mathsf{P}(Y = k) = \binom{n}{k} q^k (1 - q)^{n-k},$$

where $n \in \mathbb{Z}^+, 0 < q < 1$, and

$$\binom{n}{k} \equiv \frac{n!}{k!(n-k)!}. \tag{1.5}$$

That is, $\binom{n}{k}$ is "n choose k," see Example 1.4. It is easy to see that, by the binomial theorem, $\sum_{k=0}^{n} \mathsf{P}(Y = k) = 1$, i.e.,

$$\sum_{k=0}^{n} \binom{n}{k} q^k (1-q)^{n-k} = (q + (1-q))^n = 1.$$

Also,

$$m(\theta) = \sum_{k=0}^{n} \binom{n}{k} q^k (1-q)^{n-k} e^{\theta k}$$

$$= (qe^\theta + (1-q))^n.$$

■ **EXAMPLE 1.2**

If we are given n independent Bernoulli distributed random variables, X_i, each having the same parameter q, then $Y = \sum_{i=1}^{n} X_i$ is binomially distributed with parameters n and q. That is, for $k \in \{0, 1, 2, ..., n\}$, the event $\{Y = k\}$ can be written as a union on disjoint component events, where k of the X_i equal 1 and $n - k$ of the X_i equal 0. Each such component event occurs with probability $p^k(1-p)^{n-k}$. The number of such events, i.e., the number of ways the random vector $(X_1, X_2, ..., X_n)$ has exactly k ones, is

$$\frac{n!}{k!(n-k)!} = \binom{n}{k},$$

where $n!$ is the number of *permutations* (ordered arrangements) of n different objects and the factors $k!$ and $(n - k)!$ in the denominator account for the k ones being indistinguishable and the $n - k$ zeros being indistinguishable.

1.4.4 The Poisson distribution

A random variable X is *Poisson* distributed with parameter $\lambda > 0$ if $R_X = \mathbb{Z}^+$ and the PMF is

$$p(i) = \frac{\lambda^i}{i!} e^{-\lambda}$$

for $i \in \mathbb{Z}^+$. We can check that $\mathsf{E}X = \lambda$ as in the geometric case. The MGF is

$$m(\theta) = \sum_{i=0}^{\infty} e^{\theta n} \frac{\lambda^n}{n!} e^{-\lambda}$$

$$= e^{-\lambda} \sum_{i=0}^{\infty} \frac{(e^\theta \lambda)^n}{n!}$$

$$= \exp((e^\theta - 1)\lambda).$$

1.4.5   The discrete uniform distribution

A discrete random variable X is *uniformly* distributed on a *finite* range

$$R_X \quad \subset \quad \mathbb{R}$$

if

$$P(X = x) \quad = \quad \frac{1}{|R_X|}$$

for all $x \in R_X$, where $|R_X|$ is the size of (the number of elements in) R_X. Clearly, therefore, for any $A \subset R_X$,

$$P(X \in A) \quad = \quad \frac{|A|}{|R_X|},$$

i.e., to compute this probability, one needs to *count* the number of elements in A and R_X.

■ **EXAMPLE 1.3**

Suppose that a random experiment consists of tossing two different six-sided dice on the floor. Consider the events consisting of all outcomes having the same numbers (d_1, d_2) on the upturned faces of the dice. Note that there are $6 \times 6 = 36$ such events. Assume that the probability of each such event is $\frac{1}{36}$, i.e., the dice are "fair." This implies that the random variables d_i are independent and uniformly distributed on their state space $\{1, 2, 3, 4, 5, 6\}$.

Suppose that we are interested in $P(X \in \{7, 11\})$, where the random variable

$$X \quad \equiv \quad d_1 + d_2.$$

That is, we are interested in the event

$$(d_1, d_2) \in \{(1,6), (2,5), (3,4), (4,3), (5,2), (6,1), (5,6), (6,5)\}$$

with eight members. So, $P(X \in \{7, 11\}) = \frac{8}{36}$.

■ **EXAMPLE 1.4**

Suppose that five cards (a poker hand) are drawn, without replacement, from a standard deck of 52 different playing cards. The random variable X enumerates each *combination* (not considering the order in which the individual cards were drawn) of poker hands beginning with 1 and ending with the total number of different poker hands possible, $\binom{52}{5}$, where $\binom{n}{k}$ is given in (1.5). That is, $|R_X| = \binom{52}{5}$. Assume X is uniformly distributed (i.e., a fair hand is drawn) and suppose we wish to find the probability that a flush is drawn, i.e., $P(X \in \text{flushes})$. As there are four suits each having 13 cards, the number of poker hands that are flushes is $4\binom{13}{5}$. So,

$$P(X \in \text{flushes}) \quad = \quad \frac{4\binom{13}{5}}{\binom{52}{5}}.$$

Similarly, the probability of a drawing a poker hand with a pair of aces from a fair deck is

$$\frac{\binom{4}{2}\binom{48}{3}}{\binom{52}{4}},$$

where the term $\binom{4}{2} = 6$ is the number of ways to form a pair of aces and term $\binom{48}{3}$ is the number of ways to form the balance of the hand (i.e., 3 more cards) without using aces.

■ **EXAMPLE 1.5**

Consider the context of the previous example but now suppose that we care about the *order* in which the cards were drawn, again without replacement. To compute the number of different hands, we count the number of ways we can permute 5 cards chosen from a deck of 52 without replacement. This quantity is

$$52 \times 51 \times 50 \times 49 \times 48 \quad = \quad \frac{52!}{(52 - 5)!}.$$

Note that a single *combination* of 5 different cards will have $5! = 120$ different (ordered) permutations.

On the other hand, if the cards are drawn with replacement (i.e., each card is restored to the deck after it is drawn) and we continue to care about the order in which the cards are drawn, the number of possible hands is simply 52^5. Note that in this case, a hand may consist of several copies of the same card.

A group of example discrete distributions is given in Figure 1.2.

1.5 CONTINUOUSLY DISTRIBUTED RANDOM VARIABLES

The CDF of a continuously distributed (or just "continuous") random variable X has a piecewise-continuous and bounded derivative. The derivative $f = F'$ (i.e., $dF(x) = f(x)\,dx$) is known as the probability density function (PDF) of X. We clearly have

$$F(x) = \int_{-\infty}^{x} f(z)\,dz.$$

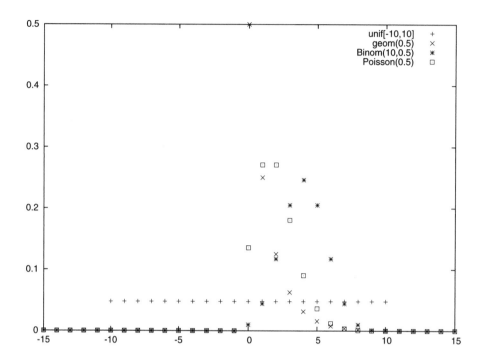

Figure 1.2   Example discrete distributions.

From this identity, we see that any PDF f is a nonnegative function satisfying

$$\int_{-\infty}^{\infty} f(z)\,\mathrm{d}z \;=\; 1.$$

Moreover,

$$\mathsf{E}g(X) \;=\; \int_{-\infty}^{\infty} g(x)f(x)\,\mathrm{d}x$$

and, in particular, if $g(X) = \mathbf{1}\{X \in B\}$, then this reduces to

$$\mathsf{P}(X \in B) \;=\; \int_B f(z)\,\mathrm{d}z.$$

Finally, note that the range $R_X = \{x \in \mathbb{R} \mid f(x) > 0\}$.

1.5.1   The continuous uniform distribution

A random variable X is *uniformly* distributed over the interval $[a, b]$ if its PDF is

$$f(x) = \begin{cases} \dfrac{1}{b-a} & \text{if } a \le x \le b, \\ 0 & \text{else,} \end{cases}$$

where $b > a$. Clearly, $\mathsf{E}X = (b + a)/2$. We can similarly define a uniformly distributed random variable X over any range $R_X \subset \mathbb{R}$ having finite total length, i.e., $|R_X| < \infty$.

1.5.2 The exponential distribution

A random variable X is *exponentially* distributed with real parameter $\lambda > 0$ if its PDF is

$$f(x) = \left\{ \begin{array}{cl} \lambda \mathrm{e}^{-\lambda x} & \text{if } x \geq 0, \\ 0 & \text{else.} \end{array} \right.$$

The CDF is $F(x) = 1 - \mathrm{e}^{-\lambda x}$ for $x \geq 0$, $\mathsf{E}X = 1/\lambda$, and the MGF is

$$m(\theta) = \frac{\lambda}{\lambda - \theta} \tag{1.6}$$

for $\theta < \lambda$; see Section 2.1.

1.5.3 The gamma distribution

A random variable X is *gamma* distributed with positive real parameters λ and r if its PDF is

$$f(x) = \left\{ \begin{array}{cl} \lambda^r x^{r-1} \mathrm{e}^{-\lambda x} / \Gamma_r & \text{if } x \geq 0, \\ 0 & \text{else,} \end{array} \right.$$

where the normalizing gamma function $\Gamma_r = \int_0^\infty z^r \mathrm{e}^{-z}\, \mathrm{d}z$. When r is a positive integer, we can integrate by parts to show that $\Gamma_r = (r - 1)!$; in this case, the gamma distribution is sometimes called the *Erlang* distribution. Let μ be the mean and σ^2 be the variance associated with this distribution. We have the following identities:

$$\lambda = \frac{\mu}{\sigma^2} \quad \text{and} \quad r = \frac{\mu^2}{\sigma^2}. \tag{1.7}$$

Finally, the MGF is

$$m(\theta) = \left(\frac{\lambda}{\lambda - \theta} \right)^r \tag{1.8}$$

for $\theta < \lambda$. We see that a gamma distributed random variable with parameters λ and $r = 1$ is just an exponentially distributed random variable.

1.5.4 The Gaussian (or normal) distribution

A *Gaussian* (or *normally*) distributed random variable X with mean μ and variance σ^2 has PDF

$$f(x) = \frac{1}{\sigma\sqrt{2\pi}} \exp\left(-\frac{(x - \mu)^2}{2\sigma^2} \right)$$

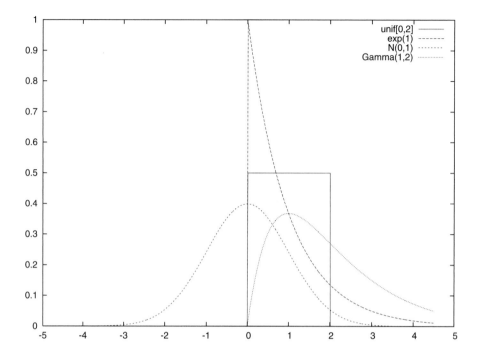

Figure 1.3   Example continuous distributions.

for $x \in \mathbb{R}$. The MGF is

$$m(\theta) = \exp(\mu\theta + \tfrac{1}{2}\sigma^2\theta^2).\tag{1.9}$$

See Figure 1.3 for example continuous distributions.

1.6   SOME USEFUL INEQUALITIES

Clearly, if the event $A_1 \subset A_2$, then $\mathsf{P}(A_1) \leq \mathsf{P}(A_2) = \mathsf{P}(A_1) + \mathsf{P}(A_2 \backslash A_1)$. For any collection of events $A_1, A_2, ..., A_n$, Boole's inequality holds:

$$\mathsf{P}\left(\bigcup_{i=1}^{n} A_i\right) \leq \sum_{i=1}^{n} \mathsf{P}(A_i).$$

Note that when the A_i are disjoint, equality holds simply by the additivity property of a probability measure P.

If two random variables X and Y are such that $\mathsf{P}(X \geq Y) = 1$ (i.e., $X \geq Y$ *almost surely*), then $\mathsf{E}X \geq \mathsf{E}Y$.

Consider a random variable X with $E|X| < \infty$ and a real number $x > 0$. Since

$$|X| \geq |X|\mathbf{1}\{|X| \geq x\} \geq x\mathbf{1}\{|X| \geq x\} \text{ almost surely,}$$

we arrive at Markov's inequality:

$$E|X| \geq Ex\mathbf{1}\{|X| \geq x\} = xE\mathbf{1}\{|X| \geq x\} = xP(|X| \geq x).$$

An alternative explanation for continuously distributed random variables X is

$$
\begin{aligned}
E|X| &= \int_{-\infty}^{\infty} |z| f(z)\, \mathrm{d}z \geq \int_{-\infty}^{-x} (-z) f(z)\, \mathrm{d}z + \int_{x}^{\infty} z f(z)\, \mathrm{d}z \\
&\geq \int_{-\infty}^{-x} x f(z)\, \mathrm{d}z + \int_{x}^{\infty} x f(z)\, \mathrm{d}z = xP(|X| \geq x).
\end{aligned}
$$

Now take $x = \varepsilon^2$, where $\varepsilon > 0$, and argue Markov's inequality with $(X - EX)^2$ in place of $|X|$ to get Chebyshev's inequality

$$\mathrm{var}(X) \equiv E[(X - EX)^2] \geq \varepsilon^2 P(|X - EX| \geq \varepsilon),$$

i.e.,

$$P(|X - EX| \geq \varepsilon) \leq \varepsilon^{-2}\mathrm{var}(X). \tag{1.10}$$

Noting that, for all $\theta > 0$, $\{X \geq x\} = \{e^{\theta X} \geq e^{\theta x}\}$ and arguing as for Markov's inequality gives the Chernoff (or Cramér) inequality:

$$
\begin{aligned}
Ee^{\theta X} &\geq e^{\theta x} P(X \geq x) \\
\Rightarrow P(X \geq x) &\leq \exp\left(-[x\theta - \log Ee^{\theta X}]\right) \\
&\leq \exp\left(-\max_{\theta > 0}[x\theta - \log Ee^{\theta X}]\right), \tag{1.11}
\end{aligned}
$$

where we have simply sharpened the inequality by taking the maximum over the free parameter θ. Note the log-MGF of X in the Chernoff bound.

The Cauchy-Schwarz inequality states that

$$E|XY| \leq \sqrt{E(X^2)}\sqrt{E(Y^2)}$$

for all random variables X and Y with the inequality strict whenever $X \neq cY$ or $Y = 0$ almost surely for some constant c. This inequality is an immediate consequence of the fact that

$$E\left(\frac{X}{\sqrt{E(X^2)}} - \frac{Y}{\sqrt{E(Y^2)}}\right)^2 \geq 0$$

whenever $X \neq 0$ and $Y \neq 0$ almost surely. Also, note that if we take $Y = 1$ almost surely, the Cauchy-Schwarz simply states that the variance of a random variable X is not negative, i.e., that

$$E(X^2) - (EX)^2 \geq 0.$$

This is also an immediate consequence of Jensen's inequality. A real-valued function g on $\mathbb{R}$ is said to be *convex* if

$$g(px + (1-p)y) \;\leq\; pg(x) + (1-p)g(y) \tag{1.12}$$

for any $x, y \in \mathbb{R}$ and any real fraction $p \in [0,1]$. If the inequality is reversed in this definition, the function g would be *concave*. For any convex function g and random variable X, we have Jensen's inequality:

$$g(\mathsf{E}X) \;\leq\; \mathsf{E}(g(X)). \tag{1.13}$$

1.7 JOINT DISTRIBUTION FUNCTIONS

For the case of two random variables X and Y the *joint* CDF is

$$F_{X,Y}(x,y) = \mathsf{P}(X \leq x, Y \leq y) \ \text{ for } x, y \in \mathbb{R}.$$

We can similarly define a joint CDF for more than two random variables.

1.7.1 Joint PDF

If X and Y are both continuously distributed, we can define their joint PDF as

$$f_{X,Y} \;=\; \frac{\partial^2 F_{X,Y}}{\partial x\, \partial y}.$$

For any (Borel measurable) real-valued function g over $\mathbb{R}^2$,

$$\mathsf{E}g(X,Y) \;=\; \int_{-\infty}^{\infty} \int_{-\infty}^{\infty} g(x,y) f_{X,Y}(x,y)\, \mathrm{d}x\, \mathrm{d}y$$

and, in particular, if

$$g(X,Y) = \mathbf{1}\left\{ \begin{pmatrix} X \\ Y \end{pmatrix} \in A \right\},$$

for some (Borel) $A \subset \mathbb{R}^2$, then this reduces to

$$\mathsf{P}\left(\begin{pmatrix} X \\ Y \end{pmatrix} \in A \right) \;=\; \iint_A f_{X,Y}(x,y)\, \mathrm{d}x\, \mathrm{d}y.$$

1.7.2   Marginalizing a joint distribution

Beginning with the joint CDF $F_{X,Y}$, we can obtain either *marginal* CDF F_Y or F_X by simply taking limits:

$$F_X(x) = \lim_{y \to \infty} F_{X,Y}(x,y) \quad \text{and} \quad F_Y(y) = \lim_{x \to \infty} F_{X,Y}(x,y).$$

To see why, note that

$$
\begin{aligned}
\lim_{x \to \infty} F_{X,Y}(x,y) &= \mathsf{P}(X \le x, Y < \infty) \\
&= \mathsf{P}(\{\omega \in \Omega \mid X(\omega) \le x\} \cap \Omega) \\
&= \mathsf{P}(X \le x),
\end{aligned}
$$

where we used the fact that, by definition of a (real-valued) random variable, the event $Y < \infty$ is the whole sample space Ω. Similarly, one can recover either *marginal* PDF from the joint PDF:

$$f_X(x) = \int_{-\infty}^{\infty} f_{X,Y}(x,y)\,dy \quad \text{and} \quad f_Y(y) = \int_{-\infty}^{\infty} f_{X,Y}(x,y)\,dx.$$

Marginal PMFs are similarly obtained by summation of a joint PMF.

1.8   CONDITIONAL EXPECTATION

Consider an event A such that $\mathsf{P}(A) > 0$ and a random variable X. The *conditional expected value of X given A*, denoted $\mu(X|A)$, is computed by simply using the conditional distribution of X given A:

$$F_{X|A}(z) \equiv \mathsf{P}(X \le z|A),$$

i.e.,

$$\mu(X|A) = \int_{-\infty}^{\infty} x\,dF_{X|A}(x).$$

In the case of a discretely distributed random variable X, simply

$$\mu(X|A) = \sum_{j=1}^{\infty} a_j \mathsf{P}(X = a_j|A),$$

where $\{a_j\}_{j=1}^{\infty} = R_X$. The conditional PMF of X given A is denoted $p_{X|A}$, i.e., $p_{X|A}(a_j) = \mathsf{P}(X = a_j|A)$ for all j.

In a similar way we can define the conditional PDF of a continuously distributed random variable X given the event A,

$$f_{X|A}(x) \equiv \frac{d}{dx} F_{X|A}(x),$$

and thereby compute

$$\mu(X|A) \;=\; \int_{-\infty}^{\infty} x f_{X|A}(x)\,\mathrm{d}x. \tag{1.14}$$

Consider now two discretely distributed random variables X and Y. We will define the *conditional expectation of X given the random variable Y* denoted $\mathsf{E}(X|Y)$. The quantity $\mathsf{E}(X|Y)$ is a random variable itself. Indeed, suppose $\{b_j\}_{j=1}^{\infty} = R_Y$ and, for *all* samples

$$\omega_j \;\in\; \{\omega \in \Omega \mid Y(\omega) = b_j\} \;\equiv\; B_j$$

define

$$\mathsf{E}(X|Y)(\omega_j) \;\equiv\; \mu(X|B_j),$$

where the conditional expected value on the right-hand side can be denoted $\mu(X|Y = b_j)$. That is, the conditional expectation $\mathsf{E}(X|Y)$ maps all samples in the event B_j to the conditional expected value $\mu(X|B_j)$. Therefore, the random variable $\mathsf{E}(X|Y)$ is almost surely a *function of Y*.[1]

Now consider two random variables X and Y which are continuously distributed with joint PDF $f_{X,Y}$. For $f_Y(y) > 0$, we can define the conditional *density*:

$$f_{X|Y}(x|y) \;\equiv\; \frac{f_{X,Y}(x,y)}{f_Y(y)}$$

for all $x \in \mathbb{R}$. Note that $f_{X|Y}(\cdot|y)$ is itself a PDF and, with this conditional density, the following conditional expected value can be computed

$$\mu(X|Y = y) \;=\; \int_{-\infty}^{\infty} x f_{X|Y}(x|y)\,\mathrm{d}x,$$

where, unlike (1.14), the event $\{Y = y\}$ has zero probability. Again, note that $\mu(X|Y = y)$ is a function of y, say $h(y)$, and that the conditional expectation $\mathsf{E}(X|Y) = h(Y)$.

When X and Y are independent, the conditional distribution of X given Y is just the distribution of X and, therefore, $\mathsf{E}(X|Y) = \mathsf{E}X$. In other words, if X and Y are independent, then knowledge of Y (i.e., *given Y*) does not affect the *remaining uncertainty* of the random variable X.

■ **EXAMPLE 1.6**

For the purposes of a simple graphical example, suppose that the sample space $\Omega = [0,1] \subset \mathbb{R}$ (but recall that, in general, Ω can be a completely abstract space without ordering). In Figure 1.4, the previous case of jointly discrete random variables X, Y and $\mathsf{E}(X|Y)$ are plotted as functions from Ω to $\mathbb{R}$. To further simplify the graph, we assume that these random variables are piecewise constant functions over Ω and that the probability P is the (Lebesgue) measure corresponding to Euclidean length.

---

[1]Equivalently, $\mathsf{E}(X|Y)$ is $\sigma(Y)$-*measurable*, where $\sigma(Y)$ is the smallest σ-algebra over Ω containing the events B_j. In this concrete way, $\sigma(Y)$ quantifies the information content of Y.

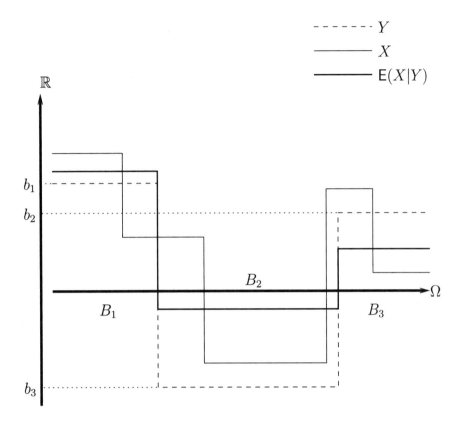

Figure 1.4 Smoothing effect of conditional expectation.

Figure 1.4 shows that $\mathsf{E}(X|Y)$ is a *smoothed* (less "uncertain") version of X. Also $\mathsf{E}(X|Y)$ depends on Y only through the events

$$B_j \;\; \equiv \;\; \{Y = b_j\},$$

i.e., the extent to which the random variable Y discriminates the samples $\omega \in \Omega$. That is, consider a discrete random variable Z with range $R_Z = \{c_j\}_{j=1}^{\infty}$ and define the events

$$C_j \;\; \equiv \;\; \{Z = c_j\}$$

for all j. If the collections of events $\{B_j\}_{j=1}^{\infty}$ and $\{C_j\}_{j=1}^{\infty}$ are the same (allowing for differences of probability zero), then $\mathsf{E}(X|Y) = \mathsf{E}(X|Z)$ almost surely. Note that R_Y can be different from R_Z, in which case

$$\mathsf{E}(X|Y) \;\; = \;\; h(Y) \;\; = \;\; \mathsf{E}(X|Z) \;\; = \;\; g(Z) \;\; \text{almost surely,}$$

with $g \not\equiv h$.

In general, $E(X|Y)$ is the function of Y which minimizes the *mean-square error* (MSE),

$$E[(X - h(Y))^2],$$

among all (measurable) functions h. So, $E(X|Y)$ is the best approximation of X given Y. Again, $E(X|Y)$ and X have the same expectation in particular, i.e.,

$$E(E(X|Y)) = EX.$$

It is left as a simple exercise to check this property for the cases of jointly discrete or jointly continuous random variables X and Y considered above.

1.9 INDEPENDENT RANDOM VARIABLES

A collection of continuously distributed random variables $X_1, X_2, ..., X_n$ are said to be *mutually independent* (or just "independent") if and only if their joint PDF is equal to the product of the marginal PDFs, i.e.,

$$f_{X_1, X_2, ..., X_n}(x_1, x_2, ..., x_n) = \prod_{i=1}^{n} f_{X_i}(x_i)$$

for all real $x_1, x_2, ..., x_n$. This definition is consistent with that at the end of Section 1.2.

When X and Y are both discretely distributed, we can similarly define their joint PMF $p_{X,Y}$ and there is a similar condition for independence (the joint PMF is the product of the marginal PMFs). In general, a condition for independence is that the joint CDF is the product of the marginal CDFs.

If the random variables $\{X_i\}_{i=1}^{n}$ are independent, then

$$E \prod_{i=1}^{n} X_i \quad = \quad \prod_{i=1}^{n} EX_i. \tag{1.15}$$

In particular, for $n = 2$, this means that if X_1 and X_2 are independent, then they are *uncorrelated*, i.e., their *covariance* equals zero:

$$0 \quad = \quad \text{cov}(X_1, X_2) \equiv E\left((X_1 - EX_1)(X_2 - EX_2)\right) \quad = \quad E(X_1 X_2) - EX_1 EX_2.$$

The converse is, however, not true in general; see Problem 1.4 at the end of the chapter.

1.9.1 Sums of independent random variables

In this section we will consider sums of mutually independent continuous random variables. Our objective is to find the PDF of the sum given the PDF of the component random variables.

To this end, consider two independent random variables X_1 and X_2 with PDFs f_1 and f_2 respectively; so, $f_{X_1,X_2} = f_1 f_2$. Thus, the CDF of the sum is

$$F(z) = \mathsf{P}(X_1 + X_2 \le z) = \int_{-\infty}^{\infty} \int_{-\infty}^{z-x_1} f_1(x_1) f_2(x_2) \, dx_2 \, dx_1.$$

Exchanging the first integral on the right-hand side with a derivative with respect to z, the PDF of $X_1 + X_2$ is

$$f(z) = \frac{d}{dz} F(z) = \int_{-\infty}^{\infty} f_1(x_1) f_2(z - x_1) \, dx_1 \quad \text{for all } z \in \mathbb{R}.$$

Thus, f is the *convolution* of f_1 and f_2 which is denoted $f = f_1 * f_2$.

In this context, moment generating functions can be used to simplify calculations. Let the MGF of X_i be

$$m_i(\theta) = \mathsf{E}e^{\theta X_i} = \int_{-\infty}^{\infty} f_i(x) e^{\theta x} \, dx.$$

Note that m_i is basically the (bilateral) Laplace transform [164] of f_i. The MGF of $X_1 + X_2$ is

$$m(\theta) = \mathsf{E}e^{\theta(X_1+X_2)} = \mathsf{E}e^{\theta X_1} e^{\theta X_2} = m_1(\theta) m_2(\theta), \tag{1.16}$$

where the last equation holds because of the independence of X_1 and X_2. So, convolution of PDFs corresponds to simple multiplication of MGFs (which, in turn, corresponds to addition of independent random variables).

■ **EXAMPLE 1.7**

As an example, suppose X_1 and X_2 are independent and both exponentially distributed with parameter λ. The PDF of $X_1 + X_2$ is f, where $f(z) = 0$ for $z < 0$ and, for $z \ge 0$,

$$f(z) = \int_0^z f_1(x_1) f_2(z - x_1) \, dx_1 = \lambda^2 z e^{-\lambda z}.$$

The MGF of $X_1 + X_2$ is, by (1.6) and (1.16),

$$m(\theta) = \left(\frac{\lambda}{\lambda - \theta} \right)^2,$$

which is consistent with the PDF just computed. There is a one-to-one relationship between PDFs and MGFs of nonnegative random variables.[2] We can therefore use the MGF approach to find the PDF of the sum of n independent random variables $\{X_i\}_{i=1}^n$ each having an exponential distribution with parameter λ. Indeed, the MGF of $\sum_{i=1}^n X_i$ is easily computed as

$$m(\theta) = \left(\frac{\lambda}{\lambda - \theta} \right)^n. \tag{1.17}$$

---

[2]In this case, the MGF is a *unilateral* Laplace transform [164]: $m(\theta) = \int_0^{\infty} f(z) e^{\theta z} \, dz$.

This is the MGF of a gamma (Erlang) distributed random variable with parameters λ and $n \in \mathbb{Z}^+$ and PDF

$$f_n(z) = \frac{\lambda^n z^{n-1} e^{-\lambda z}}{(n-1)!} \tag{1.18}$$

for $z \geq 0$.

■ **EXAMPLE 1.8**

Suppose that, for $i = 1, 2$, the random variable X_i is Gaussian distributed with mean μ_i and variance σ_i^2. Also suppose that X_1 and X_2 are independent. By (1.9) and (1.16), the MGF of $X_1 + X_2$ is

$$
\begin{aligned}
m(\theta) &= \exp\left(\mu_1\theta + \tfrac{1}{2}\sigma_1^2\theta^2\right) \times \exp\left(\mu_2\theta + \tfrac{1}{2}\sigma_2^2\theta^2\right) \\
&= \exp\left((\mu_1 + \mu_2)\theta + \tfrac{1}{2}(\sigma_1^2 + \sigma_2^2)\theta^2\right),
\end{aligned}
$$

which we recognize as a Gaussian MGF. Thus, $X_1 + X_2$ is Gaussian distributed with mean $\mu_1 + \mu_2$ and variance $\sigma_1^2 + \sigma_2^2$; see Problems 1.5 and 1.6.

1.10 CONDITIONAL INDEPENDENCE

If

$$\mathsf{P}(A \mid B, C) = \mathsf{P}(A \mid B), \tag{1.19}$$

the events A and C are said to be independent *given* B. This is a natural extension of the unqualified notion of independent events, i.e., events A and C are (unconditionally) independent if

$$\mathsf{P}(A \mid C) = \mathsf{P}(A).$$

Note that (1.19) implies $\mathsf{P}(C \mid B, A) = \mathsf{P}(C \mid B)$.

Similarly, random variables X and Y are conditionally independent given Z if

$$\mathsf{P}(X \in A \mid Z \in B, \, Y \in C) = \mathsf{P}(X \in A \mid Z \in B)$$

for all $A, B, C \subset \mathbb{R}$. Conditional independence does not imply (unqualified) independence, as we will see in the following chapter.

1.11 A LAW OF LARGE NUMBERS

In this section, we describe the basic connection between statistics and probability through the laws of large numbers (LLNs) [44, 62, 63]. Suppose we have an IID sequence of random variables $X_1, X_2, X_3, \dots$. Also suppose that the common distribution has finite variance, i.e.,

$$
\begin{aligned}
\sigma^2 &\equiv \mathrm{var}(X) \\
&\equiv \mathsf{E}(X - \mathsf{E}X)^2 \\
&< \infty,
\end{aligned}
$$

where $X \sim X_i$. Finally, suppose that the mean exists and is finite, i.e.,

$$
\mu \equiv \mathsf{E}X < \infty.
$$

Define the sum

$$
S_n = X_1 + X_2 + \cdots + X_n
$$

for $n \geq 1$ and note that $\mathsf{E}S_n = n\mu$ and $\mathrm{var}(S_n) = n\sigma^2$. The quantity S_n/n is called the *empirical* mean of X after n samples and is an *unbiased* estimate of μ, i.e.,

$$
\mathsf{E}\left(\frac{S_n}{n}\right) = \mu.
$$

Also, because of the following *weak* LLN, S_n/n is said to be a *weakly consistent* estimator of μ.

Theorem 1.11.1. *For all $\varepsilon > 0$,*

$$
\lim_{n \to \infty} \mathsf{P}\left(\left|\frac{S_n}{n} - \mu\right| \geq \varepsilon\right) = 0.
$$

Proof: By Chebyshev's inequality (1.10),

$$
\mathsf{P}\left(\left|\frac{S_n}{n} - \mu\right| \geq \varepsilon\right) \leq \frac{\mathrm{var}(S_n/n)}{\varepsilon^2} = \frac{\sigma^2}{n\varepsilon^2}.
$$

Therefore,

$$
\lim_{n \to \infty} \mathsf{P}\left(\left|\frac{S_n}{n} - \mu\right| \geq \varepsilon\right) = 0
$$

as desired. $\qquad\qquad\Box$

The *strong* LLN asserts that, if $\mathsf{E}|X| < \infty$, then

$$
\mathsf{P}\left(\lim_{n \to \infty} \frac{S_n}{n} = \mu\right) = 1.
$$

In other words, $S_n/n \to \mu$ almost surely. So, S_n/n is said to be a *strongly consistent* estimator of μ. A proof of the strong LLN, which implies the weak LLN, is given in [44, 62].

1.12 FIRST-ORDER AUTOREGRESSIVE ESTIMATORS

Given a series of samples X_n at "times" $n \in \{0, 1, 2, ...\}$, one may wish to iteratively estimate their mean. To this end, we can define $\overline{X}_n$ as the "current" estimate of the mean. A typical problem in this context is that the underlying distribution of the samples is slowly changing with time. For example, the Transmission Control Protocol (TCP) estimates average packet round-trip times (RTTs) [139] (and "absolute" variation about the estimated average) to calibrate a time-out mechanism for acknowledgements of transmitted packets. Also, for packet queues in Internet routers, proposed active queue management (AQM) techniques such as [105, 165, 231] estimate packet backlogs and the number of long-term active TCP sessions.

Since the distribution of X_n is changing, one could want to more significantly weight the recent samples X_k (i.e., $k \leq n$ and $k \approx n$) in the computation of $\overline{X}_n$. For example, one might use a *moving average* (MA) of order 2, i.e., for $n \geq 2$,

$$\overline{X}_n = \beta_0 X_n + \beta_1 X_{n-1} + \beta_2 X_{n-2},$$

where $0 < \beta_i$ for all i and $\sum_i \beta_i = 1$ (e.g., all $\beta_i = \frac{1}{3}$); clearly, no older samples X_k with $k < n - 2$ affect the MA $\overline{X}_n$.

Alternatively, an order 1 autoregressive (AR) estimate could be used, i.e., for $n > 1$,

$$\begin{aligned} \overline{X}_n &= \alpha \overline{X}_{n-1} + (1 - \alpha) X_n \\ \Rightarrow \overline{X}_n - \overline{X}_{n-1} &= (1 - \alpha)(X_n - \overline{X}_{n-1}), \end{aligned} \qquad (1.20)$$

where $0 < \alpha < 1$ is the "forgetting factor" and $\overline{X}_0 = X_0$. Note that all past values of X contribute to the current value of this autoregressive processes according to weights that exponentially diminish:

$$\overline{X}_n = \alpha^n \overline{X}_0 + (1 - \alpha)[\alpha^{n-1} X_1 + \alpha^{n-2} X_2 + ... + \alpha X_{n-1} + X_n].$$

Also note that if $1 - \alpha$ is a power of 2, then the autoregressive update (1.20) is simply implemented with two additive operations and one bit-shift (the latter to multiply by $1 - \alpha$). There is a simple trade-off in the choice of α. A small α implies that $\overline{X}_n$ is more responsive to the current samples X_k, but this can lead to undesirable oscillations in the AR process $\overline{X}$. A large value of α means that the AR process will have diminished oscillations ("low-pass" filter) but will be less responsive to changes in the distribution of the samples X_k [136, 164].

■ **EXAMPLE 1.9**

Consider a sequence of independent random variables X_n. Initially, the distribution is uniform on the interval [0,1] (i.e., $EX = 0.5$), but for $n \geq 20$ the distribution is uniform on the interval [3,4] (i.e., EX changes to 3.5). We see from Figure 1.5 that for forgetting factor $\alpha = 0.2$, a sample path of the first-order AR process $\overline{X}$ responds much more quickly to the change in mean (at $n = 20$) but is more oscillatory than the corresponding sample path of the AR process using forgetting factor $\alpha = 0.8$.

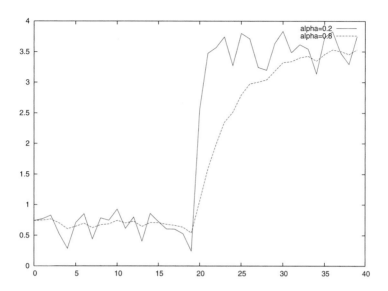

Figure 1.5 Performance of first order AR estimators.

1.13 MEASURES OF SEPARATION BETWEEN DISTRIBUTIONS

Consider two cumulative distribution functions F_1 and F_2. Suppose we wish to measure the degree to which they are different. More formally, we wish to stipulate a kind of *metric* $m(F_1, F_2) \in \mathbb{R}^+$ on the set of such distributions satisfying certain properties:

- $m(F_1, F_2) = 0$ when $F_1 \equiv F_2$ and

- m increases as the amount of "separation" between F_1 and F_2 increases.

In networking, such metrics have recently been proposed (in, e.g., [67]) to detect anomalous activity. That is, suppose a CDF F_1 representing the nominal distribution of an attribute of a flow of packets (e.g., of their destination port number attributes [41]) is known. The CDF F_2 represents the corresponding distribution as measured online. When $m(F_1, F_2)$ exceeds a certain threshold, the network operator (or some automatic intrusion detection system (IDS)) may deem that the packet flow is exhibiting abnormal behavior and decide to take action (e.g., filter-out/firewall any identified offending packets).

Some specific ways to measure the separation between two distributions include the Kolmogorov-Smirnov distance between two CDFs:

$$m(F_1, F_2) \quad = \quad \max_{x \in \mathbb{R}} |F_1(x) - F_2(x)|.$$

For a parameter $\alpha \geq 1$, we can also define

$$m(F_1, F_2) \quad = \quad \left(\int_{-\infty}^{\infty} |F_1(x) - F_2(x)|^\alpha \, dx \right)^{1/\alpha},$$

where we note that, as $\alpha \to \infty$, this metric converges to that of Kolmogorov-Smirnov.

Given two PMFs p_1 and p_2 on the same state space we can define their *chi-squared separation* as

$$\sum_x \frac{(p(x) - q(x))^2}{p(x)}.$$

A similar definition exists for PDFs, i.e., for continuous distributions.

Given the means μ and variances σ of two distributions, the Fisher separation between them is

$$\frac{|\mu_1 - \mu_2|}{\sigma_1^2 + \sigma_2^2};$$

alternatively, the standard deviation could be used instead of the variance in the denominator leading to a dimensionless Fisher separation metric. Note how the Fisher separation is increasing in the difference of the means but decreasing in either variance. There are other potentially significant features of a distribution besides the mean and variance, e.g., median and mode that can be used as a basis of a measure of separation ([106], p. 185).

In [67], the *entropy* of a distribution was argued to be a significant feature for detection of distributed denial-of-service (DDoS) attacks. The entropy of a PMF p with strict range R is defined to be

$$\sum_{x \in R} p(x) \log p(x).$$

Thus one can consider the difference between the entropies of two distributions with the same range R, p_1 and p_2, as a measure of their separation. Another useful measure of separation is the Kullback-Leibler distance [49]:

$$\sum_{x \in R} p_1(x) \log \frac{p_1(x)}{p_2(x)}.$$

Again, similar definitions exist for PDFs.

1.14 STATISTICAL CONFIDENCE

Central limit theorems (CLTs) date back to Laplace and DeMoivre. They demonstrated that scaled sums of IID random variables of rather *arbitrary* distribution converge *in distribution* to a Gaussian. Convergence in distribution does not necessarily involve the existence of a limiting random variable and is a notion of convergence that is weaker than that of the weak LLN. A common use of the CLT is to evaluate the degree of "confidence" in the result of a group of experimental trials such as those obtained from a simulation study or a poll.

1.14.1 A central limit theorem

Suppose we have an IID sequence of random variables $X_1, X_2, X_3, \dots$. Also, as in the case of the weak LLN, suppose that the common distribution has finite variance, i.e.,

$$\sigma^2 \equiv \text{var}(X) \equiv \mathsf{E}(X - \mathsf{E}X)^2 < \infty,$$

where $X \sim X_i$ and $\sigma > 0$. Finally, suppose that the mean exists and is finite, i.e.,

$$\mu \ \equiv \ \mathsf{E}X \ < \ \infty.$$

Define the cumulative sum

$$S_n \ = \ X_1 + X_2 + \cdots + X_n$$

for $n \geq 1$ and note again that $\mathsf{E}S_n = n\mu$ and $\mathrm{var}(S_n) = n\sigma^2$. Thus, for all n,

$$\mathsf{E}\left(\frac{S_n - n\mu}{\sigma\sqrt{n}}\right) \ = \ 0$$

and

$$\mathrm{var}\left(\frac{S_n - n\mu}{\sigma\sqrt{n}}\right) \ = \ 1.$$

Theorem 1.14.1. *For all $x \in \mathbb{R}$,*

$$\lim_{n\to\infty} \mathsf{P}\left(\frac{S_n - n\mu}{\sigma\sqrt{n}} \leq x\right) \ = \ \int_{-\infty}^{x} \frac{1}{\sqrt{2\pi}} e^{-z^2/2} \, \mathrm{d}z.$$

That is,

$$\frac{S_n - n\mu}{\sigma\sqrt{n}}$$

converges in distribution to a standard (mean 0 and variance 1) Gaussian. A proof for this central limit theorem is given in Section 5.2 of [63]; see Problem 1.16 at the end of this chapter.

1.14.2 Confidence intervals

Suppose that n identically distributed samples X_1, X_2, X_3, ..., X_n have been generated by repeated trials of some experiment. Let μ and $\sigma > 0$ be the mean and standard deviation, respectively, of X_k. Assuming a central limit theorem for the sequence $\{X_k\}$, we have that

$$\frac{\sqrt{n}}{\sigma}(\overline{X}_n - \mu) \tag{1.21}$$

is approximately distributed as a standard Gaussian random variable, where the *sample mean* (or *empirical mean*) is

$$\overline{X}_n \ \equiv \ \frac{1}{n}\sum_{k=1}^{n} X_k.$$

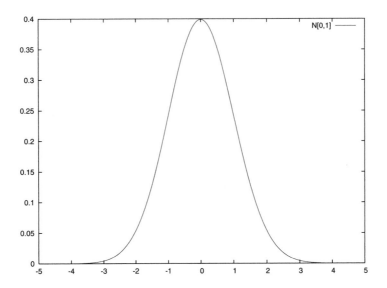

Figure 1.6 PDF of a standard Gaussian random variable $\exp(-z^2/2)/\sqrt{2\pi}$.

The mean μ is taken to be an *unknown quantity* that is to be estimated from the samples X_k. Note that the sample mean is an *unbiased* estimate of μ, i.e.,

$$\mathsf{E}\overline{X}_n \;=\; \mu.$$

This, in turn, allows us to assume that the quantity in (1.21) is Gaussian distributed for relatively small n and use this to compute "error bounds" on the law of large numbers. If Y is a standard Gaussian random variable,

$$
\begin{aligned}
\mathsf{P}(|Y| \le 2) \;&=\; \Phi(2) - \Phi(-2)\\
&=\; \int_{-2}^{2} \frac{1}{\sqrt{2\pi}} \mathrm{e}^{-z^2/2}\, \mathrm{d}z\\
&\approx\; 0.95;
\end{aligned}
$$

see Figure 1.6. Assuming that the standard deviation σ is known, by the central limit approximation, for all sufficiently large n,

$$0.95 \approx \mathsf{P}\left(\left|\frac{\sqrt{n}}{\sigma}(\overline{X}_n - \mu)\right| \le 2\right) = \mathsf{P}\left(\mu \in \left[\overline{X}_n - \frac{2\sigma}{\sqrt{n}},\, \overline{X}_n + \frac{2\sigma}{\sqrt{n}}\right]\right). \quad (1.22)$$

So, with probability 0.95 (i.e., "19 times out of 20"), the true mean μ resides in the interval

$$\left[\overline{X}_n - \frac{2\sigma}{\sqrt{n}},\, \overline{X}_n + \frac{2\sigma}{\sqrt{n}}\right].$$

Consequently, this interval is called the *95% confidence interval* for μ.

Typically, in practice, the standard deviation σ is also not known and must also be estimated from the samples X_k. The *sample variance* is

$$
\begin{aligned}
\overline{\sigma_n^2} &\equiv \frac{1}{n}\sum_{k=1}^{n}(X_k - \overline{X}_n)^2 \\
&= \left(\frac{1}{n}\sum_{k=1}^{n}X_k^2\right) - (\overline{X}_n)^2.
\end{aligned}
$$

The implicit assumption is that a more general form of central limit theorem holds when the sample standard deviation,

$$
\overline{\sigma}_n \equiv \sqrt{\overline{\sigma_n^2}} \geq 0,
$$

is used instead of the true, but unknown, standard deviation σ above [194]. That is, the 95% confidence interval for μ is taken to be

$$
\left[\overline{X}_n - \frac{2\overline{\sigma}_n}{\sqrt{n}}, \ \overline{X}_n + \frac{2\overline{\sigma}_n}{\sqrt{n}}\right]. \tag{1.23}
$$

It turns out that the sample variance defined above is a consistent but *biased* estimator for σ^2. In fact,

$$
\mathsf{E}\overline{\sigma_n^2} = \frac{n-1}{n}\sigma^2. \tag{1.24}
$$

Thus, for a small number n of samples, it may prove more accurate to use

$$
\sqrt{\frac{n}{n-1}\overline{\sigma_n^2}}
$$

instead of $\overline{\sigma}_n$ in the 95% confidence interval formulation above. That is,

$$
\frac{n}{n-1}\overline{\sigma_n^2}
$$

is both a consistent and unbiased estimator of σ^2. Note that this quantity and $\overline{\sigma_n^2}$ are both *consistent* estimators of σ^2, i.e., by the LLN, they both converge to σ^2 as $n \to \infty$.

When the number of available samples n is small (less than 30), the quantity in (1.21) approximately follows a Student's t distribution [106]. Thus, instead of (1.22), the following is used to define the confidence interval for small sample sizes:

$$
\mathsf{P}\left(\left|\frac{\sqrt{n}}{\sigma}(\overline{X}_n - \mu)\right| \leq \zeta_n(0.95)\right) = 0.95, \tag{1.25}
$$

where the function ζ_n is defined by the Student's t distribution with n degrees of freedom (samples).

Confidence intervals are discussed in [155, 194], Section 5.3 of [63], and Section 2.3 of [74].

1.14.3 Recursive formulas and a stopping criterion

In terms of simulation code, a simple *recursive* formula in the number of observed samples for the sample mean and sample standard deviation may be convenient [194]. For the sample mean, we clearly have

$$\overline{X}_n = \frac{1}{n}((n-1)\overline{X}_{n-1} + X_n).$$

Also, the sample variance satisfies

$$\overline{\sigma_n^2} = \overline{\sigma^2}_{n-1} + \frac{1}{n}\left(-\overline{\sigma^2}_{n-1} + (X_n - \overline{X}_n)^2\right). \tag{1.26}$$

Let

$$\gamma_n \equiv \frac{n}{n-1}\overline{\sigma_n^2}$$

be the *unbiased* estimate of the variance. From (1.26), one can derive the following identity:

$$\gamma_n = \gamma_{n-1} - \frac{1}{n-1}\gamma_{n-1} + \frac{1}{n}(X_n - \overline{X}_{n-1})^2. \tag{1.27}$$

Recall that a basic assumption in the computation of the confidence interval above was that the sample points X_i are independent. In practice, a simulation may produce sequences of highly dependent X_i. In this case, several independent *batches* of consecutive samples may be obtainable by simulation [106]. The confidence interval is taken using the sample mean and standard deviation of each batch; note that the "straight" sample mean $\overline{X}_n$ would equal that obtained from the batches.

Finally, in order to arrive at a criterion to terminate a simulation, define the *relative error*

$$\xi_n \equiv \frac{\sqrt{\text{var}(\overline{X}_n)}}{|\overline{X}_n|} \tag{1.28}$$

$$= \frac{\overline{\sigma}_n}{\sqrt{n}|\overline{X}_n|}. \tag{1.29}$$

Here we have assumed $\mu \neq 0$ and $\sigma^2 < \infty$. A simulation may be terminated when the relative error reaches, say, 0.1, i.e., the variance of the sample standard deviation is 10% of the sample mean. Note that we can express the statement of the confidence interval (1.23) as

$$P\left(\frac{\mu}{\overline{X}_n} \in [1 - 2\xi_n, \ 1 + 2\xi_n]\right) \approx 0.95, \tag{1.30}$$

where we could use $\zeta_n(0.95)$, defined using the Student's t distribution in (1.25), instead of "2" in (1.30) if the number of samples n is small. So, using the stopping criterion $\xi_n \leq 0.1$, the claim is then made that the sample mean $\overline{X}_n$ is accurate to within 20% of the true mean with 95% probability. Also, for a relative error of 0.1, the *number of required samples* is, by (1.28),

$$n = 100\left(\frac{\overline{\sigma}_n}{\overline{X}_n}\right)^2 \approx 100\left(\frac{\sigma}{\mu}\right)^2. \tag{1.31}$$

In summary, a simulation produces IID samples X_i from which a sequence of sample means $\overline{X}_n$ and sample variances $\overline{\sigma^2}_n$ are computed. The simulation may be terminated when the computed relative error ξ_n reaches a predefined threshold. The accuracy of the resulting estimate $\overline{X}_n$ of the quantity of interest μ can be interpreted in terms of a confidence interval (implicitly invoking a central limit theorem or Student's t distribution).

■ **EXAMPLE 1.10**

A great deal of current research activity in networking involves *comparisons* of the performance of competing mechanisms (devices, algorithms, protocols, etc.) by simulation or through prototypical deployment on the Internet. Suppose that n trials are conducted for each of two mechanisms in order to compare their performance, leading to a dataset

$$\{D_{k,i}\}_{i=1}^{n}$$

for mechanism $k \in \{1, 2\}$. Also suppose that, for all i, the ith trial (yielding data $D_{1,i}$ and $D_{2,i}$) was conducted under arguably equal environmental conditions for both mechanisms. Let

$$X_i \;\equiv\; D_{1,i} - D_{2,i}$$

be the difference in the performance of the two mechanisms for the common environmental conditions of trial i. That is, for each trial, an "apple-to-apple" comparison is made using *coupled* or *paired* observations.

To assess whether $\mathsf{E}X > 0$ (respectively, $\mathsf{E}X = 0$), we simply compute the confidence interval according to (1.22) or (1.25) and determine whether the origin is to the left of it (respectively, contained by it).

Given uncoupled observations that are different in number, a procedure for deciding whether $\mathsf{E}X = 0$ (i.e., a "t test") is summarized in Section 13.4.2 of [106].

1.15 DECIDING BETWEEN TWO ALTERNATIVE CLAIMS

Suppose that a series of measurements X_i are drawn from the Internet. A problem is that the Internet may be in different "states" of operation leading to samples X_i that are independent but *not* identically distributed. As a great simplification, suppose that the network can be in only one of two states indexed by $j \in \{1, 2\}$. Also suppose that a batch of n samples X_i, $1 \le i \le n$, is taken while the network is in a single state but that state is not known. Finally, suppose it is known that the probability that the network is in state 1 is p_1 and that

$$\mu_j \;=\; \mathsf{E}(X_i \mid \text{network state } j)$$

for *known* values μ_j, $j \in \{1, 2\}$. Without loss of generality, take $\mu_1 < \mu_2$.

We wish to infer from the sample data X_i the state of the network. More specifically, we wish to minimize the probability of error P_e in our decision. To do this, note that by the central limit theorem, *given* that the network is in state j, the sample mean

$$\overline{X}_n \;=\; \frac{1}{n}\sum_{i=1}^{n} X_i$$

is approximately normally distributed with mean μ_j and variance $\sigma_{j,n}^2$. An unbiased, consistent estimate of this variance is

$$\overline{\sigma_{j,n}^2} \;\equiv\; \frac{1}{n-1}\sum_{i=1}^{n}(X_i - \overline{X}_n)^2.$$

To determine the probability of decision error, we will condition on the state of the network:

$$P_e \;=\; \sum_{k=1}^{2} P(\text{error} \mid \text{network state } k)p_k, \tag{1.32}$$

where $p_2 = 1 - p_1$. To this point, we have not described the method by which a decision on the network state is made. Consider a decision based on the comparison of the sample mean $\overline{X}_n$ with a threshold θ, where

$$\mu_1 \le \theta \le \mu_2,$$

so that the network is deemed to be in state 2 (having the higher mean) if $\overline{X}_n > \theta$; otherwise, the network is deemed to be in state 1. So, a more concrete expression for the error probability (1.32) ensues because we can approximate

$$P(\text{error} \mid \text{network in state 2}) \;=\; P(\overline{X}_n \le \theta \mid \text{network in state 2})$$

$$\approx \; \Phi\left(\frac{\mu_2 - \theta}{\sqrt{\sigma_{2,n}^2}}\right),$$

where Φ is 1 minus the CDF of a standard Gaussian distribution. Using a similar argument when conditioning on the network being in state 1, we arrive at the following expression:

$$P_e \;=\; \Phi\left(\frac{\theta - \mu_1}{\sqrt{\sigma_{1,n}^2}}\right)p_1 + \Phi\left(\frac{\mu_2 - \theta}{\sqrt{\sigma_{2,n}^2}}\right)p_2. \tag{1.33}$$

Thus, to determine the optimal value of θ, we need to minimize P_e over θ. This approach can be easily generalized to make decisions among more than two alternative (mutually exclusive) hypotheses. In [113], Wald's classical framework to decide between two alternative claims based on *sequential* independent observations is used on failed scan (connection set-up attempt) data to detect the presence of Internet worms.

Problems

1.1   For any two events A and B show that

$$P(A) \;\le\; P(A \cap B) + P(\overline{B}).$$

1.2   Prove the law of total probability (1.1).

1.3   Consider two independent random variables X_1 and X_2.

(a) Show that they are uncorrelated, i.e., $\text{cov}(X_1, X_2) = 0$.

(b) Show that $\text{var}(X_1 + X_2) = \text{var}(X_1) + \text{var}(X_2)$.

1.4   Suppose that X is a continuous random variable uniformly distributed on the interval $[-1, 1]$ and that $Y = X^2$. Show that X and Y are uncorrelated but that they are (clearly) dependent.

1.5   Two random variables X_1 and X_2 are said to be *jointly Gaussian* distributed if their joint PDF is

$$f_{X_1, X_2}(x_1, x_2) \;=\; \frac{1}{2\pi \, \det(\mathbf{C})} \exp\!\big(-(\underline{x} - \underline{\mu})^{\mathrm{T}} \mathbf{C}^{-1} (\underline{x} - \underline{\mu})\big), \qquad (1.34)$$

where the (symmetric) *covariance matrix* is

$$\mathbf{C} = \begin{bmatrix} \text{var}(X_1) & \text{cov}(X_1, X_2) \\ \text{cov}(X_1, X_2) & \text{var}(X_2) \end{bmatrix}, \qquad \mu = \begin{bmatrix} \mathsf{E}X_1 \\ \mathsf{E}X_2 \end{bmatrix}$$

and $\det(\mathbf{C})$ is the *determinant* of $\mathbf{C}$. Show that if two jointly Gaussian random variables are uncorrelated, then they are also independent.[3]

1.6   For *jointly* Gaussian X_1 and X_2 show:

(a) For scalars α_1 and $\alpha 2$, $\alpha_1 X_1 + \alpha_2 X_2$ (a "linear combination" of Gaussian random variables) is Gaussian distributed.

(b) $\mathsf{E}(X|Y)$ is Gaussian distributed.

1.7   Show that a Bernoulli random variable X with $R_X = \{0, 1\}$ can always be represented as an indicator function $\mathbf{1}_A$ for some event A (express A in terms of X). Prove Jensen's inequality (1.13) for a Bernoulli random variable.

1.8   Prove Jensen's inequality for any discretely distributed random variable.

1.9   Find the MGF of a geometrically distributed random variable and verify the expression given for the MGF corresponding to a Poisson distribution.

1.10   Compute the variance of the distributions described in Sections 1.4 and 1.5.

1.11   If $\mathsf{P}(X \geq 0) = 1$ (i.e., X is nonnegative almost surely), show

$$\mathsf{E}X = \int_0^\infty \mathsf{P}(X > x)\,\mathrm{d}x.$$

1.12   Suppose X is Cauchy distributed with PDF

$$f(x) = \frac{1}{\pi(1 + x^2)}$$

[3]The joint PDF of $n > 2$ jointly Gaussian random variables has the same form as (1.34) except that the 2π term is replaced by the more general term $(2\pi)^{n/2}$.

for $x \in \mathbb{R}$.

(a) Verify that $\mathsf{E}(X\mathbf{1}\{X > 0\}) = \infty$ and that $\mathsf{E}(-X\mathbf{1}\{X < 0\}) = \infty$

(b) Conclude that $\mathsf{E}X$ does not exist. Note that the question of *existence* is different from the question of *finiteness*.

1.13   The *linear least square error* (LLSE) estimator of a random variable X given a random variable Y is a linear function $h(Y) = aY + b$ which minimizes the MSE

$$\mathsf{E}[(X - h(Y))^2];$$

i.e., for the LLSE estimator, the constants a and b are chosen so as to minimize the MSE. Show that the LLSE estimator is the conditional expectation $\mathsf{E}(X|Y)$ when the random variables X and Y are jointly Gaussian with $\mathrm{var}(Y) > 0$ (so, in this case, the best estimator is a linear one).

1.14   For the gamma distribution, verify (1.7) and (1.8) and show that

$$\Gamma_r \;=\; (r-1)!$$

when $r \in \mathbb{Z}^+$.

1.15   Use MGFs to prove that the binomial distribution with parameters n and q converges to the Poisson distribution with parameter λ as $q \to 0$ and $n \to \infty$ in such a way that $nq \to \lambda$. This is Poisson's theorem (sometimes called the law of small numbers). Hint: $(1 + x)^{1/x} \to e$ as $x \downarrow 0$.

1.16   Consider a random variable Y_λ that is Poisson distributed with parameter λ, i.e., $\mathsf{E}Y_\lambda = \lambda$.

(a) Show that $\mathrm{var}(Y_\lambda) = \lambda$ too.

(b) Using MGFs, show that, as $\lambda \to \infty$, the distribution of

$$\frac{Y_\lambda - \lambda}{\sqrt{\lambda}}$$

converges to a standard (mean 0 and variance 1) Gaussian distribution.

This is a kind of CLT for Poisson processes; see Chapter 2. The CLT has been generalized to many other contexts, including functional CLTs on the convergence of stochastic processes to Brownian motion, see [21].

1.17   Prove (1.24).

1.18   Prove (1.26) and (1.27).

1.19   If U is a continuous random variable that is uniformly distributed over $[0, 1]$, show that $F^{-1}(U)$ has CDF F, where

$$F^{-1}(u) \;\equiv\; \inf\{x \mid F(x) = u\}.$$

1.20   Suppose a group of (distinct) persons each has an independent birthday among the 365 possible ones. Determine the minimum number n of such persons required so that the

probability that at least two share a birthday is greater than or equal to 0.5.
Hints: Compute the probability of the complementary event and the answer is between 20
and 25.
The surprisingly small result is known as the birthday paradox.

1.21   Suppose a hacker wishes to have a domain name server (DNS) associate the domain
name www.kesidis.com with one of his own 32-bit Internet Protocol (IP) addresses so that
he can intercept some of the critically important correspondences that are directed to this
site. The hacker simultaneously transmits q identical queries for www.kesidis.com to the
targeted DNS. Further suppose that the targeted DNS naively forwards each query to an
authoritative DNS using IID transaction identifiers (used to authenticate the authoritative
DNS's response) which are 16 bits long and not known to the hacker. Shortly thereafter,
and before the authoritative DNS can reply, the hacker also transmits s responses to the
targeted DNS spoofing those of the authoritative DNS, where each such response associates
www.kesidis.com with the hacker's chosen IP address and contains a guess at one of the
transaction identifiers generated by the targeted DNS. Assuming

$$s \;=\; q \equiv n,$$

find the value of n so that the probability that a forwarded query and spoofed response have
the same transaction identifier is 0.5, i.e., the probability that the hacker guesses correctly
and thereby poisons the targeted DNS's cache.

1.22   In an idealized network using ALOHA medium access control, each of n nodes
attempts to transmit a packet in a time slot with probability p, after the initial packet
transmission failed due to interference from another host. Such retransmission decisions
are independent. Suppose all hosts are synchronized to common time slot boundaries and
that they are always in "retransmission" mode (with a packet to transmit).

(a) Find the probability that a packet is successfully transmitted in a given time slot by
a given node.

(b) Find the probability that a packet is successfully transmitted in a given time slot by
any node.

(c) Find the expected number of successfully transmitted packets per time slot by the
group of nodes, i.e., the network's throughput.

(d) Show that the throughput is maximized by the choice of $p = 1/n$ and that, as $n \to \infty$,
the throughput converges to $1/e \approx 0.37$ packets per time slot.

(d) Show that the maximum throughput of *uns*lotted ALOHA is $1/(2e)$.

1.23   Show that the minimizing value of the decision threshold θ in (1.33) is $(\mu_1 + \mu_2)/2$
when the sample variances are equal, i.e., $\overline{\sigma_{1,n}^2} = \overline{\sigma_{2,n}^2}$.

1.24   Consider a link carrying packets to a Web server. Suppose that, under normal
operating conditions, the link will subject the Web server to a data rate of 4 Mbps. However,
when the Web server is under a DDoS attack, the link will carry an average of 6 Mbps to the
server. An IDS samples the link's data rate and determines whether the server is under attack.
Assume known standard deviations in the data rate of 1 Mbps under normal conditions and

of 1.5 Mbps under attack conditions. Finally, assume attack conditions exist 25% of the time. Find the value of the optimal decision threshold θ (compared against the sample mean) that minimizes the probability of decision error.

1.25   In the previous problem, instead of minimizing the probability of decision error, suppose the probability that it was decided that the network is under attack when, in fact, it was not can be no more than 0.10, i.e.,

$$P_n(\theta) \equiv P(\text{decision error} \mid \text{no attack}) \leq 0.10.$$

Again, this decision is based on the sample mean. Note that this event is called a *false positive* or *type II* error. Such false positives can be caused by legitimate "flash crowds" of temporary but excessive demand. Subject to this bound we wish to minimize the probability of missed detection ("type I" error) of an actual attack:

$$P_a(\theta) \equiv P(\text{decision error} \mid \text{attack}).$$

That is, find

$$\arg \min_{\theta \mid P_n(\theta) \leq 0.10} P_a(\theta).$$

This is called a *Neyman-Pearson test* [174] (of the sample mean with the computed value of θ).

1.26   Consider a simple *binary symmetric channel* model wherein a single bit $X \in \{0, 1\}$ is transmitted and a single bit Y is received such that the transmission error probabilities are equal, i.e., $P(Y = 1 | X = 0) = P(Y = 0 | X = 1) \equiv c_e$. For $i \in \{0, 1\}$, find $P(X = i | Y = i)$ (i.e., the probability that bit i was transmitted given bit i was received) in terms of c_e and $s_0 \equiv P(X = 0)$.

1.27   Suppose that the reported outcome of a poll regarding a presidential race is, "Candidate X will collect 48% of the vote with an error of $\pm 2\%$ 19 times out of 20." Explain this outcome in the terms previously used to describe statistical confidence based on the CLT. Also, what are the basic underlying assumptions about which specific individuals, among the entire voting population, were polled for this statement to hold?

1.28   In the context of Example 1.10, suppose that we have compiled only the separate empirical distributions p_1 and p_2, respectively, based on the data sets $\{D_{1,i}\}_{i=1}^n$ and $\{D_{2,i}\}_{i=1}^n$, but *not* the empirical distribution of $X = D_1 - D_2$ on a trial-by-trial basis. Given p_1 and p_2:

(a) Can we obtain the empirical mean $\overline{X}_n$ of X?

(b) Can we obtain the empirical variance of X?

CHAPTER 2

MARKOV CHAINS

A stochastic (or *random*) process is a collection of random variables indexed by a parameter in a domain. In this book, this parameter will be interpreted as *time* (stochastic processes describing images can be indexed by more than one *spatial* parameter and those describing video will have joint spatial and temporal indexes). If the time parameter takes values only in $\mathbb{Z}^+$ (or any other countable subset of $\mathbb{R}$), the stochastic process is said to be discrete time; i.e.,

$$\{X(t) \mid t \in \mathbb{Z}^+\}$$

is a discrete time stochastic process when $X(t)$ is a random variable for all $t \in \mathbb{Z}^+$. If the time parameter t takes values over $\mathbb{R}$ or $\mathbb{R}^+$ (or any real interval), the stochastic process is said to be *continuous time*.

The dependence on the sample $\omega \in \Omega$ can be explicitly indicated by writing $X_\omega(t)$. For a given sample ω, the random object mapping $t \to X_\omega(t)$, for all $t \in \mathbb{R}^+$ say, is called a *sample path* of the stochastic process X.

The *state space* of a stochastic process is simply the union of the strict ranges of the random variables $\{X(t) \mid t \in \mathbb{Z}^+\}$. In this book, we will restrict our attention to stochastic processes with countable state spaces. In this chapter and for the majority of the examples that follow, we will take the state space to be $\mathbb{Z}$, $\mathbb{Z}^+$, or a finite subset $\{0, 1, 2, ..., K\}$. Of course, this means that the random variables $X(t)$ are all discretely distributed.

Most of the queuing systems studied in this book are substantially simpler to analyze when they are considered operating in continuous time. So, we focus our attention on continuous-time Markov chains in this chapter. Discrete-time Markov chains are briefly covered at the end of the chapter. Refer to [20, 118, 119, 161, 193] for further details concerning Markov processes.

2.1 MEMORYLESS PROPERTY OF THE EXPONENTIAL DISTRIBUTION

In this section, the salient properties of exponentially distributed random variables are discussed. These properties are fundamental to the subsequent construction of Markov chains.

Theorem 2.1.1. *If X is exponentially distributed,*

$$P(X > x + y \mid X > y) = \mathsf{P}(X > x).$$

This is the *memoryless* property and its simple proof is left as an exercise. For example, if X represents the duration of the lifetime of a light bulb, the memoryless property implies that, given that $X > y$, the probability that the *residual* lifetime $(X - y)$ is greater than x is equal to the probability that the *unconditioned* lifetime is greater than x. So, in this sense, given $X > y$, the lifetime has "forgotten" that $X > y$. Only exponentially distributed random variables have this property among all continuously distributed random variables (see Problem 2.3 at the end of the chapter) and only geometrically distributed random variables have this property among all discretely distributed random variables.

Now suppose that X_1 and X_2 are *independent* and exponentially distributed random variables with parameters λ_1 and λ_2, respectively. The following two properties will be fundamental to our discussion of Markov processes in this chapter.

Theorem 2.1.2. $\min\{X_1, X_2\}$ *is exponentially distributed with parameter* $\lambda_1 + \lambda_2$.

Proof: Define $Z = \min\{X_1, X_2\}$ and let F_Z, F_1, and F_2 be the CDF of Z, X_1, and X_2, respectively. Clearly, $F_Z(z) = 0$ for $z < 0$. For $z \geq 0$,

$$
\begin{aligned}
1 - F_Z(z) &= \mathsf{P}(\min\{X_1, X_2\} > z) \\
&= \mathsf{P}(X_1 > z, X_2 > z) \\
&= \mathsf{P}(X_1 > z)\mathsf{P}(X_2 > z) \quad \text{by independence} \\
&= \exp(-(\lambda_1 + \lambda_2)z)
\end{aligned}
$$

as desired.   □

Theorem 2.1.3.

$$\mathsf{P}(\min\{X_1, X_2\} = X_1) = \frac{\lambda_1}{\lambda_1 + \lambda_2}.$$

Proof:

$$
\begin{aligned}
\mathsf{P}(\min\{X_1, X_2\} = X_1) &= \mathsf{P}(X_1 \le X_2) \\
&= \int_{-\infty}^{\infty} \int_{-\infty}^{x_2} \lambda_1 \mathrm{e}^{-\lambda_1 x_1}\, \mathrm{d}x_1 \; \lambda_2 \mathrm{e}^{-\lambda_2 x_2}\, \mathrm{d}x_2 \\
&= \int_{-\infty}^{\infty} \lambda_2 \mathrm{e}^{-(\lambda_1 + \lambda_2)x_2}\, \mathrm{d}x_2 \\
&= \frac{\lambda_1}{\lambda_1 + \lambda_2}
\end{aligned}
$$

as desired.   □

Two independent geometrically distributed random variables also have these properties.

2.2 FINITE-DIMENSIONAL DISTRIBUTIONS AND STATIONARITY

Consider a stochastic process

$$\{X(t) \mid t \in \mathbb{R}^+\}$$

with state space $\mathbb{Z}^+$. Let $p_{t_1, t_2, \ldots, t_n}$ be the joint PMF of $X(t_1), X(t_2), \ldots, X(t_n)$ for some finite n and different $t_k \in \mathbb{R}^+$ for all $k \in \{1, 2, \ldots, n\}$, i.e.,

$$p_{t_1, t_2, \ldots, t_n}(x_1, x_2, \ldots, x_n) = \mathsf{P}(X(t_1) = x_1, X(t_2) = x_2, \ldots, X(t_n) = x_n). \qquad (2.1)$$

This is called an *n-dimensional distribution* of X. The family of all such joint PMFs is called the set of *finite-dimensional distributions* (FDDs) of X. Note that the FDDs are *consistent* in that one can marginalize (reduce the dimension) and obtain another, e.g.,

$$p_{t_1, t_2, t_4}(x_1, x_2, x_4) \equiv \sum_{x_3 \in \mathbb{Z}^+} p_{t_1, t_2, t_3, t_4}(x_1, x_2, x_3, x_4). \qquad (2.2)$$

Beginning with a family of consistent FDDs, Kolmogorov's extension (or "consistency") theorem [104] is a general result demonstrating the existence of a stochastic process $t \to X_\omega(t)$, $\omega \in \Omega$, that possesses them. In the following sections, we will begin with a sample path definition of a Markov process and, from that, show how to derive its FDDs.

A stochastic process X is said to be *stationary* if all of its FDDs are time-shift invariant, i.e., if

$$p_{t_1, t_2, \ldots, t_n} \equiv p_{t_1 + \tau, t_2 + \tau, \ldots, t_n + \tau} \qquad (2.3)$$

for all integers $n \ge 1$, all $t_k \in \mathbb{R}^+$, and all $\tau \in \mathbb{R}$ such that $t_k + \tau \in \mathbb{R}^+$ for all k.

A weaker definition for stationarity is *wide-sense stationarity* (WSS), which only requires:

(i) $\mathsf{E}X(t)$ is a constant function of t and

(ii) the *autocorrelation* $\mathsf{E}[X(t)X(s)]$ depends on t and s only through their difference $t-s$, i.e.,

$$\mathsf{E}[X(t)X(s)] \;=\; \mathsf{E}[X(t+\tau)X(s+\tau)] \;=\; R(t-s)$$

for all τ, where R is the autocorrelation function of X.

The WSS processes are important in communication theory wherein signals are corrupted by interference and noise (in particular, additive broadband *white* noise having autocorrelation function $R = \delta$, the Dirac delta function). Such signals can be filtered by linear time-invariant systems and analyzed in the frequency domain. The Fourier transform of a WSS signal's autocorrelation is its *power spectral density* [164]. Queues are, however, highly nonlinear systems so we will not consider further the class of WSS signals in this book, but see [52] for an interesting application of linear systems theory to queues.

2.3   THE POISSON (COUNTING) PROCESS ON $\mathbb{R}^+$

A *counting process* X on $\mathbb{R}^+$ is characterized by the following properties:

(a) X has state space $\mathbb{Z}^+$,

(b) X has nondecreasing (in time) sample paths that are continuous from the right, i.e.,

$$\lim_{t\downarrow s} X(t) \;=\; X(s), \quad \text{and}$$

(c) $X(t) \le X(t-) + 1$ so that X does make a single transition of size 2 or more, where $t-$ is a time immediately prior to t, i.e.,

$$X(t-) \;\equiv\; \lim_{s\uparrow t} X(s).$$

For example, consider a post office where the ith customer arrives at time $T_i \in \mathbb{R}^+$. We take the origin of time to be zero and, clearly, $T_i \le T_{i+1}$ for all i. The *total number* of customers that arrived over the interval of time $[0, t]$ is defined to be $X(t)$. Note that $X(T_i) = i$, $X(t) < i$ if $t < T_i$, and $X(t) - X(s)$ is the number of customers that have arrived over the interval $(s, t]$. In other words,

$$X(t) = \sum_{i=1}^{\infty} \mathbf{1}\{T_i \le t\} = \max\{i \mid T_i \le t\}.$$

Of course, X is an example of a continuous-time counting process that is continuous from the right. For a sample path of X see Figure 2.1.

Consider the sequence of *interarrival* times $S_i = T_i - T_{i-1}$ for $i \in \{1, 2, 3, ...\}$, where

$$T_0 \equiv 0.$$

A *Poisson process* is a continuous-time counting process whose interarrival times $\{S_i\}_{i=1}^{\infty}$ are mutually IID *exponential* random variables. Let the parameter of the exponential distribution of the S_i's be λ, i.e., $\mathsf{E}S_i = \lambda^{-1}$ for all i. Since

$$T_n = \sum_{i=1}^{n} S_i,$$

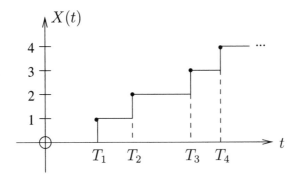

Figure 2.1 A sample path of the Poisson process.

T_n is Erlang (gamma) distributed with parameters λ and n; see Section 1.9.1.

A natural question to ask about a stochastic process X is: What is the distribution of $X(t)$ for some specified time t? In other words, what is the (one-dimensional) *marginal* distribution of the process? We will show that for the Poisson process, $X(t)$ is Poisson *distributed* with mean λt. For this reason, λ is sometimes called the *intensity* (or "mean rate" or just "rate") of the Poisson process X.

Theorem 2.3.1. $X(t)$ *is Poisson distributed with parameter* λt.

Proof: First note that, for $t \geq 0$,

$$P(X(t) = 0) \; = \; P(T_1 > t) \;\; = \;\; e^{-\lambda t}. \tag{2.4}$$

Now, for an integer $i > 0$ and a real $t \geq 0$,

$$P(X(t) \leq i) \;\; = \;\; P(T_{i+1} > t) \;\; = \;\; \int_t^\infty \frac{\lambda^{i+1} z^i e^{-\lambda z}}{i!} \, dz,$$

where we have used the gamma PDF; see Equation (1.18). By integrating by parts, we get

$$
\begin{aligned}
P(X(t) \leq i) \;\; &= \;\; \frac{\lambda^i z^i}{i!}(-e^{-\lambda z})\big|_t^\infty + \int_t^\infty \frac{\lambda^i z^{i-1} e^{-\lambda z}}{(i-1)!} \, dz \\
&= \;\; \frac{(\lambda t)^i e^{-\lambda t}}{i!} + \int_t^\infty \frac{\lambda^i z^{i-1} e^{-\lambda z}}{(i-1)!} \, dz.
\end{aligned}
$$

After successively integrating by parts in this manner, we get

$$
\begin{aligned}
P(X(t) \leq i) \;\; &= \;\; \frac{(\lambda t)^i e^{-\lambda t}}{i!} + \cdots + \frac{(\lambda t)^1 e^{-\lambda t}}{1!} + \int_t^\infty \lambda e^{-\lambda z} \, dz \\
&= \;\; \sum_{j=0}^{i} \frac{(\lambda t)^j e^{-\lambda t}}{j!}.
\end{aligned}
$$

Now note that $\{X(t) = i\}$ and $\{X(t) \le i - 1\}$ are disjoint events and

$$\{X(t) = i\} \cup \{X(t) \le i - 1\} \;=\; \{X(t) \le i\}.$$

Thus,

$$
\begin{aligned}
\mathsf{P}(X(t) = i) &= \mathsf{P}(X(t) \le i) - \mathsf{P}(X(t) \le i - 1) \\
&= \sum_{j=0}^{i} \frac{(\lambda t)^j e^{-\lambda t}}{j!} - \sum_{j=0}^{i-1} \frac{(\lambda t)^j e^{-\lambda t}}{j!} \\
&= \frac{(\lambda t)^i e^{-\lambda t}}{i!},
\end{aligned}
$$

which is the Poisson PMF as desired. $\qquad\square$

Now consider k disjoint intervals of real time $(s_1, t_1]$, $(s_2, t_2]$, ..., $(s_k, t_k]$ with

$$s_1 < t_1 < s_2 < t_2 < \cdots < s_k < t_k. \tag{2.5}$$

Here, X is a Poisson process if and only if, for all k, all $s_1, t_1, s_2, t_2, \ldots, s_k, t_k \in \mathbb{R}^+$ satisfying (2.5), and all $n_1, n_2, \ldots, n_k \in \mathbb{Z}^+$,

$$
\begin{aligned}
&\mathsf{P}(X(t_1) - X(s_1) = n_1, \; X(t_2) - X(s_2) = n_2, \; ..., \; X(t_k) - X(s_k) = n_k) \\
&= \prod_{i=1}^{k} \frac{[\lambda(t_i - s_i)]^{n_i}}{n_i!} e^{-\lambda(t_i - s_i)}.
\end{aligned}
\tag{2.6}
$$

Note that $X(t_i) - X(s_i)$ (which is called an *increment* of X) is the number of transitions of the Poisson process in the interval of time $(s_i, t_i]$. Thus, (2.6) states that the Poisson process has *independent (nonoverlapping) increments*. Also, the increment over a time interval of length τ is Poisson distributed with parameter $\lambda \tau$ (a slight generalization of Theorem 2.3.1). The Poisson process is the only counting process that

- has Poisson distributed independent increments, or

- has IID exponentially distributed interarrival times, or

- possesses the *conditional uniformity* property [55, 183]; see Problem 2.14.

That is, all of these properties are equivalent. The memoryless property of the exponential distribution is principally responsible for the independent increments property of a Poisson process, as will be argued in a more general Markovian context in the next section.

We will now drive the k-dimensional marginal distribution of a Poisson process by using the independent increments property. So, consider times $0 \le t_1 < t_2 < \cdots < t_k$ and

$$\mathsf{P}(X(t_1) = m_1, \; X(t_2) = m_2, \; ..., \; X(t_k) = m_k), \tag{2.7}$$

where $m_1, m_2, ..., m_k \in \mathbb{Z}$ and $m_i \le m_{i+1}$ for all i (otherwise the probability above would be zero). Defining $\Delta m_i \equiv m_i - m_{i-1}$ and $\Delta X_i \equiv X(t_i) - X(t_{i-1})$, the quantity in (2.7) equals

$$
\begin{aligned}
&\mathsf{P}(X(t_1) = m_1, \; \Delta X_2 = \Delta m_2, \; ..., \; \Delta X_k = \Delta m_k) \\
&= \mathsf{P}(\Delta X_2 = \Delta m_2, \; ..., \; \Delta X_k = \Delta m_k \mid X(t_1) = m_1) \, \mathsf{P}(X(t_1) = m_1) \\
&= \mathsf{P}(\Delta X_2 = \Delta m_2, \; ..., \; \Delta X_k = \Delta m_k) \, \mathsf{P}(X(t_1) = m_1),
\end{aligned}
$$

where the last equality is by the independent increments property. By repeating this argument, we get that the quantity in (2.7) equals

$$P(X(t_1) = m_1) \prod_{i=2}^{k} P(X(t_i) - X(t_{i-1}) = m_i - m_{i-1})$$

$$= \frac{(\lambda t_1)^{m_1}}{m_1!} e^{-\lambda t_1} \prod_{i=2}^{k} \frac{(\lambda(t_i - t_{i-1}))^{m_i - m_{i-1}}}{(m_i - m_{i-1})!} e^{-\lambda(t_i - t_{i-1})},$$

which is in agreement with (2.6).

2.4 CONTINUOUS-TIME, TIME-HOMOGENEOUS MARKOV PROCESSES WITH COUNTABLE STATE SPACE

We will now define a kind of stochastic process called a *Markov* process of which the Poisson process is an example; more specifically, a Poisson process is a variety of (transient) *pure birth* Markov process. A Markov process over a countable state space Σ is sometimes called a Markov *chain*. Without loss of generality, we will subsequently take $\Sigma = \mathbb{Z}^+$. A Markov chain is a kind of *random walk* on Σ. It visits a state, stays there for an exponentially distributed amount of time, then makes a transition at random to another state, stays at this new state for an exponentially distributed amount of time, then makes a transition at random to another state, etc. All of these visit times and transitions are independent in a way that will be more precisely explained in the following.

2.4.1 The Markov property

Definition 2.4.1. *If, for all integers $k \geq 1$, all subsets $A, B, B_1, ..., B_k \subset \Sigma$, and all times $t, s, s_1, ..., s_k \in \mathbb{R}^+$ such that $t > s > s_1 > \cdots > s_k$,*

$$P(X(t) \in A \mid X(s) \in B, \, X(s_1) \in B_1, \, \cdots, \, X(s_k) \in B_k)$$
$$= P(X(t) \in A \mid X(s) \in B), \qquad (2.8)$$

then the stochastic process X is said to possess the Markov property.

If we identify $X(t)$ as a *future* value of the process, $X(s)$ as the *present* value, and *past* values as $X(s_1), ..., X(s_k)$, then the Markov property asserts that the *future and the past are conditionally independent given the present*. In other words, given the present *state* $X(s)$ of a Markov process, one does not require knowledge of the past to determine its future evolution. Any stochastic process (on any state space with any time domain) that has the Markov property is called a Markov process. As such, the Markov property is a "stochastic extension" of notions of state associated with finite-state machines and linear time-invariant systems.

The property (2.8) is an immediate consequence of a slightly stronger and more succinctly stated Markov property: for all times $s < t$ and any (measurable) function f,

$$\mathsf{E}(f(X_t) \mid X_r,\ 0 \le r \le s) \ =\ \mathsf{E}(f(X_t) \mid X_s). \qquad (2.9)$$

2.4.2 Sample path construction of a time-homogeneous, continuous-time Markov chain

In this section, how a Markov chain X makes transitions from state to state will be described. For a *time-homogeneous* Markov chain, consider each state $n \in \mathbb{Z}^+$ and let

$$\frac{1}{-q_{n,n}} \ >\ 0$$

be the mean visiting time of the Markov process, i.e., $q_{n,n} < 0$. That is, a Markov chain is said to enter state n at time T and subsequently visit state n for S seconds if $X(T-) \ne n$, $X(t) = n$ for all $T \le t < S + T$, and $X(S + T) \ne n$. Also, define the assumed finite set of states

$$\mathcal{T}_n \ \subset\ \mathbb{Z}^+\backslash\{n\}$$

to which a transition is possible directly from n. For all $m \in \mathcal{T}_n$, define $q_{n,m} > 0$ such that the probability of a transition from n to m is

$$-\frac{q_{n,m}}{q_{n,n}} \ >\ 0.$$

Thus, we clearly need to require that

$$\sum_{m \in \mathcal{T}_n} -\frac{q_{n,m}}{q_{n,n}} \ =\ 1,$$

i.e., for all $n \in \mathbb{Z}^+$,

$$\sum_{m \in \mathbb{Z}^+} q_{n,m} \ =\ 0, \qquad (2.10)$$

where $q_{n,m} \equiv 0$ for all $m \notin \mathcal{T} \cup \{n\}$.

Now let T_i be the time of the ith *state transition* with $T_0 \equiv 0$, i.e., the process X is constant on intervals $[T_{i-1}, T_i)$ and

$$X(T_{i-1}) \ =\ X(T_i-) \ne X(T_i)$$

for all $i \in \mathbb{Z}^+$. Let the column vector $\underline{\pi}(0)$ represent the distribution of $X(0)$ on $\mathbb{Z}^+$, so that entry in the nth row is

$$\pi_n(0) \ =\ \mathsf{P}(X(0) = n),$$

i.e., $\underline{\pi}(0)$ is the *initial distribution* of the stochastic process X.

An alternative description of how a Markov chain X with time domain $\mathbb{R}^+$ makes transitions from state to state will now be given. Suppose that $X(T_i) = n \in \mathbb{Z}^+$. To the states $m \in \mathcal{T}_n$, associate an *exponentially* distributed random variable $S_i(n, m)$ with parameter $q_{n,m} > 0$ (recall this means $\mathsf{E}S_i(n, m) = 1/q_{n,m}$). Given $X(T_i) = n$, the *smallest* of the random variables

$$\{S_i(n, m) \mid m \in \mathcal{T}_n\}$$

determines $X(T_{i+1})$ and the intertransition time $T_{i+1} - T_i$. That is, $X(T_{i+1}) = j$ if and only if

$$T_{i+1} - T_i \;=\; S_i(n, j) \;=\; \min_{m \in \mathcal{T}_n} S_i(n, m).$$

The entire collection of exponential random variables

$$\{S_i(n, m) \mid i \in \mathbb{Z}^+, n \in \mathbb{Z}^+, m \in \mathcal{T}_n\}$$

are assumed mutually independent. Therefore, by Theorem 2.1.2 and (2.10), the intertransition time $T_{i+1} - T_i$ is exponentially distributed with parameter

$$-q_{n,n} \;\equiv\; \sum_{m \in \mathcal{T}_n} q_{n,m}, \tag{2.11}$$

so that

$$\mathsf{E}(T_{i+1} - T_i) \;=\; \frac{1}{-q_{n,n}} > 0$$

in particular. Also, the state transition probabilities

$$\begin{aligned} \mathsf{P}(X(T_{i+1}) = j \mid X(T_i) = n) \;&=\; \mathsf{P}(S_i(n, j) = \min_{m \in \mathcal{T}_n} S_i(n, m)) \\ &=\; -\frac{q_{n,j}}{q_{n,n}}, \end{aligned} \tag{2.12}$$

where the last equality is by Theorem 2.1.3 and definition (2.11). Note again that if a transition from state n to state j is impossible (has probability zero), $q_{n,j} = 0$.

In this book, we will always assume that

$$-q_{n,n} \;<\; \infty \text{ for all states } n,$$

i.e., the Markov chain is *conservative*. Also, we have assumed that the Markov chain is *temporally (time) homogeneous*, i.e., for all times $s, t \geq 0$ and all states n, m:

$$\mathsf{P}(X(s + t) = n \mid X(s) = m) = \mathsf{P}(X(t) = n \mid X(0) = m). \tag{2.13}$$

In summary, assuming the initial distribution $\pi(0)$ and the parameters

$$\{q_{n,m} \mid n, m \in \mathbb{Z}^+\}$$

are known, we have described how to construct a sample path of the Markov chain X from a collection of independent random variables

$$\{S_i(n, m) \mid i \in \mathbb{Z}^+, \, n \in \Sigma = \mathbb{Z}^+, \, m \in \mathcal{T}_n\},$$

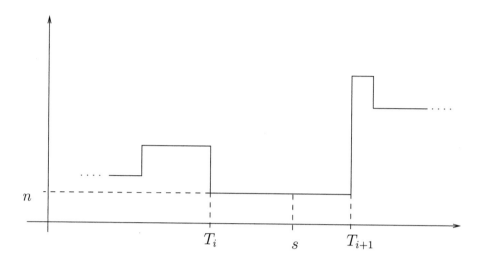

Figure 2.2   A sample path of a Markov chain.

where $S_i(n, m)$ is an exponentially distributed with parameter $q_{n,m}$. When a Markov chain visits state n, it stays an exponentially distributed amount of time with mean $-1/q_{n,n}$ and then makes a transition to another state $m \in \mathcal{T}_n$ with probability $-q_{n,m}/q_{n,n}$.

To prove that the processes thus constructed are Markovian (i.e., satisfy the Markov properties (2.8) and (2.9)), let $n = X(s)$ and let i be the number of transitions of X prior to the present time s. Clearly, the random variables i, n, and T_i (the last transition time prior to s) can be discerned from $\{X_r, \ 0 \le r \le s\}$ and can therefore be considered "given" as well. The memoryless property of the random variable $T_{i+1} - T_i$, distributed exponentially with parameter $-q_{n,n}$, implies that

$$
\begin{aligned}
&\mathsf{P}(T_{i+1} - s > x \mid T_{i+1} - T_i > s - T_i) \\
&= \quad \mathsf{P}(T_{i+1} - T_i > x + (s - T_i) \mid T_{i+1} - T_i > s - T_i) \\
&= \quad \mathsf{P}(T_{i+1} - T_i > x) \\
&= \quad \exp(q_{n,n}x)
\end{aligned}
$$

for all $x > 0$; see Figure 2.2. Note that $\exp(q_{n,n}x)$ depends on $\{X_r, \ 0 \le r \le s\}$ only through $n = X(s)$. So, $T_{i+1} - s$ is exponentially distributed with parameter $-q_{n,n}$ and conditionally independent of $s - T_i$ given $\{X_r, \ 0 \le r \le s\}$. Furthermore, $\{X_r, \ 0 \le r < T_i\}$ is similarly conditionally independent of $\{X_r, \ r \ge T_{i+1}\}$ given $X(s) = n$ (by the assumed mutual independence of the $\{S_i(n, m)\}$ random variables).

Since the exponential distribution is the only continuous one that possesses the memoryless property,[1] one can show the converse statement, i.e., that the previous constructions are implied by (2.8) and (2.9).

---

[1] Again, the proof of this statement is left as an exercise; see Problem 2.3 at the end of the chapter.

■ **EXAMPLE 2.1**

Clearly, a Poisson process with intensity λ is an example of a Markov chain with transition rates

$$q_{n,m} = \begin{cases} \lambda & \text{if } m = n+1, \\ -\lambda & \text{if } m = n, \\ 0 & \text{else.} \end{cases}$$

2.4.3 The transition rate matrix and transition rate diagram

The matrix $\mathbf{Q}$ having $q_{n,m}$ as its entry in the nth row and mth column is called the *transition rate matrix* (or just "rate matrix") of the Markov chain X. Note that, by (2.10), the sum of the entries in any row of the matrix $\mathbf{Q}$ equals zero. The nth row of $\mathbf{Q}$ corresponds to state n *from* which transitions occur, and the mth column of $\mathbf{Q}$ corresponds to states m *to* which transitions occur. For $n \neq m$, the parameter $q_{n,m}$ is called a *transition rate* because, for any $i \in \mathbb{Z}^+$, $\mathsf{E}S_i(n,m) = 1/q_{n,m}$. Thus, we expect that, if $q_{n,m} > q_{n,j}$, then transitions from state n to m will tend to be made more frequently (at a higher *rate*) by the Markov chain than transitions from state n to j.

■ **EXAMPLE 2.2**

For example, the transition matrix of a Poisson process with intensity $\lambda > 0$ is

$$\mathbf{Q} = \begin{bmatrix} -\lambda & \lambda & 0 & 0 & 0 & \cdots \\ 0 & -\lambda & \lambda & 0 & 0 & \cdots \\ 0 & 0 & -\lambda & \lambda & 0 & \cdots \\ \vdots & \vdots & \vdots & \vdots & \vdots & \ddots \end{bmatrix}$$

■ **EXAMPLE 2.3**

As another example, suppose the strict state space of X is $\{0, 1, 2\}$ and the rate matrix is

$$\mathbf{Q} = \begin{bmatrix} -5 & 2 & 3 \\ 0 & -4 & 4 \\ 1 & 0 & -1 \end{bmatrix} \tag{2.14}$$

Note how we use just a 3×3 rate matrix $\mathbf{Q}$ since the *strict* state space is just a 3-tuple $\{0, 1, 2\}$ rather than all of the nonnegative integers, $\mathbb{Z}^+$. Similarly, the stationary distribution π would be a three-dimensional vector. Also note that, in this example, a direct transition from state 2 to state 1 is impossible (as is a direct transition from state 1 to state 0). Also, each visit to state 0 lasts an exponentially distributed amount

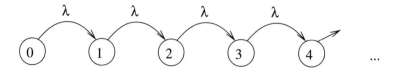

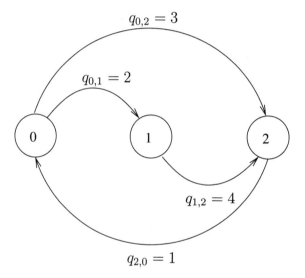

Figure 2.3   The transition rate diagram of the Poisson process.

Figure 2.4   A transition rate diagram on state space $\{0, 1, 2\}$.

of time with parameter 5 (i.e., with mean 0.2); a transition to state 1 then occurs with probability $\frac{2}{5}$ or a transition to state 2 occurs with probability $\frac{3}{5}$.

We can also represent the transition rates graphically by what is called a *transition rate diagram*. The states of the Markov chain are circled and arrows are used to indicate the possible transitions between states. The transition rate itself labels the corresponding arrow (transition). The transition rate diagrams of the previous two examples are given in Figures 2.3 and 2.4, respectively. When an arrow is drawn and labeled with a transition rate q, the transition rate is assumed to be strictly positive.

2.4.4 The Kolmogorov equations

Consider again the Markov chain X with rate matrix $\mathbf{Q}$. For $\tau \in \mathbb{R}^+$ and $n, m \in \mathbb{Z}^+$, define

$$p_{n,m}(\tau) \;=\; \mathsf{P}(X(s+\tau) = m \mid X(s) = n).$$

Note again that we are assuming that the chain is temporally homogeneous so that the right-hand side of the above equation does not depend on time s. The matrix $\mathbf{P}(\tau)$ whose entry in the nth row and mth column is $p_{n,m}(\tau)$ is called the *transition probability matrix*. Finally, for each time $s \in \mathbb{R}^+$, define the sequence

$$\pi_n(s) \;\equiv\; \mathsf{P}(X(s) = n) \ \text{ for } n \in \mathbb{Z}^+.$$

So, the column vector $\underline{\pi}(s)$, whose ith entry is $\pi_i(s)$, is the marginal distribution of X at time s, i.e., the distribution (PMF) of $X(s)$.

Conditioning on $X(s)$ and using the law of total probability (1.1),

$$\mathsf{P}(X(s+\tau) = m) \;=\; \sum_{n=0}^{\infty} \mathsf{P}(X(s+\tau) = m \mid X(s) = n)\mathsf{P}(X(s) = n)$$

for all $m \in \mathbb{Z}^+$, i.e.,

$$\pi_m(s+\tau) \;=\; \sum_{i=0}^{\infty} p_{n,m}(\tau)\pi_n(s) \ \text{ for all } m \in \mathbb{Z}^+.$$

We can write these equations compactly in matrix form:

$$\underline{\pi}^{\mathrm{T}}(s+\tau) \;=\; \underline{\pi}^{\mathrm{T}}(s)\mathbf{P}(\tau), \tag{2.15}$$

where $\underline{\pi}^{\mathrm{T}}(s)$ is the *transpose* of the column vector $\underline{\pi}(s)$, i.e., $\underline{\pi}^{\mathrm{T}}(s)$ is a row vector.

Moreover, any FDD of the Markov chain can be computed from the transition probability functions and the initial distribution. For example, for times $t > s > r > 0$,

$$
\begin{aligned}
&\mathsf{P}(X(t) = n, \ X(s) = m, \ X(r) = k) \\
&= \ \mathsf{P}(X(t) = n \mid X(s) = m, \ X(r) = k)\mathsf{P}(X(s) = m, \ X(r) = k) \\
&= \ \mathsf{P}(X(t) = n \mid X(s) = m)\mathsf{P}(X(s) = m \mid X(r) = k)\mathsf{P}(X(r) = k) \\
&= \ p_{m,n}(t - s)p_{k,m}(s - r)\sum_{i} \mathsf{P}(X(r) = k \mid X(0) = i)\mathsf{P}(X(0) = i) \\
&= \ p_{m,n}(t - s)p_{k,m}(s - r)\sum_{i} \mathsf{P}(X(r) = k \mid X(0) = i)\mathsf{P}(X(0) = i) \\
&= \ p_{m,n}(t - s)p_{k,m}(s - r)\sum_{i} p_{i,k}(r)\pi_i(0) \tag{2.16}
\end{aligned}
$$

where the second equality is the Markov property. In the second-to-last expression, we clearly see the transition from some initial state to k at time r, then to state m at time s ($s - r$ seconds later), and finally to to state n at time t ($t - s$ seconds later).

Our objective in the remainder of this section is to compute the transition probability matrix $\mathbf{P}(t)$ in terms of the known transition rate matrix $\mathbf{Q}$. First note that

$$p_{n,m}(0) = \mathbf{1}\{n = m\}$$

(a transition in an interval of time of length zero occurs with probability zero), which can be written in matrix form as

$$\mathbf{P}(0) = \mathbf{I}, \tag{2.17}$$

where $\mathbf{I}$ is the (multiplicative) identity matrix, i.e., the square matrix with 1's in every diagonal entry and 0's in every off-diagonal entry. Now consider the quantity

$$p_{n,m}(\varepsilon) = \mathrm{P}(X(s+\varepsilon) = m \mid X(s) = n)$$

for $n \neq m$, a *small* amount of time $0 < \varepsilon \ll 1$, and an arbitrarily chosen time $s \in \mathbb{R}^+$. Let V_n be the *residual* holding time in state n after time s, i.e., $X(t) = n$ for all $t \in [s, s+V_n)$ and $X(s+V_n) \neq n$. The total holding time in state n is exponentially distributed with parameter $-q_{n,n}$ and therefore, by the memoryless property, V_n is also exponentially distributed with parameter $-q_{n,n}$. Thus,

$$p_{n,m}(\varepsilon) = \mathrm{P}(V_n \leq \varepsilon) \times \frac{q_{n,m}}{-q_{n,n}} + \mathrm{o}(\varepsilon). \tag{2.18}$$

We will now explain the terms of the right-hand side. The first term represents the probability that the Markov chain X makes only a single transition (from n to m) in interval of time $(s, s + \varepsilon]$. Recall that the probability that X makes a transition to state m from state n is $-q_{n,m}/q_{n,n}$. The symbol $\mathrm{o}(\varepsilon)$ ("little oh of ε") represents a function satisfying

$$\lim_{\varepsilon \to 0} \frac{\mathrm{o}(\varepsilon)}{\varepsilon} = 0.$$

In (2.18), the term $\mathrm{o}(\varepsilon)$ represents the probability that the Markov chain has *two or more* transitions in the interval of time $(s, s + \varepsilon]$; see Problem 2.5 at the end of this chapter.

Now note that

$$\begin{aligned}
\mathrm{P}(V_n \leq \varepsilon) &= 1 - \exp(\varepsilon q_{n,n}) \\
&= -\varepsilon q_{n,n} + \mathrm{o}(\varepsilon),
\end{aligned}$$

so that, after substituting into (2.18), we get

$$p_{n,m}(\varepsilon) = q_{n,m}\varepsilon + \mathrm{o}(\varepsilon), \tag{2.19}$$

which implies that

$$\frac{p_{n,m}(\varepsilon) - p_{n,m}(0)}{\varepsilon} = q_{n,m} + \frac{\mathrm{o}(\varepsilon)}{\varepsilon},$$

where we recall that $p_{n,m}(0) = 0$ for all $n \neq m$. Letting $\varepsilon \to 0$, we get

$$\dot{p}_{n,m}(0) = q_{n,m}, \tag{2.20}$$

where the left-hand side is the *time derivative* of $p_{n,m}$ at time 0. Finally, since

$$p_{n,n}(\varepsilon) = 1 - \sum_{m \in \mathbb{Z}^+, \, m \neq n} p_{n,m}(\varepsilon),$$

we get, after differentiating with respect to time,

$$\dot{p}_{n,n}(0) = -\sum_{m \neq n} q_{n,m} = q_{n,n} < 0, \tag{2.21}$$

where we have used the *definition* of $q_{n,n}$. In matrix form, (2.20) and (2.21) are

$$\dot{\mathbf{P}}(0) = \mathbf{Q}. \tag{2.22}$$

In fact, this statement can be generalized to obtain the *Kolmogorov backward equations*:

Theorem 2.4.1. *For all* $s \geq 0$,

$$\dot{\mathbf{P}}(s) = \mathbf{P}(s)\mathbf{Q}. \tag{2.23}$$

Proof: By (2.22) and (2.17),

$$\dot{\mathbf{P}}(0) = \mathbf{I}\mathbf{Q} = \mathbf{P}(0)\mathbf{Q},$$

which gives the desired result for $s = 0$. For $s > 0$, take a real ε such that

$$0 < \varepsilon \ll \min\{s, 1\}.$$

So,

$$
\begin{aligned}
p_{n,m}(s) &= \mathsf{P}(X(s) = m \mid X(0) = n) \\
&= \frac{\mathsf{P}(X(s) = m,\, X(0) = n)}{\mathsf{P}(X(0) = n)} \\
&= \sum_{k=0}^{\infty} \frac{\mathsf{P}(X(s) = m,\, X(s - \varepsilon) = k,\, X(0) = n)}{\mathsf{P}(X(0) = n)} \\
&\quad \times \frac{\mathsf{P}(X(s - \varepsilon) = k,\, X(0) = n)}{\mathsf{P}(X(s - \varepsilon) = k,\, X(0) = n)} \\
&= \sum_{k=0}^{\infty} \mathsf{P}(X(s - \varepsilon) = k \mid X(0) = n) \\
&\quad \times \mathsf{P}(X(s) = m \mid X(s - \varepsilon) = k,\, X(0) = n) \\
&= \sum_{k=0}^{\infty} \mathsf{P}(X(s - \varepsilon) = k \mid X(0) = n) \\
&\quad \times \mathsf{P}(X(s) = m \mid X(s - \varepsilon) = k) \\
&= \sum_{k=0}^{\infty} p_{n,k}(s - \varepsilon) p_{k,m}(\varepsilon),
\end{aligned}
$$

where the second-to-last equality is the Markov property. So, by (2.19),

$$
\begin{aligned}
p_{n,m}(s) &= p_{n,m}(s - \varepsilon) p_{m,m}(\varepsilon) + \varepsilon \sum_{k \neq m} p_{n,k}(s - \varepsilon) q_{k,m} + \mathrm{o}(\varepsilon) \\
&= p_{n,m}(s - \varepsilon) \left(1 - \sum_{i \neq m} p_{m,i}(\varepsilon) \right) + \varepsilon \sum_{k \neq m} p_{n,k}(s - \varepsilon) q_{k,m} + \mathrm{o}(\varepsilon) \\
&= p_{n,m}(s - \varepsilon) \left(1 - \varepsilon \sum_{i \neq m} q_{m,i} \right) + \varepsilon \sum_{k \neq m} p_{n,k}(s - \varepsilon) q_{k,m} + \mathrm{o}(\varepsilon) \\
&= p_{n,m}(s - \varepsilon)(1 + \varepsilon q_{m,m}) + \varepsilon \sum_{k \neq m} p_{n,k}(s - \varepsilon) q_{k,m} + \mathrm{o}(\varepsilon).
\end{aligned}
$$

After a simple rearrangement we get

$$\frac{p_{n,m}(s) - p_{n,m}(s-\varepsilon)}{\varepsilon} = p_{n,m}(s-\varepsilon)q_{m,m} + \sum_{k \neq m} p_{n,k}(s-\varepsilon)q_{k,m} + \frac{o(\varepsilon)}{\varepsilon}$$

$$= \sum_{k=0}^{\infty} p_{n,k}(s-\varepsilon)q_{k,m} + \frac{o(\varepsilon)}{\varepsilon}.$$

So, letting $\varepsilon \to 0$ in the previous equation, we get, for all $n, m \in \mathbb{Z}^+$ and all real $s > 0$,

$$\dot{p}_{n,m}(s) = \sum_{k=0}^{\infty} p_{n,k}(s)q_{k,m}$$

as desired. □

Using a similar argument, one can condition on the distribution of $X(\varepsilon)$, i.e., move forward in time from the origin (see Section 2.5.3), and then arrive at the Kolmogorov *forward* equations [20, 118, 161]:

$$\dot{\mathbf{P}}(s) = \mathbf{Q}\mathbf{P}(s). \tag{2.24}$$

Recall that

$$\mathbf{P}(0) = \mathbf{I}.$$

Equipped with this *initial condition*, we can solve the Kolmogorov equations (2.23) for the case of a finite state space to get, for all $t \geq 0$,

$$\mathbf{P}(t) = e^{\mathbf{Q}t}, \tag{2.25}$$

where the *matrix exponential*

$$\exp(\mathbf{Q}t) \equiv \mathbf{I} + \mathbf{Q}t + \frac{1}{2!}\mathbf{Q}^2 t^2 + \frac{1}{3!}\mathbf{Q}^3 t^3 + \cdots. \tag{2.26}$$

Note that the terms $t^k/k!$ are scalars and the terms $\mathbf{Q}^k$ (including $\mathbf{Q}^0 = \mathbf{I}$) are all square matrices of the same dimensions. Indeed, clearly $\exp(\mathbf{Q}0) = I$ and, for all $t > 0$,

$$\frac{\mathrm{d}}{\mathrm{d}t}\exp(\mathbf{Q}t) = \mathbf{Q} + \mathbf{Q}^2 t + \frac{1}{2!}\mathbf{Q}^3 t^2 + \cdots$$

$$= [\mathbf{I} + \mathbf{Q}t + \frac{1}{2!}\mathbf{Q}^2 t^2 + \cdots]\mathbf{Q}$$

$$= \exp(\mathbf{Q}t)\mathbf{Q},$$

where, in the second equality, we could have instead factored $\mathbf{Q}$ out to the left to obtain the forward equations.

In summary, for all $s, t \in \mathbb{R}^+$ such that $s \leq t$, the distribution of $X(t)$ is

$$\underline{\pi}^{\mathrm{T}}(t) = \underline{\pi}^{\mathrm{T}}(s)\,\mathbf{P}(t-s)$$

$$= \underline{\pi}^{\mathrm{T}}(s)\,\exp(\mathbf{Q}(t-s)).$$

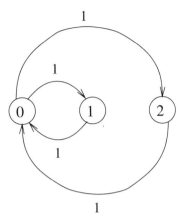

Figure 2.5   An example transition rate diagram.

■ **EXAMPLE 2.4**

In this example, we will give an overview of a simple way to compute the matrix exponential $\exp(\mathbf{Q}t)$ for the case where $\mathbf{Q}$ has distinct real eigenvalues. Consider the transition rate matrix (TRM)

$$
\mathbf{Q} \;=\; \begin{bmatrix} -2 & 1 & 1 \\ 1 & -1 & 0 \\ 1 & 0 & -1 \end{bmatrix}. \tag{2.27}
$$

The corresponding transition rate diagram (TRD) is given in Figure 2.5.

We first compute the eigenvalues and eigenvectors of $\mathbf{Q}$. The eigenvalues are the roots of $\mathbf{Q}$'s characteristic polynomial:

$$
\det(z\mathbf{I} - \mathbf{Q}) \;\equiv\; z(z+1)(z+3).
$$

Thus, the eigenvalues of $\mathbf{Q}$ are 0, -1 and -3. Taking $z \in \{0, -1, -3\}$ and then solving

$$
\mathbf{Q}\underline{x} \;=\; z\underline{x} \tag{2.28}
$$

for $\underline{x}$ (to determine the *right* eigenvectors corresponding to the eigenvalues) gives:

- $[1 \;\; 1 \;\; 1]^{\mathrm{T}}$ is an eigenvector corresponding to eigenvalue 0,

- $[0 \;\; 1 \; -1]^{\mathrm{T}}$ is an eigenvector corresponding to eigenvalue -1, and

- $[2 \; -1 \; -1]^{\mathrm{T}}$ is an eigenvector corresponding to eigenvalue -3.

Combining these three statements in matrix form, as (2.28) for a single eigenvector, gives

$$
\mathbf{Q} \times \begin{bmatrix} 1 & 0 & 2 \\ 1 & 1 & -1 \\ 1 & -1 & -1 \end{bmatrix} \;=\; \begin{bmatrix} 1 & 0 & 2 \\ 1 & 1 & -1 \\ 1 & -1 & -1 \end{bmatrix} \times \begin{bmatrix} 0 & 0 & 0 \\ 0 & -1 & 0 \\ 0 & 0 & -3 \end{bmatrix}.
$$

Let the diagonal matrix of eigenvalues of $\mathbf{Q}$ be

$$\mathbf{\Lambda} \equiv \begin{bmatrix} 0 & 0 & 0 \\ 0 & -1 & 0 \\ 0 & 0 & -3 \end{bmatrix},$$

and let the matrix whose rows are the eigenvectors of $\mathbf{Q}$ in the same positions as the corresponding eigenvalues are in $\mathbf{\Lambda}$ be

$$\mathbf{V} \equiv \begin{bmatrix} 1 & 0 & 2 \\ 1 & 1 & -1 \\ 1 & -1 & -1 \end{bmatrix}.$$

Thus, we arrive at a *Jordan decomposition* of the matrix $\mathbf{Q}$ [30]:

$$\mathbf{Q} = \mathbf{V}\mathbf{\Lambda}\mathbf{V}^{-1}.$$

Note that, for all integers $k \geq 1$,

$$\mathbf{Q}^k = \mathbf{V}\mathbf{\Lambda}^k\mathbf{V}^{-1},$$

where

$$\mathbf{\Lambda}^k = \begin{bmatrix} 0 & 0 & 0 \\ 0 & (-1)^k & 0 \\ 0 & 0 & (-3)^k \end{bmatrix}.$$

Substituting into (2.26) gives

$$\exp(\mathbf{Q}t) = \mathbf{V}\exp(\mathbf{\Lambda}t)\mathbf{V}^{-1}$$

$$= \mathbf{V}\begin{bmatrix} 1 & 0 & 0 \\ 0 & e^{-t} & 0 \\ 0 & 0 & e^{-3t} \end{bmatrix}\mathbf{V}^{-1}.$$

Note that we could have developed this example using left eigenvectors instead of right; for example, the stationary distribution $\underline{\sigma}^{\mathrm{T}}$ is the left eigenvector corresponding to eigenvalue 0; see (2.29) below.

Ways to compute the matrix exponential $\exp(\mathbf{Q}t)$ for TRMs $\mathbf{Q}$ with nondistinct or complex eigenvalues are discussed in Chapter 8 of [30] or Chapter IV of [20].

2.4.5   The balance equations for the stationary distribution

Suppose there exists a distribution $\underline{\sigma}$ on the state space $\Sigma = \mathbb{Z}^+$ that satisfies

$$\underline{\sigma}^{\mathrm{T}}\mathbf{Q} = \underline{0}^{\mathrm{T}}, \tag{2.29}$$

i.e.,

$$\sum_{n=0}^{\infty} \sigma_n q_{n,m} = 0 \quad \text{for all } m \in \mathbb{Z}^+, \tag{2.30}$$

so that $\underline{\sigma}$ is a nonnegative left eigenvector of $\mathbf{Q}$ with eigenvalue zero. Clearly therefore, for all integers $k > 0$,

$$\underline{\sigma}^{\mathrm{T}} \mathbf{Q}^k \;=\; \underline{0}^{\mathrm{T}}.$$

Thus, by (2.25),

$$\underline{\sigma}^{\mathrm{T}} \mathbf{P}(t) \;=\; \underline{\sigma}^{\mathrm{T}} \mathbf{I} \;=\; \underline{\sigma}^{\mathrm{T}}$$

for all $t \in \mathbb{R}^+$. Now consider the Markov chain X described above and recall that $\underline{\pi}(t)$ is defined to be the distribution of $X(t)$. Therefore, if $\underline{\pi}(0) = \underline{\sigma}$, then $\underline{\pi}(t) = \underline{\sigma}$ *for all* real $t > 0$. This is why $\underline{\sigma}$ is called a *stationary* or *invariant* distribution of the Markov chain X with rate matrix $\mathbf{Q}$. The Markov chain X itself is said to be stationary if $\underline{\pi}(0) = \underline{\sigma}$.

■ **EXAMPLE 2.5**

For the example TRM of Equation (2.27), the invariant distribution is

$$\sigma^{\mathrm{T}} \;=\; \begin{bmatrix} \frac{1}{3} & \frac{1}{3} & \frac{1}{3} \end{bmatrix}.$$

■ **EXAMPLE 2.6**

The generation of Asynchronous Transfer Mode (ATM) packets from a human speech source can be modeled by a two-state Markov chain. First let the *talkspurt* state be denoted by 1 and the *silent* state be denoted by 0. That is, our modeling assumption is that successive talkspurts and silent periods are independent and exponentially distributed. In steady state, the mean duration of a talkspurt is 352 ms and the mean duration of a silence period is 650 ms [53]. The mean number of packets generated per second is 22, i.e., 22 48-byte payloads, or about 8 kbits per second on average. Solving (2.29) for a two-state Markov chain gives the invariant distribution:

$$\sigma_0 = \frac{q_{1,0}}{q_{0,1} + q_{1,0}} \quad \text{and} \quad \sigma_1 = \frac{q_{0,1}}{q_{0,1} + q_{1,0}}.$$

From the above information, we get

$$q_{1,0} = \frac{1}{0.352} \quad \text{and} \quad q_{0,1} = \frac{1}{0.650}.$$

Finally, the transmission rate r packets per second during a talkspurt is determined by (2.36):

$$0 \cdot \sigma_0 + r \cdot \sigma_1 = 22.$$

2.4.6 Transience and recurrence

We now consider the properties of Markov chains that have bearing on the issues of existence and uniqueness of stationary distributions, i.e., of solutions to the balance equations $\underline{\sigma}^T \mathbf{Q} = 0$ and

$$\sum_{i=0}^{\infty} \sigma_i = 1. \tag{2.31}$$

Note that, by the definition of its diagonal entries, the sum of the columns of a rate matrix $\mathbf{Q}$ is the zero vector. Thus, the equations $\underline{\sigma}^T \mathbf{Q} = \underline{0}^T$ are dependent, thereby requiring another equation (i.e., (2.31)) if a unique solution $\underline{\sigma}$ is to exist. That is, we replace one of the columns of $\mathbf{Q}$, say the ith, with a column *all* of whose entries are 1, resulting in the matrix $\tilde{\mathbf{Q}}_i$. We then attempt to solve $\underline{\sigma}^T \tilde{\mathbf{Q}}_i = \underline{e}_i^T$, where $\underline{e}_i$ is a column vector whose entries are all zero except that the ith entry is 1. Thus, we are interested in conditions on the rate matrix $\mathbf{Q}$ that result in the invertibility (nonsingularity) of $\tilde{\mathbf{Q}}_i$ (for all i) giving a *unique*

$$\underline{\sigma}^T = \underline{e}_i^T \tilde{\mathbf{Q}}_i^{-1}.$$

Obviously,

$$\sigma_i \geq 0 \text{ for all } i$$

is also required for $\underline{\sigma}$ to be a PMF on the state space.

First note that the quantity

$$V_X(i) \equiv \int_0^{\infty} \mathbf{1}\{X(t) = i\} \, dt$$

represents the total amount of time the stochastic process X visits state i. A state i of a Markov chain is said to be *recurrent* if

$$\mathsf{P}(V_X(i) = \infty \mid X(0) = i) = 1, \tag{2.32}$$

i.e., the Markov chain will visit state i infinitely often with probability 1. On the other hand, if

$$\mathsf{P}(V_X(i) = \infty \mid X(0) = i) = 0, \tag{2.33}$$

i.e., $\mathsf{P}(V_X(i) < \infty) = 1$ so that the Markov chain will visit state i only finitely often, then i is said to be a *transient* state. All states are recurrent in the example of Figure 2.4, whereas all states are transient for the Poisson process. If all of the states of a Markov chain are recurrent, then the Markov chain itself is said to be recurrent.

Suppose that i is a recurrent state. Let $\tau_i > 0$ be the time of the first *transition back into* state i by the Markov chain. The state i is said to be *positive recurrent* if

$$\mathsf{E}(\tau_i \mid X(0) = i) < \infty. \tag{2.34}$$

On the other hand, if the state i is recurrent and

$$\mathsf{E}(\tau_i \mid X(0) = i) = \infty,$$

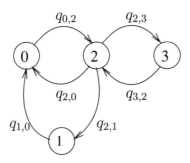

Figure 2.6 An irreducible chain.

then it is said to be *null recurrent*; see Section 2.5.3 for an example. If *all* of the states of the (temporally homogeneous) Markov chain are positive recurrent, then the Markov chain itself is said to be positive recurrent. Examples will be given in Section 2.5.

Consider the transition rate diagram associated with the rate matrix $\mathbf{Q}$ of a Markov chain X. A rate matrix $\mathbf{Q}$ is *irreducible* if there is a path *from* any state of the transition rate diagram *to* any other state of the diagram. In Figure 2.6, an irreducible transition rate diagram is depicted.

In Figure 2.7, a transition rate diagram is depicted that does not have a path *from* state 2 *to* state 0; therefore, the associated Markov chain is reducible in this example. The state space of a reducible Markov chain can be partitioned into one transient class (subset) and a number of recurrent (or "communicating") classes. If a Markov chain begins somewhere in the transient class, it will ultimately leave it if there are one or more recurrent classes. Once in a recurrent class, the Markov chain never leaves it (when a single state constitutes an entire recurrent class, it is sometimes called an *absorbing* state of the Markov chain). For the example of Figure 2.7, $\{0, 5\}$ is the transient class and $\{1, 2\}$ and $\{3, 4\}$ are recurrent classes. Note that irreducibility is a property only of the transition rate diagram (i.e., whether the transition rates are zero or not); irreducibility is otherwise not dependent on the values of transition rates. Finally, note that if the Markov chain has a finite number of states, then all recurrent states are positive recurrent and the recurrent and transient states can be determined by the TRD's structure, as in Figure 2.7.

Theorem 2.4.2. *If the continuous-time Markov chain X is irreducible and positive recurrent, there exists a unique stationary distribution $\underline{\sigma}$.*

For a proof of this theorem see, for example, Chapter 3 of [161] or Chapter IV of [20]. Again, example stationary distributions will be computed in Section 2.5.

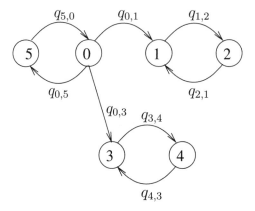

Figure 2.7   A reducible chain.

2.4.7   Convergence in distribution to steady state

In the following theorem, the associated Markov chain $X(t) \sim \underline{\pi}(t)$ is not necessarily stationary.

Theorem 2.4.3. *For any irreducible and positive recurrent TRM* **Q** *and any initial distribution* $\underline{\pi}(0)$,

$$\lim_{t \to \infty} \underline{\pi}^{\mathrm{T}}(t) \;=\; \lim_{t \to \infty} \underline{\pi}^{\mathrm{T}}(0) \exp(\mathbf{Q}t) \;=\; \underline{\sigma}^{\mathrm{T}}. \tag{2.35}$$

That is, the Markov chain will converge in distribution to its stationary $\underline{\sigma}$; see [20, 161]. For this reason, $\underline{\sigma}$ is also known as the *steady-state* distribution of the Markov chain X with rate matrix **Q**; see Problem 2.6(a) at the end of this chapter. More generally, for any *summable* function g on $\mathbb{Z}^+$

$$\mathsf{E}g(X(t)) \;=\; \sum_{i=0}^{\infty} \pi_i(t)g(i) \;\to\; \sum_{i=0}^{\infty} \sigma_i g(i) \tag{2.36}$$

as $t \to \infty$ [20].

2.4.8   Time reversibility and the detailed balance equations

Consider a Markov chain X with transition rate matrix **Q** and unique stationary distribution $\underline{\sigma}$. Take the entire real line $\mathbb{R}$ to be the time domain. Also consider the stochastic process that is X *reversed in time*, i.e., define

$$Y(t) \;\equiv\; X(-t)$$

for $t \in \mathbb{R}$.

Theorem 2.4.4. *The time-reversed Markov chain of X, Y, is itself a Markov chain and, if X is stationary, the transition rate matrix of Y is $\mathbf{R}$ whose entry in the mth row and nth column is*

$$r_{m,n} \;=\; q_{n,m}\frac{\sigma_n}{\sigma_m}, \tag{2.37}$$

where $q_{n,m}$ are the transition rates of X.

Proof: First note that the balance equations (2.29) ensure that

$$\sum_{n=0}^{\infty} r_{m,n} \;=\; 0, \tag{2.38}$$

so that $\mathbf{R}$ is indeed a transition rate matrix.

Consider an arbitrary integer $k \geq 1$, arbitrary subsets $A, B, B_1, ..., B_k$ of $\mathbb{Z}^+$, and arbitrary times $t, s, s_1, ..., s_k \in \mathbb{R}^+$ such that $t < s < s_1 < \cdots < s_k$, i.e.,

$$-t > \;-s > \;-s_1 > \cdots > \;-s_k.$$

The transition probabilities for the reverse-time chain Y are

$$
\begin{aligned}
& \mathsf{P}(Y(-t) \in A \mid Y(-s) \in B, \; Y(-s_1) \in B_1, \; ..., \; Y(-s_k) \in B_k) \\
&= \; \mathsf{P}(X(t) \in A \mid X(s) \in B, \; X(s_1) \in B_1, \; ..., \; X(s_k) \in B_k) \\
&= \; \frac{\mathsf{P}(X(t) \in A, \; X(s) \in B, \; X(s_1) \in B_1, \; ..., \; X(s_k) \in B_k)}{\mathsf{P}(X(s) \in B, \; X(s_1) \in B_1, \; ..., \; X(s_k) \in B_k)} \\
&= \; \frac{\mathsf{P}(X(s_k) \in B_k \mid X(t) \in A, \; ..., \; X(s_{k-1}) \in B_{k-1})}{\mathsf{P}(X(s_k) \in B_k \mid X(s) \in B, \; ..., \; X(s_{k-1}) \in B_{k-1})} \\
& \qquad \times \frac{\mathsf{P}(X(t) \in A, \; ..., \; X(s_{k-1}) \in B_{k-1})}{\mathsf{P}(X(s) \in B, \; ..., \; X(s_{k-1}) \in B_{k-1})} \\
&= \; \frac{\mathsf{P}(X(s_k) \in B_k \mid X(s_{k-1}) \in B_{k-1})}{\mathsf{P}(X(s_k) \in B_k \mid X(s_{k-1}) \in B_{k-1})} \\
& \qquad \times \frac{\mathsf{P}(X(t) \in A, \; ..., \; X(s_{k-1}) \in B_{k-1})}{\mathsf{P}(X(s) \in B, \; ..., \; X(s_{k-1}) \in B_{k-1})} \\
&= \; \frac{\mathsf{P}(X(t) \in A, \; X(s) \in B, \; X(s_1) \in B_1, \; ..., \; X(s_{k-1}) \in B_{k-1})}{\mathsf{P}(X(s) \in B, \; X(s_1) \in B_1, \; ..., \; X(s_{k-1}) \in B_{k-1})},
\end{aligned}
$$

where the second-to-last equality is a result of the Markov property of X. We can repeat this argument $k-1$ more times to get

$$
\begin{aligned}
& \mathsf{P}(Y(-t) \in A \mid Y(-s) \in B, \; Y(-s_1) \in B_1, \; ..., \; Y(-s_k) \in B_k) \\
&= \; \frac{\mathsf{P}(X(t) \in A, \; X(s) \in B)}{\mathsf{P}(X(s) \in B)} \\
&= \; \mathsf{P}(X(t) \in A \mid X(s) \in B) \\
&= \; \mathsf{P}(Y(-t) \in A \mid Y(-s) \in B).
\end{aligned}
$$

So, we have just shown that Y is Markovian.

We now want to find $\mathbf{R}$ in terms of $\mathbf{Q}$ and $\underline{\sigma}$. For $t < s$ (i.e., $-s < -t$), note that

$$
\begin{aligned}
&\mathsf{P}(Y(-t) = n \mid Y(-s) = m) \\
&= \ \mathsf{P}(X(t) = n \mid X(s) = m) \\
&= \ \frac{\mathsf{P}(X(t) = n, \ X(s) = m)}{\mathsf{P}(X(s) = m)} \times \frac{\mathsf{P}(X(t) = n)}{\mathsf{P}(X(t) = n)} \\
&= \ \mathsf{P}(X(s) = m \mid X(t) = n) \times \frac{\mathsf{P}(X(t) = n)}{\mathsf{P}(X(s) = m)}.
\end{aligned}
$$

Since X is stationary by assumption, this implies that

$$
p_{m,n}^{Y}(-t - (-s)) \ = \ p_{n,m}^{X}(s - t)\frac{\sigma_n}{\sigma_m},
$$

where $n \neq m$ and the left-hand side is the transition probability function for Y. By (2.22), differentiating this equation with respect to $s - t = -t - (-s)$ and then evaluating the result at $s - t = 0$ gives

$$
r_{m,n} \ = \ q_{n,m}\frac{\sigma_n}{\sigma_m} \tag{2.39}
$$

as desired. $\qquad\qquad\qquad\qquad\qquad\qquad\qquad\qquad\qquad\qquad\qquad\qquad\qquad\square$

Given the TRD R, it is easy to show that the reverse-time chain $Y(t) \equiv X(-t)$ also has stationary distribution $\underline{\sigma}$. Clearly, this should be true since the fraction of of time that Y visits any given state would be the same as the forward-time chain X.

A Markov chain X is said to be *time reversible* if

$$
r_{m,n} \ = \ q_{m,n} \ \text{ for all } n \neq m. \tag{2.40}
$$

Many of the Markov chains subsequently considered will be time reversible. As we will now see, there is a simplified set of balance equations to compute the stationary distribution for time reversible Markov chains. Equations (2.37) and (2.40) together give the *detailed balance equations* for a time-reversible Markov chain:

$$
\sigma_m q_{m,n} \ = \ \sigma_n q_{n,m} \ \text{ for all } n \neq m. \tag{2.41}
$$

So, X is time reversible if the average rate at which transitions from state m to n occur in reverse time equals the average rate at which transitions from state n back to m occur forward in time.

If a distribution $\underline{\sigma}$ satisfies the detailed balance equations (2.41) for a rate matrix $\mathbf{Q}$, clearly it also satisfies the balance equations (2.30) for the invariant distribution of $\mathbf{Q}$. Verifying this is left as an exercise. Given an irreducible and positive recurrent rate matrix $\mathbf{Q}$, if one finds a distribution $\underline{\sigma}$ that satisfies (2.41), then the associated Markov chain is time reversible. That is, time reversibility is a property that holds *if and only if* the detailed balance equations (2.41) are satisfied.

Note that all two-state Markov chains are time reversible since the single balance equation is also a detailed balance equation.

■ **EXAMPLE 2.7**

Clearly, the TRM of Equation (2.27) is time reversible since the invariant is uniform ($\sigma_i = \sigma_j$ for all $i \neq j$) and the TRM is symmetric ($q_{i,j} = q_{j,i}$ for all $i \neq j$).

■ **EXAMPLE 2.8**

Consider the following TRM:

$$\mathbf{Q} \;=\; \begin{bmatrix} -3 & 1 & 2 \\ 1 & -2 & 1 \\ 1 & 1 & -2 \end{bmatrix}.$$

Its invariant distribution is

$$\underline{\sigma}^{\mathrm{T}} \;=\; \begin{bmatrix} \frac{3}{12} & \frac{4}{12} & \frac{5}{12} \end{bmatrix},$$

so that

$$\sigma_1 q_{1,2} = \tfrac{3}{12} \cdot 1 \;\neq\; \tfrac{4}{12} \cdot 1 = \sigma_2 q_{2,1}.$$

Other examples of TRMs that are not time reversible are easily constructed by considering positive recurrent states $i \neq j$ (i.e., σ_i, $\sigma_j > 0$) with $q_{i,j} = 0$ and $q_{j,i} \neq 0$.

2.5 BIRTH-DEATH MARKOV CHAINS

We now define an important class of Markov chains on $\Sigma = \mathbb{Z}^+$ that are called birth-death processes [20, 118]. From state zero, a birth-death process can only make a transition to state 1; let the rate of this transition be $q_{0,1}$. From state $i > 0$, a birth-death process can only make a transition to state $i - 1$ (at rate $q_{i,i-1}$) or state $i + 1$ (at rate $q_{i,i+1}$). The terminology comes from Markovian population models wherein $X(t)$ is the number of living individuals at time t, a state change from i to $i+1$ represents a birth, and a state change from i to $i - 1$ represents a death.

To simplify notation, we define

$$\lambda_i \;=\; q_{i,i+1} \quad \text{for } i \geq 0$$

and

$$\mu_i \;=\; q_{i,i-1} \quad \text{for } i \geq 1.$$

2.5.1 Birth-death processes with finite state space

In this book, we will consider two kinds of birth-death processes. One kind has a finite state space

$$\Sigma = \mathbb{Z}_K^+ \equiv \{0, 1, 2, ..., K\}$$

and transition rates $\lambda_i > 0$ for all $i \in \{0, 1, 2, ..., K-1\}$ and $\mu_i > 0$ for all $i \in \{1, 2, ..., K\}$ but $\lambda_K = 0$. So, the finite birth-death process has an $(K+1) \times (K+1)$ transition rate matrix

$$\mathbf{Q} = \begin{bmatrix} -\lambda_0 & \lambda_0 & 0 & 0 & 0 & \cdots & 0 \\ \mu_1 & -\mu_1 - \lambda_1 & \lambda_1 & 0 & 0 & \cdots & 0 \\ 0 & \mu_2 & -\mu_2 - \lambda_2 & \lambda_2 & 0 & \cdots & 0 \\ \vdots & \vdots & \vdots & \ddots & \ddots & & \vdots \\ 0 & 0 & \cdots & 0 & \mu_{K-1} & -\mu_{K-1} - \lambda_{K-1} & \lambda_{K-1} \\ 0 & 0 & \cdots & 0 & 0 & \mu_K & -\mu_K \end{bmatrix}. \quad (2.42)$$

Note that this rate matrix is irreducible. The finiteness of the state space implies that the birth-death process is also positive recurrent. We will now compute the stationary distribution $\underline{\sigma}$ which is a vector of size $K+1$. Our objective is to solve

$$\underline{\sigma}^{\mathrm{T}} \mathbf{Q} = 0,$$

which is a compact representation for the following system of $K+1$ balance equations:

$$-\lambda_0 \sigma_0 + \mu_1 \sigma_1 = 0,$$
$$\lambda_{i-1} \sigma_{i-1} - (\mu_i + \lambda_i)\sigma_i + \mu_{i+1}\sigma_{i+1} = 0 \quad \text{for } 0 < i < K,$$
$$\lambda_{K-1}\sigma_{K-1} - \mu_K \sigma_K = 0.$$

The solution to these equations[2] is given by

$$\sigma_i = \sigma_0 \prod_{j=1}^{i} \frac{\lambda_{j-1}}{\mu_j}$$

for $0 < i \leq K$ and σ_0 is chosen as a normalizing term (to satisfy (2.31)),

$$\sigma_0 = \left(1 + \sum_{i=1}^{K} \prod_{n=1}^{i} \frac{\lambda_{n-1}}{\mu_n}\right)^{-1}.$$

It is left as a simple exercise to determine whether this Markov chain is time reversible and detailed balance holds.

---

[2]For a systematic method to solve balance equations (which are difference equations), see the material on Z-transforms in [164] or the material on moment generating functions in [226].

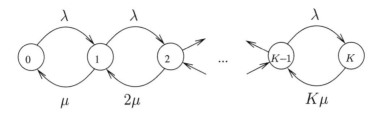

Figure 2.8 The transition rate diagram of an example finite birth-death process.

■ **EXAMPLE 2.9**

We consider the example where

$$\lambda_i = \lambda \quad \text{and} \quad \mu_i = i \cdot \mu$$

for some positive constants λ and μ. The transition rate diagram is depicted in Figure 2.8. Define the constant

$$\rho \equiv \frac{\lambda}{\mu}.$$

In this case

$$\sigma_i = \sigma_0 \frac{\rho^i}{i!} \quad \text{for } 1 \le i \le K \tag{2.43}$$

and

$$\sigma_0 = \left(\sum_{n=0}^{K} \frac{\rho^n}{n!} \right)^{-1}.$$

Thus, the stationary distribution in this example is a *truncated* Poisson distribution.

2.5.2 Birth-death processes with infinite state space

The other kind of birth-death process considered in this book has an infinite state space $\mathbb{Z}^+$ with transition rates $\lambda_i > 0$ for all $i \ge 0$ and $\mu_i > 0$ for all $i \ge 1$. The transition rate diagram is depicted in Figure 2.9. In this case, the balance equations are

$$-\lambda_0 \sigma_0 + \mu_1 \sigma_1 = 0$$

and, for $i > 0$,

$$\lambda_{i-1}\sigma_{i-1} - (\mu_i + \lambda_i)\sigma_i + \mu_{i+1}\sigma_{i+1} = 0.$$

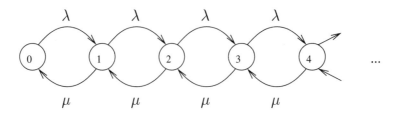

Figure 2.9   The transition rate diagram of an example infinite birth-death process.

As for the finite case, the infinite birth-death process is irreducible.

Assuming for the moment that it is positive recurrent as well, we can solve the balance equations to get

$$\sigma_i = \sigma_0 \prod_{j=1}^{i} \frac{\lambda_{j-1}}{\mu_j}$$

for $0 < i \leq K$. Choosing σ_0 in order to satisfy (2.31), we get

$$\sigma_0 = \left(1 + \sum_{i=1}^{\infty} \prod_{n=1}^{i} \frac{\lambda_{n-1}}{\mu_n}\right)^{-1}.$$

The condition for positive recurrence is that

$$\sum_{i=1}^{\infty} \prod_{n=1}^{i} \frac{\lambda_{n-1}}{\mu_n} < \infty$$

because $\sigma_0 > 0$ under this condition and, therefore, $\underline{\sigma}$ is a well-defined distribution.

■ EXAMPLE 2.10

We now consider the example where $\lambda_i = \lambda$ and $\mu_i = \mu$ for all i and positive constants λ and μ. Again define the constant

$$\rho \equiv \frac{\lambda}{\mu}.$$

In the case where $\rho < 1$,

$$\sigma_i = (1-\rho)\rho^i \quad \text{for } i \geq 1. \tag{2.44}$$

Note that

$$\sigma_0 = \left(\sum_{i=0}^{\infty} \rho^i\right)^{-1},$$

which converges (to $1 - \rho$) if and only if $\rho < 1$; this is the condition for positive recurrence in this example. Thus, the stationary distribution when $\rho < 1$ is geometric with parameter ρ. The issue of recurrence for this birth-death Markov chain is further explored in the next section.

2.5.3 Applications of the forward equations

Consider an interval $J = \{i, i + 1, ..., j - 1, j\} \subset \mathbb{Z}$ of states, where $i < j$. Suppose a birth-death Markov chain X makes a transition into the interval at state i at time t, i.e., $X(t) = i$ and $X(t-) = i - 1 \notin J$. Let Z_k be the first *time* that X makes a transition to state k after time t, i.e.,

$$Z_k = \inf\{s \geq t \mid X(s) = k\}.$$

Note that $Z_i = t$ by the definition of t above. Also, by the assumed temporal homogeneity, the distribution of $Z_i - t$ does not depend on t; so we take $t = 0$ to simplify notation in the following. Assume that the birth-death process is such that there is a positive probability that it will *exit* the interval J at either end. In this section, we will show how the Kolmogorov equations can be used to compute the probability that the Markov chain *exits* the interval J at i. For $k = i - 1, i, ..., j, j + 1$, define

$$g(k) = \mathsf{P}(Z_{i-1} < Z_{j+1} \mid X(0) = k).$$

So, we are interested in computing the quantities $g(i)$ or $g(j)$.

First note that $g(i - 1) = 1$ and $g(j + 1) = 0$. Now consider a positive real number $\varepsilon \ll 1$ and note that, by a forward-conditioning argument, for $i \leq k \leq j$,

$$
\begin{aligned}
g(k) &= \sum_m \mathsf{P}(Z_{i-1} < Z_{j+1} \mid X(0) = k, \ X(\varepsilon) = m) \\
&\quad \times \mathsf{P}(X(\varepsilon) = m \mid X(0) = k) \\
&= \sum_m \mathsf{P}(Z_{i-1} < Z_{j+1} \mid X(\varepsilon) = m)\mathsf{P}(X(\varepsilon) = m \mid X(0) = k) \\
&= g(k)(1 + \varepsilon q_{k,k}) + \sum_{m \neq k} g(m)q_{k,m}\varepsilon + \mathrm{o}(\varepsilon),
\end{aligned}
$$

where the second equality above is just the Markov property itself. Recall that

$$\exp(\varepsilon \mathbf{Q}) = \mathbf{I} + \varepsilon \mathbf{Q} + \mathrm{o}(\varepsilon)\mathbf{U},$$

where $\mathbf{U}$ is a square matrix in which every entry is 1. Also recall that

$$q_{k,k} = -\sum_{m \neq k} q_{k,m} = -q_{k,k-1} - q_{k,k+1}.$$

Therefore,

$$\sum_{m=k-1}^{k+1} g(k)q_{k,m} = 0 \quad \text{for } i \leq k \leq j. \tag{2.45}$$

Note that (2.45) constitutes a set of $j - i + 1$ equations in as many unknowns ($g(k)$ for $i \le k \le j$) with boundary conditions $g(i-1) = 1$ and $g(j+1) = 0$. The unique solution of these equations can be found by, for example, the systematic method of Z-transforms [164, 226]. In particular, the desired quantity $g(i)$ can be found.

Consider the example where $q > 0$ such that, for all $k \in J$,

$$q_{k,k+1} \;=\; q \;=\; q_{k,k-1}$$

for some constant $q > 0$. In this case, the solution of (2.45) is

$$g(k) = Ak + B$$

for all $k \in J$ and for some constants A and B. These constants can be determined from the boundary conditions, i.e.,

$$
\begin{aligned}
1 &= g(i-1) = A(i-1) + B,\\
0 &= g(j+1) = A(j+1) + B.
\end{aligned}
$$

Therefore, $A = -1/(j-i+2)$, $B = (j+1)/(j-i+2)$, and

$$g(k) = \frac{j - k + 1}{j - i + 2}.$$

Now consider the problem of computing the mean *time* until the return to a state i for the birth-death Markov chain with $q_{k,k+1} \equiv \lambda$ and $q_{k,k-1} \equiv \mu$. Considering that there are only finitely many states less than a given state i, state i is positive recurrent only if $h_i(i+1) < \infty$, where

$$h_i(j) \;\equiv\; \mathsf{E}(Z_i \mid X(0) = j).$$

By using a forward-equation argument similar to that used to derive (2.45), we can obtain

$$
\begin{aligned}
h_i(j) &= \frac{1}{q_{j,j+1} + q_{j,j-1}} + \frac{q_{j,j+1}}{q_{j,j+1} + q_{j,j-1}} h_i(j+1)\\
&\quad + \frac{q_{j,j-1}}{q_{j,j+1} + q_{j,j-1}} h_i(j-1)\\
&= \frac{1}{\lambda + \mu} + \frac{\lambda}{\lambda + \mu} h_i(j+1) + \frac{\mu}{\lambda + \mu} h_i(j-1) \qquad (2.46)
\end{aligned}
$$

for all $j > i$, with

$$h_i(i) \;\equiv\; 0$$

by definition. One can see that this equation must be true intuitively by noticing that the first term on the right-hand side is the mean visiting time of state j and that the coefficient of $h_i(j \pm 1)$ is the probability of transitioning from j to $j \pm 1$ in one step. If we define

$$\eta_i(j) \;\equiv\; h_i(j) - h_i(j+1),$$

then (2.46) becomes

$$
\begin{aligned}
\eta_i(j) &= \frac{1}{q_{j,j+1}} + \frac{q_{j,j-1}}{q_{j,j+1}} \eta_i(j-1)\\
&= \frac{1}{\lambda} + \frac{1}{\rho} \eta_i(j-1).
\end{aligned}
$$

Iterating, we get

$$
\begin{aligned}
\eta_i(j) &= \frac{1}{\lambda}\left(1 + \frac{1}{\rho}\right) + \frac{1}{\rho^2}\eta_i(j-2) \\
&= \frac{1}{\lambda}\sum_{k=0}^{j-i-1}\frac{1}{\rho^k} + \frac{1}{\rho^{j-i}}\eta_i(i).
\end{aligned}
$$

Multiplying through by ρ^{j-i} and then rewriting in terms of h_i gives

$$
\rho^{j-i}(h_i(j) - h_i(j+1)) = -h_i(i+1) + \frac{1}{\lambda}\sum_{k=1}^{j-i}\rho^k, \tag{2.47}
$$

where we note that $\eta_i(i) = h_i(i) - h_i(i+1) = -h_i(i+1)$. Now consider this equation as $j \to \infty$. First note that the difference $h_i(j) - h_i(j+1) \to 0$. Now if $\rho = 1$, clearly (2.47) requires that $h_i(i+1) = \infty$ since the summation on the right-hand side is tending to infinity, i.e., state i and, by the same argument, all other states are not positive recurrent. If $\rho < 1$, the summation on the right-hand side converges and the left-hand side tends to zero as $j \to \infty$ so that

$$
0 = -h_i(i+1) + \frac{1}{\lambda}\cdot\frac{\rho}{1-\rho},
$$

i.e.,

$$
h_i(i+1) = \frac{1}{\mu - \lambda}.
$$

A more general statement along these lines for birth-death Markov chains is given at the end of Section 4.7 of [118].

2.6 MODELING TIME-SERIES DATA USING A MARKOV CHAIN

Consider a single sample path $X_\omega(t)$, $t \in [0, T]$, of a stationary process, where $T \gg 1$. We may be interested in estimating its marginal mean,

$$
\mu \equiv \mathrm{E}X(t),
$$

by

$$
\frac{1}{T}\int_0^T X_\omega(t)\,\mathrm{d}t. \tag{2.48}
$$

If this quantity converges to the mean as $T \to \infty$ (for almost all sample paths X_ω) then X is said to be ergodic in the mean. If the stationary distribution of X, $\underline{\sigma}$, can be similarly approximated because

$$
\sigma_n = \lim_{T\to\infty}\frac{1}{T}\int_0^T \mathbf{1}\{X_\omega(t) = n\}\,\mathrm{d}t, \tag{2.49}
$$

then X is said to be ergodic in distribution. In practice, estimates like (2.48) and (2.49) are sometimes used even when the process X is known not to be stationary *assuming* that the *transient* portion of the sample path will be negligible, i.e., the duration of the entire sample path T is much larger than the transient portion [85].

Given data (either from a physical system or a simulation) constituting a single sample path of a stochastic process, we would like to infer attributes of the probability "law" that governs it. We can perform such computations for processes X that are *ergodic* in some sense [207].

So far in this chapter, we have assumed that the TRM $\mathbf{Q}$ of a Markov chain is known. In this section, we describe a simple way to estimate transition rates from data. More specifically, the objective of this section is to obtain the most likely TRM $\mathbf{Q}$ given one or more measured sample paths (time series) of the physical process to be modeled, i.e., obtain the TRM for which the given sample paths are most likely (or "typical" [129]).

We first assume that the states themselves are readily discernible from the data. Quantization of the physical states would be required to obtain a discrete state space if the physical state space is uncountable. Even if the physical state space is already discrete, it may be further simplified by quantization (state aggregation). In the following, we assume that the physical process is positive recurrent and irreducible (leading to a unique invariant distribution).

Given a space of N defined states, one can glean the following information from sample-path data, X_ω:

- the total time duration of the sample path, T,

- the total time spent in state i, τ_i, for each element i of the defined state space, i.e.,

$$\tau_i = \int_0^T \mathbf{1}\{X(t) = i\}\, \mathrm{d}t,$$

- the total number of jumps taken *out of* state i, J_i, and

- the total number of jumps out of state i to state j, $J_{i,j}$.

Clearly,

$$T = \sum_i \tau_i$$

and, for all states i,

$$J_i = \sum_i J_{i,j}.$$

From this information, we can derive:

- the sample occupation time for each state i,

$$\sigma_i = \frac{\tau_i}{T},$$

- the sample probability of transiting to state j from i,

$$r_{i,j} = \frac{J_{i,j}}{J_i}.$$

From this derived information, we can directly estimate the "most likely" transition rates of the process:

$$q_{i,j} = r_{i,j}(-q_{i,i}) \quad \text{for all } i \neq j. \tag{2.50}$$

This leaves us with the N unknowns $q_{i,i}$ for $1 \leq i \leq N$. We would like to use the N quantities σ_i to determine the residual N unknowns $q_{i,i}$, but in order to do, so we need to assume that the physical process is stationary. If the physical process is indeed stationary, we can identify $\underline{\sigma}$ as approximately equal to the stationary distribution of the Markov chain and therefore the balance equations hold:

$$\underline{\sigma}^{\mathrm{T}}\mathbf{Q} = \underline{0}.$$

Given that the substitution (2.50) is used for all $i \neq j$ in the balance equations, the result is only $N - 1$ linearly independent equations in N unknowns $q_{i,i}$ (recall that the columns of Q are dependent because they sum to zero). We note that the derived information σ_i and $r_{i,j}$ are all "relative" in nature. So, to obtain a final independent equation in the $-q_{i,i}$ so as to specify them completely, we consider the total "speed" of the Markov chain, i.e., the aggregate mean rate of jumps:

$$\sum_i \sigma_i(-q_{i,i}) = \frac{1}{T}\sum_i J_i.$$

■ **EXAMPLE 2.11**

Consider the following numerical example of process with $N = 3$ states with sample path data leading to the following information. The time-duration and occupation times were observed to be:

T	τ_0	τ_1	τ_2
100	20	50	30

The total number of transitions out of each state were observed to be:

J_0	J_1	J_2
10	40	30

The specific transition counts $J_{i,j}$ were observed to be:

from\to	0	1	2
0	—	5	5
1	10	—	30
2	20	10	—

So, finding $q_{i,j}$ for all $i \neq j$ as above gives

$$
\mathbf{Q} \;=\;
\begin{bmatrix}
q_{1,1} & -\frac{5}{10}q_{1,1} & -\frac{5}{10}q_{1,1} \\[6pt]
-\frac{10}{40}q_{2,2} & q_{2,2} & -\frac{30}{40}q_{2,2} \\[6pt]
-\frac{20}{30}q_{3,3} & -\frac{10}{30}q_{3,3} & q_{3,3}
\end{bmatrix}.
$$

Now the $q_{i,i}$ can be solved from the first two (independent) balance equations,

$$
\frac{20}{100}q_{1,1} - \frac{50}{100}\cdot\frac{10}{40}q_{2,2} - \frac{30}{100}\cdot\frac{20}{30}q_{3,3} \;=\; 0,
$$

$$
-\frac{20}{100}\cdot\frac{5}{10}q_{1,1} + \frac{50}{100}q_{2,2} - \frac{30}{100}\cdot\frac{10}{30}q_{3,3} \;=\; 0,
$$

and the total speed equation,

$$
\frac{20}{100}(-q_{1,1}) + \frac{50}{100}(-q_{2,2}) + \frac{30}{100}(-q_{3,3}) \;=\; \frac{1}{100}(10 + 40 + 30).
$$

The resulting solution is

$$
q_{1,1} = -\tfrac{72}{55}, \quad q_{2,2} = -\tfrac{128}{275}, \quad \text{and } q_{3,3} = -\tfrac{56}{55}.
$$

As mentioned previously, the state space itself can be determined from the data. In practice, a clustering algorithm could be used to decide or simplify the state space. Suppose that a histogram of transmission rates (in, say, bytes per second) of a stationary and ergodic packet flow has been empirically obtained. The individual samples of the transmission rates could, for example, be taken over a small sliding time window. The ultimate objective is to model the transmission rate process as a Markov chain. An example histogram h is given in Figure 2.10, i.e., h is a PMF so that

$$
\sum_x h(x) \;=\; 1,
$$

where the sum over the rate samples x was taken at a fine resolution (hence h is shown smooth in Figure 2.10).

To simplify the Markov model, we wish to reduce the size of the state space to some *given* number n, i.e., n is small compared to the sample space of the histogram h. That is, given n, we want to define $n-1$ thresholds θ_i such that

$$
0 \;<\; \theta_1 \;<\; \theta_2 \cdots \;<\; \theta_{n-1} \;<\; \infty.
$$

The ith state of the Markov chain could then be given by

$$
x_i^* \;\equiv\; \sum_{\theta_{i-1} \leq x < \theta_i} x\frac{h(x)}{h_i^*},
$$

where $\theta_0 \equiv 0$, $\theta_n \equiv \infty$, and the (marginal) probability that the Markov chain is in state x_i^* will be

$$
h_i^* \;\equiv\; \sum_{\theta_{i-1} \leq x < \theta_i} h(x),
$$

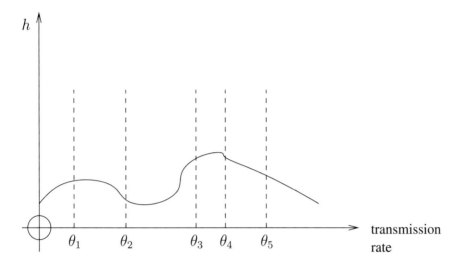

Figure 2.10   Histogram of transmission rate process with the clustering thresholds θ.

i.e., the TRM of the Markov chain will be chosen so that its invariant distribution is $\underline{h}^*$. For example, in Figure 2.11, we show a clustering with $n = 6$.

There are several approaches to choosing the thresholds $\underline{\theta}$ that, in turn, determine the state space $\underline{x}^*$ of the Markov chain. One could consider the variance of samples x within each cluster [106]. More precisely, note that the "total" variance of the raw samples is

$$\sum_x \left(x - \sum_\xi \xi h(\xi) \right)^2 h(x)$$

$$= \sum_{i=1}^n \left(x_i^* - \sum_{j=1}^n x_j^* h_j^* \right)^2 h_i^* + \sum_{i=1}^n \sum_{\theta_{i-1} \le x < \theta_i} (x - x_i^*)^2 h(x). \qquad (2.51)$$

The proof of this identity is left as an exercise. The first term on its right-hand side is the *inter*cluster variance while the second is the total *intra*cluster variance. Again, given the number of clusters n, an objective of clustering could be to select the thresholds to minimize the intracluster variance, i.e.,

$$\min_{\underline{\theta}} \sum_{i=1}^n \sum_{\theta_{i-1} \le x < \theta_i} (x - x_i^*)^2 h(x).$$

Techniques of clustering and Markov modeling are discussed briefly in [106] and in greater depth in [61, 175].

Given the state space, the data are distilled into a series of K state transition times, $T_k > 0$, where $T_0 \equiv 0$. See Figure 2.12, which depicts the quantizing/clustering operation on a sample path of trace data resulting in the sample path of the (quantized) Markov chain:

$$\{T_k,\ X(T_k)\}_{k=0}^K.$$

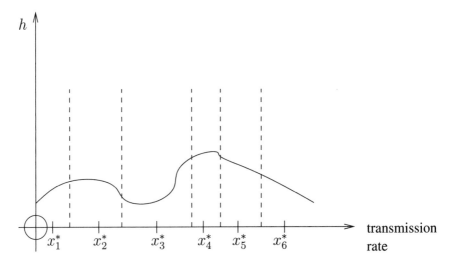

Figure 2.11   Histogram of transmission rate process with clustered states x^*.

2.7 SIMULATING A MARKOV CHAIN

Simulation is a widely used tool in performance evaluation of communication networks. Care must be taken in the reporting of simulation results so that readers can precisely repeat the described experiments and so that the results are given to a prescribed degree of confidence [168]. In general, simulations are most effective in evaluating performance when they are combined with intuition obtained from the sorts of calculations that form the remainder of this book and from practical experience. Currently, popular simulation platforms for networking include OpNet (http://www.opnet.com), the open-source NS-2 package (http://www.isi.edu/nsnam/ns), and the public Emulab (http://www.emulab.net).

In this section, we describe a simple way to generate a sample path of a Markov chain by simulation. Suppose the state space is $\mathbb{Z}^+$, the initial distribution is $\underline{\pi}(0)$, and the transition rate matrix is $\mathbf{Q} = [q_{n,m}]$. To find the initial state $X(0)$, simply generate a uniform random variable U_0 and compute $F_0^{-1}(U_0)$, where F_0 is the CDF corresponding to $\underline{\pi}(0)$, i.e.,

$$F_0(x) = \begin{cases} 0 & \text{if } x < 0, \\ \sum_{j=0}^{\lfloor x \rfloor} \pi_j(0) & \text{if } x \geq 0, \end{cases}$$

where $\lfloor x \rfloor$ is the integer part of $x \in \mathbb{R}$; recall Problem 1.19.

Now, the first transition of the Markov chain occurs at time T_1, where T_1 is exponentially distributed with parameter $-q_{X(0),X(0)} > 0$. We can generate another uniform $[0,1]$

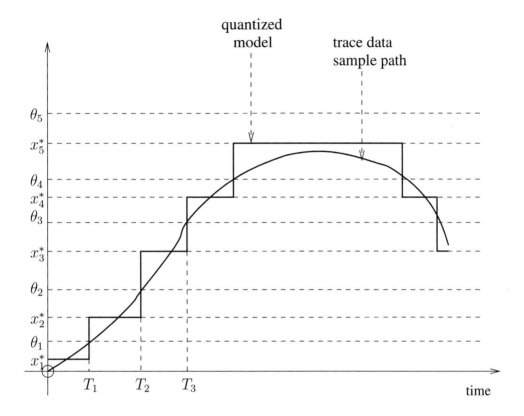

Figure 2.12 Sample path as empirically derived from quantized states.

random variable V_1 (independent of U_0) and take

$$T_1 \quad = \quad \frac{1}{q_{X(0),X(0)}} \log(V_1).$$

As discussed in Chapter 2, the distribution $\pi(T_1)$ of $X(T_1)$ is given by

$$\pi_m(T_1) \quad = \quad \frac{q_{X(0),m}}{-q_{X(0),X(0)}}$$
$$= \quad \mathsf{P}(X(T_1) = m \mid X(0))$$

for $m \neq X(0)$ and $\pi_{X(0)}(T_1) = 0$.

The second transition time occurs at time T_2, where $T_2 - T_1$ is an exponentially distributed random variable with parameter

$$-q_{X(T_1),X(T_1)}.$$

The distribution $\underline{\pi}(T_2)$ of X at time T_2 is given by

$$
\begin{aligned}
\pi_m(T_2) &= \frac{q_{X(1),m}}{-q_{X(1),X(1)}} \\
&= \mathsf{P}(X(T_2) = m \mid X(T_1))
\end{aligned}
$$

for $m \neq X(1)$ and $\pi_{X(1)}(T_2) = 0$. We can simply repeat this procedure to iteratively generate successive state transitions and intertransition times.

Finally, the Markov chain itself could be a component in a more complex event-driven simulation. In this context, the (temporally ordered) event list would have a single entry for each Markov chain. The execution time of the entry would be the *next* transition time of the Markov chain. The entry is processed as described above: the state to which the Markov chain makes a transition and the intertransition time are computed, and the next entry for the Markov chain is inserted into the event list according to the latter. There are alternative simulation techniques for Markov chains including uniformization [35].

2.8 OVERVIEW OF DISCRETE-TIME MARKOV CHAINS

In this section, we review concepts previously discussed but now for Markov processes in discrete time on countable state spaces, i.e., discrete-time Markov chains. We will highlight differences in the two contexts. Derivations that are completely analogous to the continuous-time case will be left as exercises. A follow-up section to this one, on discrete-time queues, concludes the following chapter. For further details on discrete-time Markov chains; see Chapter 3 of [118].

Recall that a stochastic process X is said be "discrete time" if its time domain is countable, e.g., $\{X(n) \mid n \in D\}$ for $D = \mathbb{Z}^+$ or for $D = \mathbb{Z}$, where, in discrete time, we will typically use n instead of t to denote time. Finite-dimensional distributions and the consistency and stationarity properties of a discrete-time stochastic process X are defined just as in (2.1), (2.2), and (2.3), respectively, but with the time values restricted to the discrete domain D, of course. The Markov property in discrete-time is also the same as that stated in continuous time in (2.8). In discrete time, the Markov property relies on the memoryless property of the (discrete) geometric distribution rather than on the (continuous) exponential distribution.

If the random variables $B(n)$ are IID Bernoulli distributed for, say, $n \in \mathbb{Z}^+$, then B is said to be a Bernoulli process on $\mathbb{Z}^+$. Let $q \equiv \mathsf{P}(B_n = 1)$. Thus, the duration of time B visits state 1 (respectively, state 0), is geometrically distributed with mean $1/(1-q)$ (respectively mean $1/q$).

The analog to the Poisson counting process on $\mathbb{Z}^+$ can be constructed:

$$
X(n) = \sum_{m=0}^{n} B(m).
$$

The marginal distribution of X follows a binomial distribution: for $k \in \{0, 1, 2, ..., n\}$,

$$
P(X(n-1) = k) = \binom{n}{k} q^k (1-q)^{n-k}.
$$

Both B and X are Markov chains.

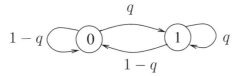

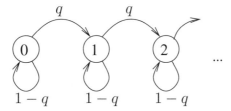

Figure 2.13 The transition probability diagram for the Bernoulli process B.

Figure 2.14 The transition probability diagram for the counting process X.

The one-step transition probabilities of a discrete-time Markov chain Y are defined to be

$$P(Y(n+1) = a \mid Y(n) = b), \qquad (2.52)$$

where a, b are, of course, taken from the countable state space of Y. The one-step transition probabilities of a *time-homogeneous* Markov chain[3] can be graphically depicted in a transition probability diagram (TPD). The transition *probability* diagrams of B and X are given in Figure 2.13 and 2.14, respectively. Note that the nodes are labeled with elements in the state space and the branches are labeled with the one-step transition probabilities. Graphicly unlike TRDs, TPDs may have "self-loops", e.g., $P(X(n+1) = 1 \mid X(n) = 1) = q > 0$.

From one-step transition probabilities of a discrete-time, time-homogeneous Markov chain, one can construct its transition *probability* matrix (TPM), i.e., the entry in the ath column and bth row of the TPM for Y is (2.52).   For example, the Bernoulli process B has state space $\{0, 1\}$ and TPM

$$\mathbf{P}_B \;=\; \begin{bmatrix} 1-q & q \\ 1-q & q \end{bmatrix}. \qquad (2.53)$$

That of the counting process X defined above is

$$\mathbf{P}_X \;=\; \begin{bmatrix} 1-q & q & 0 & 0 & 0 & \cdots \\ 0 & 1-q & q & 0 & 0 & \cdots \\ 0 & 0 & 1-q & q & 0 & \cdots \\ \vdots & \vdots & \vdots & \vdots & \vdots & \ddots \end{bmatrix}.$$

---

[3]That is, the quantity in the (2.52) Markov chain does not depend on time n for all states a, b.

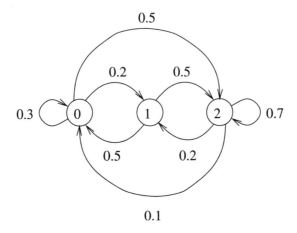

Figure 2.15 The transition probability diagram on state space $\{0, 1, 2\}$.

Another example of a discrete-time Markov chain with state space $\{0, 1, 2\}$ and TPM

$$\mathbf{P}_Y = \begin{bmatrix} 0.3 & 0.2 & 0.5 \\ 0.5 & 0 & 0.5 \\ 0.1 & 0.2 & 0.7 \end{bmatrix} \tag{2.54}$$

is given in Figure 2.15.

All TPMs $\mathbf{P}$ are *stochastic* matrices [99], i.e., they satisfy the following two properties:

- All entries are nonnegative and real (the entries are all probabilities).

- The sum of the entries of any row is 1, i.e., $\mathbf{P}\underline{1} = \underline{1}$ by the law of total probability.

Given the TPM $\mathbf{P}$ and initial distribution $\underline{\pi}(0)$ of the process Y (i.e., $\mathrm{P}(Y(0) = k) = \pi_k(0)$), one can easily compute the other marginal distributions of Y. For example, the distribution of $Y(1)$ is $\underline{\pi}^{\mathrm{T}}(1) = \underline{\pi}^{\mathrm{T}}(0)\mathbf{P}$, i.e.,

$$\begin{aligned} \pi_k(1) &\equiv \mathrm{P}(Y(1) = k) \\ &= \sum_{b \in S} \mathrm{P}(Y(1) = k \mid Y(0) = b)\mathrm{P}(Y(0) = b) \\ &= \sum_{b \in S} \mathbf{P}_{b,k}\pi_b(0) \end{aligned}$$

for all k in the state space S of Y. By induction, we can compute the distribution of $Y(n)$:

$$\underline{\pi}^{\mathrm{T}}(n) = \underline{\pi}^{\mathrm{T}}(0)\mathbf{P}^n. \tag{2.55}$$

More general finite-dimensional distributions of a discrete-time Markov chain can be computed as Equation (2.16). Also, the quantity $\mathbf{P}^n$ can be computed using the same approach as that described for the TRM (2.27). In this case, however, $\mathbf{P}$ will have an eigenvalue 1 instead of zero corresponding to the eigenvector that is the invariant distribution, and powers $\mathbf{\Lambda}^n$ of the diagonal matrix $\mathbf{\Lambda}$ are likewise simple to compute when all eigenvalues are distinct.

Note that a time-*in*homogeneous discrete-time Markov chain will simply have time-dependent one-step transition probabilities, i.e., denote by $\mathbf{P}(n)$ the TPM made up of entries (2.52), so that (2.55) would become

$$\underline{\pi}^{\mathrm{T}}(n) \quad = \quad \underline{\pi}^{\mathrm{T}}(0)\mathbf{P}(1)\mathbf{P}(2)\cdots\mathbf{P}(n). \tag{2.56}$$

For a time-inhomogeneous Markov chain Y, the forward Kolmogorov equations in discrete-time can be obtained by conditioning on $Y(1)$:

$$
\begin{aligned}
(\mathbf{P}(0,n))_{a,b} &\equiv P(Y(n) = a \mid Y(0) = b) \\
&= \sum_k \frac{P(Y(n) = a, Y(0) = b, Y(1) = k)}{P(Y(0) = b)} \\
&= \sum_k \frac{P(Y(n) = a, Y(0) = b, Y(1) = k)}{P(Y(1) = k, Y(0) = b)} \frac{P(Y(1) = k, Y(0) = b)}{P(Y(0) = b)} \\
&= \sum_k P(Y(n) = a \mid Y(0) = b, Y(1) = k)P(Y(1) = k \mid Y(0) = b) \\
&= \sum_k P(Y(n) = a \mid Y(1) = k)P(Y(1) = k \mid Y(0) = b),
\end{aligned}
$$

where the second-to-last equality is the Markov property. The Kolmogorov forward equations in matrix form are

$$\mathbf{P}(0,n) \quad = \quad \mathbf{P}(1)\mathbf{P}(1,n). \tag{2.57}$$

Similarly, the backward Kolmogorov equations are generated by conditioning on $Y(n-1)$:

$$\mathbf{P}(0,n) \quad = \quad \mathbf{P}(0,n-1)\mathbf{P}(n). \tag{2.58}$$

Note that both (2.57) and (2.58) are consistent with (2.56), i.e.,

$$\mathbf{P}(0,n) \quad \equiv \quad \mathbf{P}(1)\mathbf{P}(2)\cdots\mathbf{P}(n).$$

Clearly, in the time-homogeneous special case, this simply reduces to $\mathbf{P}(0,n) = \mathbf{P}^n$.

For a time-homogeneous Markov chain, we can define an invariant or stationary distribution of its TPM $\mathbf{P}$ as any distribution $\underline{\sigma}$ satisfying the balance equations in discrete time:

$$\underline{\sigma}^{\mathrm{T}} \quad = \quad \underline{\sigma}^{\mathrm{T}}\mathbf{P}. \tag{2.59}$$

Clearly, by (2.55), if the initial distribution $\underline{\pi}(0) = \underline{\sigma}$ for a stationary distribution $\underline{\sigma}$, then $\underline{\pi}(1) = \underline{\sigma}$ as well and, by induction, the marginal distribution of the Markov chain is $\underline{\sigma}$ forever, i.e., $\underline{\pi}(n) = \underline{\sigma}$ for all time $n > 1$ and the Markov chain is stationary. By inspection, the stationary distribution of the Bernoulli Markov chain with TPM (2.53) is

$$\underline{\sigma} \quad = \quad \begin{bmatrix} 1-q \\ q \end{bmatrix}.$$

The stationary distribution of the TPM (2.54) can be obtained numerically by solving

$$
\begin{aligned}
\underline{\sigma}^{\mathrm{T}}(\mathbf{I} - \mathbf{P}_Y) &= \underline{0}, \\
\underline{\sigma}^{\mathrm{T}}\underline{1} &= 1.
\end{aligned}
$$

Note that the first block of equations (three in this example) are equivalent to $\underline{\sigma}^T = \underline{\sigma}^T \mathbf{P}_Y$ and are linearly dependent. So, recall the idea to replace one of columns of $\mathbf{I} - \mathbf{P}_Y$, say column 3, with all 1's (corresponding to $1 = \underline{\sigma}^T \underline{1} = \sigma_0 + \sigma_1 + \sigma_2$) and replace $\underline{0}$ with $[0\ 0\ 1]^T$ before attempting to solve these three unknowns from three equations. That is, we solve

$$\underline{\sigma}^T \begin{bmatrix} 0.7 & -0.2 & 1 \\ -0.5 & -1 & 1 \\ -0.1 & -0.2 & 1 \end{bmatrix} = [0\ 0\ 1].$$

Note that the counting process X with binomially distributed marginal does not have an invariant distribution as it is transient.

One can ask whether a given TPM has a *unique* stationary distribution. As in continuous time, individual states of a discrete-time Markov chain can be null recurrent, positive recurrent, or transient and we can call the Markov chain itself "positive recurrent" if all of its states are. Also, a discrete-time Markov chain can possess the irreducible property. Unlike continuous-time chains, all discrete-time chains also possess either a *periodic* or an *aperiodic* property through their TPDs (as with the irreducibility property). A state b of a time-homogeneous Markov chain Y is *periodic* if there is a time $n > 1$ such that:

$$P(Y(m) = b \mid Y(0) = b) > 0$$

if and only if m is a multiple of n, where n is the *period* of b. That is, given $Y(0) = b$, $Y(m) = b$ is only possible when $m = kn$ for some integer k. A Markov chain is said to be aperiodic if it has no periodic states; otherwise it is said to be periodic. The three examples of discrete-time Markov chains considered previously are all aperiodic. A Markov chain with TRD depicted in Figure 2.16 is periodic; note that $n = 2$ is the period of state 2. One can solve for the invariant distribution of this Markov chain to get the unique $\underline{\sigma} = [0, 2\ 0.3\ 0.5]^T$, but the issue here is that the stationarity property of the Markov chain (2.3) does not hold because, e.g., if $X(0) = 2$, then $X(n) = 2$ almost surely (i.e., $P(X(n) = 2 \mid X(0) = 2) = 1$) for all even n and $X(n) \neq 2$ a.s. for all odd n.

The proof of the following basic statement is given in [69].

Theorem 2.8.1. *A discrete-time Markov chain has a unique stationary distribution if and only if it is irreducible, positive recurrent and aperiodic.*

Finally, we now discuss birth-death Markov chains with state space $\mathbb{Z}^+$ because they will be used subsequently to study queues in discrete time. The counting process X defined above is a "pure birth" process. In Figure 2.17, the TRD of a birth-death process on a finite state space $\{0, 1, ..., K\}$ is depicted (naturally assuming $q_k + p_k \leq 1$ for all k, where $p_0 = 0$ and $q_K = 0$). The balance equations (2.59) are

$$\begin{aligned} (1 - q_0)\sigma_0 + p_1\sigma_1 &= \sigma_0, \\ q_{n-1}\sigma_{n-1} + (1 - q_n - p_n)\sigma_n + p_{n+1}\sigma_{n+1} &= \sigma_n \quad \text{for } 0 < n < K, \\ q_{K-1}\sigma_{K-1} + (1 - p_K)\sigma_K &= \sigma_K. \end{aligned}$$

Subtracting the right-hand sides from the left-hand sides of these equations yields a set of equations just like those of Section 2.5.1 with terms λ and μ respectively replaced by q and p. Thus, the solution of the stationary distribution here just as it was in the continuous-time

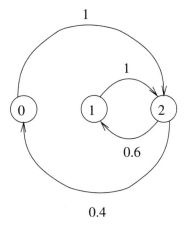

Figure 2.16   A periodic transition probability diagram.

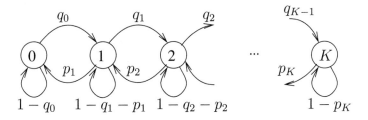

Figure 2.17   Transition probability diagram for a birth-death process.

setting:

$$\sigma_i \;=\; \sigma_0 \prod_{j=1}^{i} \frac{q_{j-1}}{p_j}$$

for $0 < i \le K$ and σ_0 is chosen as a normalizing term

$$\sigma_0 \;=\; \left(1 + \sum_{i=1}^{K} \prod_{n=1}^{i} \frac{q_{n-1}}{p_n}\right)^{-1}.$$

Also, the example with $q_n \equiv q$ and $p_n = np$ yields a truncated Poisson distribution (2.43) for σ with $\rho = q/p$.

One can also consider a discrete-time birth-death Markov chain on an infinite state space. Just as in the continuous time case, the process will be positive recurrent if and only if

$$R \;\equiv\; \sum_{i=1}^{\infty} \prod_{n=1}^{i} \frac{q_{n-1}}{p_n} \;<\; \infty,$$

in which case $\sigma_0 = (1 + R)^{-1}$ and

$$\sigma_n \;=\; \sigma_0 \prod_{j=1}^{i} \frac{q_{j-1}}{p_j}.$$

The example where $p_n = p$ and $q_n = q$ also yields a geometric, invariant stationary distribution (2.44) with $\rho = q/p < 1$. Finally, by defining g and Z as in Section 2.5.3 for a discrete-time birth-death process, one can use a similar "forward" argument to show that, for $i \leq k \leq j$,

$$g(k) \;=\; g(k+1)q_k + g(k)(1 - q_k - p_k) + g(k-1)p_k,$$

where the boundary conditions are $g(i-1) = 1$ and $g(j+1) = 0$. Note again the similarity between this equation and (2.45).

2.9   MARTINGALES ADAPTED TO DISCRETE TIME MARKOV CHAINS

Consider two discrete time stochastic processes Y and X neither of which are necessarily Markovian. The stochastic process Y is said to be a *submartingale relative to the process* X if

$$\mathsf{E}(Y(n) \mid X(n-1), X(n-2), ..., X(0)) \;\geq\; Y(n-1)$$

almost surely for all time n. Note that

$$\mathsf{E}(Y(n) \mid X(n-1)) \;\geq\; Y(n-1)$$

if X is Markovian. The proof of the following basic convergence result is beyond the scope of this book; see Section 11.5 of [225]. We will apply it to a route selection problem in Chapter 6.

Theorem 2.9.1. *If there is a constant $A < \infty$ such that $\sup_n \mathsf{E}|Y(n)| < A$, then there is a random variable Y such that*

$$\mathsf{P}\left(\lim_{n \to \infty} Y(n) = Y \right) \;=\; 1,$$

i.e., $Y(n) \to Y$ almost surely.

Problems

2.1   Verify that the theorems of Section 2.1 hold for geometrically distributed random variables.

2.2   Extend Theorems 2.1.2 and 2.1.3 to involve more than two independent, exponentially distributed random variables.

2.3   Show that exponentially distributed random variables are the *only* continuous, non-negative random variables with the memoryless property.

2.4   Show that a stationary process is wide-sense stationary but find an example where the converse does not hold.

2.5   With regard to the statement of (2.18), consider two independent and exponentially (but not necessarily identically) distributed random variables X_1 and X_2. For $\varepsilon > 0$, show that

$$P(X_1 + X_2 < \varepsilon) = o(\varepsilon).$$

2.6   For a transition rate matrix $\mathbf{Q}$ with unique invariant distribution $\underline{\sigma}$:

(a) Show that

$$\lim_{t \to \infty} \exp(t\mathbf{Q}) = \begin{bmatrix} \underline{\sigma}^{\mathrm{T}} \\ \underline{\sigma}^{\mathrm{T}} \\ \vdots \\ \underline{\sigma}^{\mathrm{T}} \end{bmatrix}.$$

Hint: Consider the statement of (2.35).

(b) Verify this numerically for Example 2.4 and for

$$\mathbf{Q} = \begin{bmatrix} -\lambda & \lambda \\ \mu & -\mu \end{bmatrix} = \mathbf{V} \begin{bmatrix} -\lambda - \mu & 0 \\ 0 & 0 \end{bmatrix} \mathbf{V}^{-1}, \qquad (2.60)$$

where V is a matrix of right eigenvectors of $\mathbf{Q}$:

$$\mathbf{V} = \begin{bmatrix} \lambda & 1 \\ -\mu & 1 \end{bmatrix}.$$

2.7   Show that the reducible Markov chain X with state space depicted in Figure 2.7 has infinitely many invariant distributions of the form

$$\underline{\sigma} = \alpha_1 \begin{bmatrix} 0 \\ q_{2,1}/(q_{2,1} + q_{1,2}) \\ q_{1,2}/(q_{2,1} + q_{1,2}) \\ 0 \\ 0 \\ 0 \end{bmatrix} + \alpha_2 \begin{bmatrix} 0 \\ 0 \\ 0 \\ q_{4,3}/(q_{3,4} + q_{4,3}) \\ q_{3,4}/(q_{3,4} + q_{4,3}) \\ 0 \end{bmatrix},$$

where α_1 and α_2 are any positive real numbers satisfying $\alpha_1 + \alpha_2 = 1$. Note that there are only two possible *steady-state* distributions to which the distribution of $X(t)$ converges as $t \to \infty$:

$$\begin{bmatrix} 0 \\ q_{2,1}/(q_{2,1} + q_{1,2}) \\ q_{1,2}/(q_{2,1} + q_{1,2}) \\ 0 \\ 0 \\ 0 \end{bmatrix} \quad \text{or} \quad \begin{bmatrix} 0 \\ 0 \\ 0 \\ q_{4,3}/(q_{3,4} + q_{4,3}) \\ q_{3,4}/(q_{3,4} + q_{4,3}) \\ 0 \end{bmatrix}.$$

2.8   Find the stationary distribution of the Markov chain with transition rate matrix given in (2.14).

2.9   Verify Equation (2.38) and show that $\underline{\sigma}$ is the invariant of the TRM R whose rates are given by (2.37).

2.10   Are the Markov chain examples of Sections 2.5.1 and 2.5.2 time reversible? That is, check whether the detailed balance equations (2.41) hold.

2.11   If a distribution $\underline{\sigma}$ satisfies the detailed balance equations (2.41) for a rate matrix **Q**, show that it also satisfies the balance equations (2.30).

2.12   Consider a Poisson process X with rate λ. Suppose that each transition time T_i is independently considered and, with probability p, is *deleted*. So, the resulting transition times $\{\tilde{T}_i\}$ are a subset of the original $\{T_i\}$. Show that the corresponding counting process

$$\tilde{X}(t) \;\equiv\; \sum_{i=1}^{\infty} \mathbf{1}\{\tilde{T}_i \le t\}$$

is a Poisson process with parameter $\lambda(1-p)$. Note: $\tilde{X}$ is said to be a *thinned* version of the Poisson process X.

2.13   Show that the examples of Figures 2.8 and 2.9 are time reversible and verify the detailed balance equations.

2.14   Consider an interval I in $\mathbb{R}$ and suppose the number of transitions of a Poisson process N in I is given. In this context, show that the distribution of the transition times is equal to that of the ordered random vector of random variables that are IID uniform on I, i.e., show that

$$\mathsf{P}(X_i \in (x_i, x_i + \mathrm{d}x_i),\ i = 1, ..., n \mid N(I) = n) = n! \prod_{i=1}^{n} \frac{\mathrm{d}x_i}{T}, \tag{2.61}$$

where X_1 is the time of the first transition of N in I and

$$T \;\equiv\; |I|.$$

This is called the *conditional uniformity property* of a Poisson process. The Poisson process is the only counting process with this property, i.e., that satisfies (2.61) for any integer n and interval I.

2.15   Describe how one could simulate the arrival times of a Poisson process over a fixed-length interval of time by using the conditional uniformity property.

2.16   Consider a collection of IID random variables $\{Y_i\}_{i=-\infty}^{\infty}$ independent of a Poisson process N on $\mathbb{R}$. That is,

$$N(B) \;\equiv\; \sum_i \mathbf{1}\{T_i \in B\}$$

for (Borel) subsets B of $\mathbb{R}$, where $N(B)$ is a Poisson distributed random variable with parameter $\lambda|B|$ and $|B|$ is the length (Lebesgue measure) of B. Let the interval $(c, d) = R_Y \subset \mathbb{R}$ be the range of Y_i, i.e., $\mathsf{P}(Y_i \in (c, d)) = 1$, where $-\infty < c < d < \infty$. Define the counting process

$$N^Y(B) \;\equiv\; \sum_i \mathbf{1}\{T_i + Y_i \in B\},$$

i.e., shift the ith point T_i of the Poisson process N by Y_i to obtain N^Y. Show that N^Y is also a Poisson process with intensity λ by showing that

$$\mathsf{E}\exp(sN^Y(I)) \;=\; \exp(\lambda|I|(e^s-1)).$$

Hint: Consider an arbitrary interval $I = (a, b)$, define $\hat{I} = (a - d, b - c)$, and note that $|\hat{I}| = |I| + |R_Y|$. Now,

$$\mathsf{E}\exp(sN^Y(I)) \;=\; \sum_{r=0}^{\infty}\mathsf{E}(\exp(sN^Y(I)) \mid N(\hat{I}) = r)\mathsf{P}(N(\hat{I}) = r)$$

and, by (2.61), the first term of the summand is

$$\mathsf{E}\left[\exp\left(s\sum_{i=1}^{r}\mathbf{1}\{X_i + Y_i \in I\}\right) \Big| N(\hat{I}) = r\right] \;=\; (\mathsf{E}\exp(s\mathbf{1}\{U + Y \in I\}))^r,$$

where U is uniformly distributed on $\hat{I}$ and independent of $Y \sim Y_i$. Finally, show that, irrespective of the distribution of Y,

$$\mathsf{P}(U + Y \in I) = \frac{|I|}{|\hat{I}|}.$$

Note: This problem represents a special case of a more general result; see [83] and Problem 4.36 of [183].

2.17 Find the stationary distribution of the finite *Engset* birth-death Markov chain having K states and transition rates $\lambda_i = (N - i + 1)\lambda$ and $\mu_i = i\mu$ for real positive constants λ and μ and positive integers K and N. Show that when $K = N$, the stationary distribution is binomial.

2.18 Show that the solution to (2.46) is

$$h_i(j) \;=\; \frac{j - i}{\mu - \lambda}$$

for all $j > i$. Hint: Consider a solution of the form $h_i(j) = \kappa j + \alpha$ and solve for scalars κ and α.

2.19 Prove (2.51).

2.20 Compute the invariant distribution of $\mathbf{P}_Y$ given in (2.54).

2.21 Prove the statement of (2.58).

2.22 Suppose a transition rate matrix $\mathbf{Q}$ on a countable state space Σ is time reversible with invariant σ. Consider a real-valued function V on Σ and define the transition rate matrix

$$\mathbf{R}_{x,y} \;=\; \mathbf{Q}_{x,y}\min\{1,\ \exp(\beta(V(y) - V(x)))\}$$

for all $x, y \in \Sigma$.

(a) Show that $\mathbf{R}$ is also time reversible with invariant

$$g_x(\beta) \;\equiv\; \frac{\sigma_x \exp(-\beta V(x))}{Z(\beta)},\quad x \in \Sigma, \tag{2.62}$$

where

$$Z(\beta) \;=\; \sum_{y \in \Sigma} \sigma_y \exp(-\beta V(y))$$

is the normalizing constant.

(b) Show that as $\beta \to \infty$, the *Gibbs distribution* $\underline{g}(\beta)$ converges to a distribution that is concentrated on the subset of points at which V is minimized over Σ.

The quantity β is interpreted as an inverse temperature, and when it decreases to zero over time in a sufficiently slow fashion, the resulting (time-inhomogeneous) Markov process, called *simulated annealing*, will converge (in probability) so as to minimize V on Σ [1, 90, 97, 177], i.e., it will "track" the time-varying Gibbs distribution $\underline{g}(\beta(t))$.

2.23   Find the transition probabilities of the discrete time Markov chain whose state transitions correspond to those of the continuous-time TRD in Figure 2.4, i.e., the "jump chain" with no self-transitions ($\mathbf{P}_{n,n} = 0$ for all $n \in \{1, 2, 3\}$).

CHAPTER 3

INTRODUCTION TO QUEUEING THEORY

This chapter introduces the theory of queues, specifically queues with a single input flow. Several topics of general scope are initially covered. A point will be made to apply these results in subsequent chapters. The second section is devoted to queues that can be described by an underlying Markov chain. The topic of the third section is the relationship between queueing delay and queue occupancy: Little's result and the notion that Poisson arrivals see time averages. We conclude the chapter with a brief overview of discrete-time queues.

3.1 ARRIVALS, DEPARTURES, AND QUEUE OCCUPANCY

A queue or buffer is simply a waiting room with an identified arrival process and departure (completed "jobs") process. *Work* is performed on jobs by *servers* according to a service policy. In some applications considered in this book, what arrives to the queue will be packets of information. In other applications, the arrivals will represent calls attempting to be set-up in the network. In this chapter, we will simply call the arrivals jobs.

Some jobs may be blocked from entering the queue (if the queue's waiting room is full) or join the queue and be expelled from the queue before reaching the server. In this book, we will consider queues in which each job will either be blocked upon arrival or enter the queue and experience a queueing delay as it waits in the queue until it gets access to a server. A job's queueing delay plus its service time is called its sojourn time, i.e., the time between the arrival of the job to the queue and its departure from the server. In this book, we will consider queues that serve jobs in the order of their arrival; these queues are known as first come, first serve (FCFS) or first in, first out (FIFO).

A counting process $\{A(0,t] \mid t \in \mathbb{R}^+\}$ represents the number of jobs arriving at the queue over the interval of time $(0,t]$. Another counting process $\{D(0,t] \mid t \in \mathbb{R}^+\}$ represents the number of departures from the queue over $(0,t]$. Finally, the counting process $\{L(0,t] \mid t \in \mathbb{R}^+\}$ represents the number of jobs blocked (lost) upon arrival over $(0,t]$. Let $Q(t)$ be the *number* of jobs in the queueing system at time t; the quantity $Q(t)$ represents the occupancy of the queue plus the number of jobs being served at time t; $Q(t)$ includes the arrivals <u>at</u> t but not the departures <u>at</u> t. Clearly, a previously "arrived" job is either queued or has departed or has been blocked, i.e.,

$$A(0,t] + Q(0) \;\; = \;\; Q(t) + D(0,t] + L(0,t].$$

If we take the origin of time to be $-\infty$, we can simply write

$$Q(t) \;\; = \;\; A(-\infty, t] - D(-\infty, t] - L(-\infty, t].$$

We will typically assume that the servers are *nonidling* (or "work conserving") in that they are busy whenever $Q(t) > 0$. Also, we assume a job's service cannot be preempted by another job. Finally, we assume that all of the servers associated with a given queue work at the same, constant rate; thus, we can unambiguously define S_i to be the service time required by the ith job. In addition, each job i will have the following two quantities associated with it: its arrival time to the queueing system T_i (assumed to be a nondecreasing sequence in i) and, if the job is not lost, its departure (service completion) time from the server V_i.

At time t, let $\mathcal{J}_Q(t) \subset \mathbb{Z}^+$ be the index set of jobs in the queue and let $\mathcal{J}_S(t) \subset \mathbb{Z}^+$ be the index set of jobs that are being served. Thus,

$$Q(t) \;\; = \;\; |\mathcal{J}_Q(t)| + |\mathcal{J}_S(t)|.$$

For $i \in \mathcal{J}_S(t)$, let $R_i(t)$ be the *residual* amount service time required by the ith job at time t. Clearly, $0 < R_i(t) \le S_i$, i.e., $R_i(t) \in (0, \le S_i]$, for all i, t. For a queue with nonidling and nonpreemptive servers, we can define the total *workload* (or remaining *work to be done*) at time t,

$$W(t) \;\; \equiv \;\; \sum_{i \in \mathcal{J}_Q(t)} S_i + \sum_{i \in \mathcal{J}_S(t)} R_i(t). \tag{3.1}$$

For jobs i that are not lost, let V_i be the *departure time* of the job from the server, i.e., from the queueing system. Clearly, $V_i - S_i$ is the time at which the ith job enters a server and, for all t and $i \in \mathcal{J}_S(t)$,

$$R_i(t) \;\; = \;\; V_i - t;$$

see Figure 3.1. Clearly, a job i is in the queue but not in service (i.e., $i \in \mathcal{J}_Q(t)$) if $T_i \le t < V_i - S_i$.

We will study lossy queues in greater detail later in this chapter. When considering a queueing system, it is useful to consider the arrival process A, queueing discipline, and departure process D separately. The arrival process A is parameterized above as $\{T_i, S_i\}_{i \in \mathbb{Z}}$ or $\mathbb{Z}^+$. The queueing discipline determines how jobs are enqueued and in which order they are served (dequeued), i.e., the dynamics of queue Q and workload W processes.

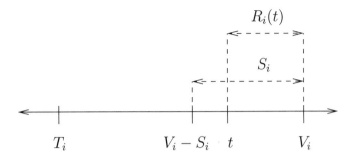

Figure 3.1 Queueing parameters associated with job i that is not lost.

The departure process, parameterized by $\{V_i, S_i\}$ is determined by both the queueing discipline and the arrival process. For a given arrival process and queueing discipline, we are typically interested in determining the "system" processes Q and W *only* in terms of the arrival parameters, i.e., not using the departure times V_i as these may not be known a priori.

3.2 LOSSLESS QUEUES

In this section, we assume that the queue we have just introduced is *lossless*, i.e., $L(-\infty, t] = 0$ for all t. Since,

$$A(s,t] = \sum_i \mathbf{1}\{T_i \in (s,t]\},$$

$$D(s,t] = \sum_i \mathbf{1}\{V_i \in (s,t]\},$$

we get that

$$Q(t) = A(-\infty, t] - D(-\infty, t] = \sum_i \mathbf{1}\{T_i \le t < V_i\}. \tag{3.2}$$

Clearly, the total delay experienced by the ith job is

$$V_i - T_i,$$

i.e., the departure time minus the arrival time. The quantity $V_i - T_i$ will also be called the *sojourn time* of the ith job. Again, this sojourn time consists of two components: the *queueing delay*, $V_i - S_i - T_i$, plus the service time, S_i.

In the following, expressions will be derived for quantities of interest such as the number of jobs in the queue, the workload, and job sojourn times. The objective is to express quantities of interest in terms of the job arrival times and service times alone.

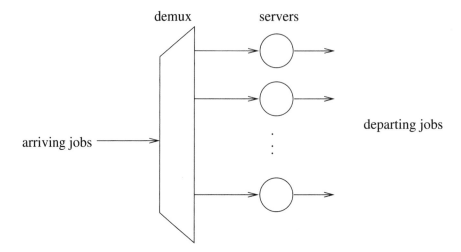

Figure 3.2 A multiserver queue with no waiting room.

3.2.1 No waiting room

Suppose the queueing system consists only of the servers and no waiting room; see Figure 3.2. Thus, if the job flow is demultiplexed (demux'ed) to one of K servers, the queueing system can only hold K jobs at any given time. Since the system is *assumed* lossless,

$$V_i \;=\; T_i + S_i$$

for all jobs i. Note that with infinitely many servers ($K = \infty$), the system is always lossless and also that an infinite server queue with Poisson arrivals was the subject of Problem 2.16. Therefore,

$$
\begin{aligned}
Q(t) &= \sum_i \mathbf{1}\{T_i \le t < T_i + S_i\} \\
&= \sum_i \mathbf{1}\{T_i \in (t - S_i, t]\}.
\end{aligned}
\tag{3.3}
$$

For this situation, clearly $\mathcal{J}_{\mathrm{Q}}(t) = \emptyset$ and $|\mathcal{J}_{\mathrm{S}}(t)| = Q(t)$ for all t. This implies that, for all t, the workload satisfies

$$
\begin{aligned}
W(t) &= \sum_{i \in \mathcal{J}_{\mathrm{S}}(t)} R_i(t) \\
&= \sum_i (T_i + S_i - t)\mathbf{1}\{T_i \in (t - S_i, t]\}.
\end{aligned}
\tag{3.4}
$$

Figure 3.3 depicts sample paths of Q and W. Note how the negative slope of the workload is proportional to the number of jobs queued.

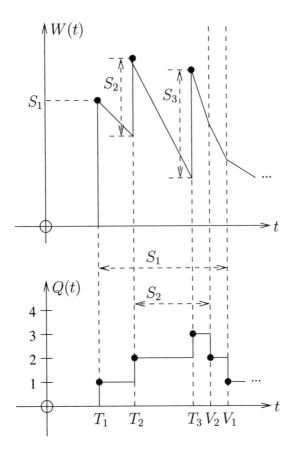

Figure 3.3 Sample paths for an infinite-server queue.

3.2.2 Single-server queue

Suppose that the queue has a waiting room and only a single server, as depicted in Figure 3.4. Clearly, if the waiting room was infinite in size, the queue would be lossless irrespective of the job arrival and service times. See Figure 3.5 for sample paths of the processes Q and W. Note that upon arrival of the ith job, Q increases by 1 and W increases by S_i. The process Q is piecewise constant and, due to the action of the server, $W(t)$ has zero time derivative if $Q(t) = 0$ (i.e., W is constant) and otherwise has time derivative -1 for any t that is not a job arrival time. Upon departure of the ith job, Q decreases by 1.

Theorem 3.2.1. *For a work-conserving, single-server, lossless FIFO queue:*

$$V_i \;=\; \max\{V_{i-1}, T_i\} + S_i \tag{3.5}$$

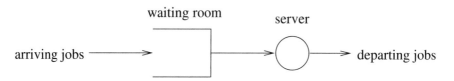

Figure 3.4   A single-server queue.

for all jobs $i \in \mathbb{Z}^+$, where

$$V_0 \;\equiv\; 0.$$

Proof: Consider the ith job arriving at the lossless queue. There are two cases. If $T_i \geq V_{i-1}$, then job $i-1$ has already departed the queue by time T_i. Consequently, $Q(T_i-) = 0$ (i.e., the queue is empty just before time T_i) and, when the ith job joins the queue, it immediately enters the server. Therefore, it departs S_i seconds after it arrives, i.e., $V_i = T_i + S_i$.

On the other hand, if $T_i < V_{i-1}$, job $i-1$ is present in the queue (and immediately ahead of the ith job) when the ith job joins the queue. Thus, the ith job will depart the queue S_i seconds after job $i-1$, i.e., $V_i = V_{i-1} + S_i$. $\square$

Note that, by subtracting T_i from both sides of (3.5), we get a statement involving the sojourn times $V_i - T_i$ and the *interarrival times* $T_i - T_{i-1}$:

$$\begin{align}
V_i - T_i &= \max\{(V_{i-1} - T_{i-1}) - (T_i - T_{i-1}),\, 0\} + S_i \tag{3.6} \\
&= \max\{V_{i-1} - T_i,\, 0\} + S_i, \tag{3.7}
\end{align}$$

where

$$T_0 \;\equiv\; 0.$$

An immediate consequence of the FIFO nature of a single-server queue is

$$V_i \;=\; T_i + W(T_i). \tag{3.8}$$

Also note that

$$\max\{V_{i-1}, T_i\}$$

is the time at which the ith job enters the server.

3.2.3   Single server and constant service times

A single-server queue is again considered. In this example, each job requires the same amount of service, i.e., for some constant $c > 0$, $S_i = 1/c$ for all i. So, the *service rate* of

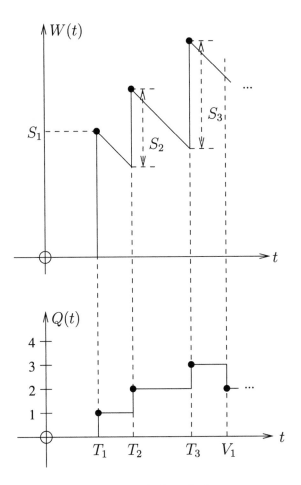

Figure 3.5 Sample paths for a single-server queue.

any server can be described as c jobs per second. Further suppose that the (assumed lossless) queue has a waiting room. In this example, we have the following simple expression for the number of jobs in the system in terms of the workload:

$$Q(t) = \lceil cW(t) \rceil \tag{3.9}$$

for all time t, where $\lceil x \rceil$ is the smallest integer greater than or equal to the real number x. This equation is an immediate consequence of the fact that each job contributes c^{-1} to the workload except for the job in service, which contributes only a fraction of c^{-1}. That is, $\lceil c(V_i - t) \rceil = 1$ when the ith job is in the server at time t, i.e., when

$$V_i - \frac{1}{c} \leq t < V_i \quad \Leftrightarrow \quad 0 < V_i - t \leq \frac{1}{c},$$

where we recall $V_i - t$ is the residual workload on the ith job.

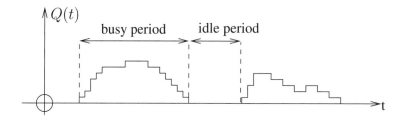

Figure 3.6 Queue busy and idle periods.

We now prove an important expression for the workload which is not recursive in nature.

Theorem 3.2.2. *For a work-conserving, single-server, lossless, initially empty ($W(0) = 0$) FIFO queue,*

$$W(t) \;=\; \max_{0 \le s \le t} \left[\frac{1}{c} A(s,t] - (t - s) \right] \tag{3.10}$$

for all times $t \ge 0$, where the maximizing value of s is t if $W(t) = 0$, else the starting time of the busy period containing t.

Proof: We first define a notion of a queue *busy period* as an interval of time $[s, t)$ with $s < t$ such that:

(a) $W(s-) = Q(s-) = 0$, i.e., the system is empty just prior to time s,

(b) $W(r) > 0$ (and $Q(r) > 0$) for all time $r \in [s, t)$, and

(c) $W(t) = Q(t) = 0$, i.e., the system is empty at time t.

Queue busy periods are separated by *idle periods*, which are intervals of time over which W (and Q) are both always zero. So, the evolution of W is an alternating sequence of busy and idle periods; see Figure 3.6. Note that a busy period is, of course, initiated with the arrival of a job to an empty queue.

Arbitrarily fix a time t somewhere in a queue busy period. Define $b(t)$ as the starting time of the busy period containing time t, so that, in particular, $b(t) \le t$ and $W(b(t-)) = 0$. The total work that arrived over $[b(t), t)$ is $A[b(t), t]/c$ and the total service done over $[b(t), t)$ was $t - b(t)$. Since $W(s) > 0$ for all $s \in [b(t), t)$,

$$W(t) \;=\; \frac{1}{c} A[b(t), t] - (t - b(t)). \tag{3.11}$$

Furthermore, for any $s \in [b(t), t)$,

$$W(t) \;=\; W(s) + \frac{1}{c} A[s, t] - (t - s)$$

$$\ge\; \frac{1}{c} A[s, t] - (t - s). \tag{3.12}$$

Now consider a time $s < b(t)$. Since $W(b(t)-) = 0$, any arrivals over $[s, b(t))$ have departed by time $b(t)$; this implies that

$$\frac{1}{c} A[s, b(t)) - (b(t) - s) \leq 0. \tag{3.13}$$

Therefore,

$$
\begin{aligned}
\frac{1}{c} A[s, t] - (t - s) &= \frac{1}{c} A[s, b(t)) - (b(t) - s) + \frac{1}{c} A[b(t), t] - (t - b(t)) \\
&\leq \frac{1}{c} A[b(t), t] - (t - b(t)) \\
&= W(t). \tag{3.14}
\end{aligned}
$$

Equation (3.11) and inequalities (3.12) and (3.14) prove the desired result for the case where $W(t) > 0$.

The other case where $Q(t) = 0$ is similarly proved using the argument behind (3.13). $\square$

Note that, by Theorem 3.2.2 and (3.9),

$$Q(t) = \left\lceil \max_{0 \leq s \leq t} A[s, t] - (t - s)c \right\rceil. \tag{3.15}$$

Also, as a kind of converse to (3.9), when the ith job is in the server at time t (i.e., $\mathcal{J}_{\mathrm{S}}(t) = \{i\}$),

$$W(t) = \frac{1}{c} \max\{Q(t) - 1, 0\} + V_i - t. \tag{3.16}$$

3.2.4 Single server and general service times

Now consider a lossless FIFO single-server queue wherein the ith arriving job has service time S_i. Let $i(t)$ be the index of the last job arriving prior to time t, i.e.,

$$i(t) \equiv \max\{j \mid T_j \leq t\}.$$

For this queue, it is left as an exercise to show that the workload is given by

$$W(t) = \left[\max_{j \leq i(t)} \left(\sum_{k=j}^{i(t)} S_k \right) - (t - T_j) \right]^{+}, \tag{3.17}$$

where $(x)^{+} \equiv \max\{x, 0\}$.

3.3 A QUEUE DESCRIBED BY AN UNDERLYING MARKOV CHAIN

A detailed survey of queues having underlying Markov chains is given in [226]. In this chapter, we will describe two of the simplest and most important examples of such queues.

The first is called the "M/M/1" queue, where the first "M" in this notation means that the job *interarrival times* are Memoryless; i.e., the job arrival process is a Poisson process which has exponential (memoryless) interarrival times $T_n - T_{n-1}$. The second "M" means that the job *service times*, S_n, are independent and identically distributed exponential (Memoryless) random variables. Also, the service times are independent of the arrival times. The "1" means that there is one work-conserving server. The queue is implicitly assumed to have an infinite capacity to hold jobs; indeed, "M/M/1" and "M/M/1/∞" specify the same queue. So, the M/M/1 queue is lossless. When a general distribution is involved, the terms "G" or "GI" are used instead of "M"; "GI" denotes general and IID. So, an M/GI/1 queue has a Poisson job arrival process and IID job service times of some distribution that is not necessarily exponential.

Let us now consider an M/M/1 queue with (Poisson) job arrivals of rate λ jobs per second and (exponentially distributed) service times with mean $1/\mu$ seconds. That is, the job interarrival times are independent and exponentially distributed with mean $1/\lambda$ seconds and, therefore, for all times $s < t$, $A(s,t)$ is a Poisson *distributed* random variable with mean $\lambda(t-s)$. The mean arrival rate of *work* is λ/μ and the service rate is one unit of work per second.

On the other hand, the mean service rate can be described as μ jobs per second. So, the queue (job) occupancy, Q, is a birth-death Markov process with infinite state space $\mathbb{Z}^+$. When the *traffic intensity*

$$\rho \equiv \frac{\lambda}{\mu} < 1,$$

Q is the positive recurrent birth-death process with transition rate diagram given in Figure 2.9. The stationary distribution of Q is geometric with parameter ρ; see Equation (2.44). The example of an M/M/K/K queue, i.e., a queue with K servers and no waiting room, is described in Section 3.5 below. The M/GI/∞ queue was the subject of Problem 2.16.

In the problems at the end of the chapter, we explore other queues with "underlying" Markov chains. In particular, from these underlying Markov chains we can derive information about the stationary mean workload of the queue. For example, one can show that the mean sojourn time of a job through an M/GI/1 queue is

$$\frac{\lambda \mathsf{E}(S^2)}{2(1 - \lambda \mathsf{E}S)}, \tag{3.18}$$

where, as above, S is distributed as the service time of a job and λ is the (Poisson) job arrival rate. This is a *Pollaczek-Khintchine* formula; see [219].

3.4 STATIONARY QUEUES

Recall that (3.6) is a statement about job *sojourn times* and Theorem 3.2.2 is a statement about queue *occupancy*. Also, in the previous section, we found the stationary distribution of the Q and W processes of the M/M/1 queue but not that of the sojourn times (delay), $V - T$, experienced by the jobs.

Consider the ith job arriving at time T_i to a FIFO single-server queue. Recall that the departure time of this job is given by

$$V_n = T_n + W(T_n). \tag{3.19}$$

Suppose the queue is stationary. In this case, (3.19) implies the sojourn times of the jobs are identically distributed. Indeed, suppose we are interested in the distribution or just the mean of the job sojourn times. Regarding (3.19), one is tempted to identify the distribution of the sojourn times $V - T$ with the stationary distribution of W; this gives the correct answer for the M/M/1 queue. In general, however, the distribution of $W(T_n)$ (i.e., the distribution of the W process *viewed* at a "typical" job arrival time T_n) is *not* equal to the stationary distribution of W (i.e., viewed at at typical time); see Section 3.4.3.

In this section, we will explore the relationship between the stationary distribution of a queueing system (i.e., as viewed from a typical time) and the distribution of the queueing system at the arrival time of a typical job. We will motivate, state, and apply Little's result and the rule that Poisson arrivals see time averages.

3.4.1   Point processes and queues on $\mathbb{R}$

A stationary Poisson process on the whole real line $\mathbb{R}$ is defined by a countable collection of points $\{\tau_i\}_{i=-\infty}^{\infty}$, where the interarrival times $\tau_i - \tau_{i-1}$ are IID exponential random variables. Alternatively, we can characterize a Poisson process on $\mathbb{R}$ by stipulating that the number of points in any interval of length t is Poisson distributed with mean λt and that the number of points in nonoverlapping intervals is independent; recall Problem 2.16 of Chapter 2.

■ **EXAMPLE 3.1**

This last characterization naturally extends to a characterization of a Poisson point process on $\mathbb{R}^n$ for all dimensions $n \geq 1$, i.e., a *spatial* Poisson process: If $v(A)$ is the volume (or area) of $A \subset \mathbb{R}^n$, then the number of points in A is Poisson distributed with mean $\lambda v(A)$.

Let $A(s, t]$ be the number of jobs arriving at a work-conserving, lossless, FIFO queue over the interval of time $(s, t]$, where $s, t \in \mathbb{R}$. Let c jobs per second be the constant service rate of the queue, i.e., each job requires $1/c$ units of work and the server can execute one unit of work per second. Assume that the point process $\{\tau_i\}_{i=-\infty}^{\infty}$ of job arrival times is stationary and not necessarily Poisson. In particular, this means that the distribution of $A(s, t]$ depends on s, t only through $t - s$, i.e., $A(s, t) \sim A(s + r, t + r)$ for all $s, t, r \in \mathbb{R}$. Clearly, we have

$$A(s, t] \;=\; \sum_{i=-\infty}^{\infty} \mathbf{1}\{s < \tau_i \leq t\}.$$

Note that some jobs have negative indices.

For any time $t \in \mathbb{R}$, the number of jobs in the queueing system at time t is given by

$$Q(t) \;=\; \left[\max_{-\infty < s \leq t} A(s, t] - c(t - s) \right] \tag{3.20}$$

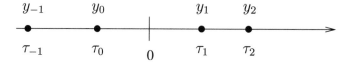

Figure 3.7   Stationary version of a marked point process **M**.

and the workload is given by

$$W(t) \quad = \quad \max_{-\infty < s \le t} \frac{1}{c} A(s,t] - (t-s); \tag{3.21}$$

see Equations (3.9) and (3.10). Again, note that the "maximums" are taken over all real times $s \le t$.

3.4.2   Stationary and synchronous versions of a marked point process

Consider again a stationary point process $\{\tau_i\}_{i=-\infty}^{\infty}$ on $\mathbb{R}$. Suppose the subscript labels are chosen so that $\tau_0 \le 0 < \tau_1$. To each point τ_i we associate a *mark* (random variable) y_i. The ensemble

$$\mathbf{M} \quad \equiv \quad \{\tau_i, y_i\}_{i=-\infty}^{\infty}$$

is called a *stationary marked point process*; see Figure 3.7. One can interpret that the marked point process is viewed at a typical time in Figure 3.7, where the typical time is the origin 0. That is, the process "began" infinitely long ago and, by time 0, has reached steady state. Alternatively, given the positions and marks on the real line, the origin of time 0 is selected "uniformly at random" (hence the term typical) and thereby fixes the indices of the marks.

Now consider the marked point process as viewed from a typical *arrival*; see Figure 3.8. That is, an arrival is chosen uniformly at random and the origin of time is set to the arrival time of that mark. To this end, define the *synchronous* marked point process

$$\mathbf{M}_0 \quad \equiv \quad \{T_i, x_i\}_{i=-\infty}^{\infty},$$

where the subscripts of the point process T_i are chosen so that $T_0 = 0$. So, x_0 is a typical mark and T_1 is the length of a typical interarrival time. As indicated above, we will interpret each point as an arrival time of a job to a queueing system. A mark associated with a job will, in some way, represent the "state" of the queueing system at the job's arrival time. A translation of a marked point process to the left by a fixed amount of time $t \in \mathbb{R}$ is denoted by

$$\mathbf{M}_0 + t \quad \equiv \quad \{T_i - t, x_i\}_{i=-\infty}^{\infty}.$$

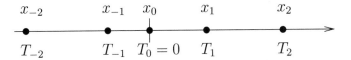

Figure 3.8 Synchronous version of a marked point process M_0.

Since $\mathbf{M}$ is stationary, it is distributed as $\mathbf{M} + t$, i.e.,

$$\mathbf{M} + t \quad \sim \quad \mathbf{M},$$

for all $t \in \mathbb{R}$.

Two basic assumptions in this book will be that the intensity of the point process

$$\lambda \quad \equiv \quad \frac{1}{\mathsf{E}T_1}$$

satisfies $0 < \lambda < \infty$ and that the processes under consideration are *ergodic* [138]; see Section 1.11. In particular, ergodicity implies that the law of large numbers for $\mathbf{M}$ (and $\mathbf{M}_0$) holds: For all times $s \in \mathbb{R}$,

$$\lim_{t \to \infty} \frac{A(s, t]}{t - s} \quad = \quad \lambda \quad \text{almost surely,}$$

and for all times $t \in \mathbb{R}$,

$$\lim_{s \to -\infty} \frac{A(s, t]}{t - s} \quad = \quad \lambda \quad \text{almost surely.}$$

Under these conditions, Loynes showed [9, 14] that there exists a stationary solution W to (3.21) with $W(0)$ distributed as the one-dimensional (stationary) marginal of W.

■ **EXAMPLE 3.2**

In this example, differences between $\mathbf{M}$ and $\mathbf{M}_0$ are demonstrated. Consider a point process on $\mathbb{R}$ whose interarrival times are discretely distributed as

$$\mathsf{P}(T_1 = 5) = \tfrac{1}{4} \quad \text{and} \quad \mathsf{P}(T_1 = 10) = \tfrac{3}{4}.$$

The distribution of $\tau_1 - \tau_0$ will now be computed. Consider a large interval of time $H \gg 1$ spanning N consecutive interarrivals. Recall that for the stationary process $\mathbf{M}$ one can interpret the origin of time as uniformly randomly selected. Thus, the probability of selecting the origin of time in an interarrival of length 10 is equal to the fraction of interarrivals of length 10 that cover H. That is, since $H \gg 1$, by the law of large numbers (Section 1.11), $H \approx N\mathsf{E}T_1 = N(5 \cdot \tfrac{1}{4} + 10 \cdot \tfrac{3}{4})$. Therefore,

$$\mathsf{P}(\tau_1 - \tau_0 = 5) \quad = \quad \frac{N \cdot 5(1/4)}{N(5(1/4) + 10(3/4))} \quad = \quad \frac{1}{7} \neq \frac{1}{4} = \mathsf{P}(T_1 = 5).$$

3.4.3 Poisson arrivals see time averages

The following is a general "conservation law" called Palm's theorem [14, 219] that we state without proof.

Theorem 3.4.1.

$$\mathsf{E} G(\mathbf{M}) \;=\; \lambda \mathsf{E} \int_0^{T_1} G(\mathbf{M}_0 + t)\, \mathrm{d}t$$

for any real-valued function G.

The following are immediate corollaries of Palm's theorem.

Lemma 3.4.1. *For all $v, w \geq 0$,*

$$\mathsf{P}(-\tau_0 > v,\, \tau_1 > w) \;=\; \lambda \int_{v+w}^{\infty} \mathsf{P}(T_1 > t)\, \mathrm{d}t. \tag{3.22}$$

Proof: Applying Palm's theorem with

$$G(\mathbf{M}) \;\equiv\; \mathbf{1}\{-\tau_0 > v,\, \tau_1 > w\}$$

results in the following right-hand side:

$$\lambda \mathsf{E} \int_0^{T_1} G(\mathbf{M}_0 + t)\, \mathrm{d}t \;=\; \lambda \mathsf{E} \int_0^{T_1} \mathbf{1}\{-(T_0 - t) > v,\, T_1 - t > w\}\, \mathrm{d}t,$$

where we note that $T_0 \equiv 0 < t < T_1$ in the integrand implies that $T_0 - t \equiv -t \leq 0 \leq T_1 - t$, i.e., the points indexed 0 and 1 of $\mathbf{M}_0 + t$ are on different sides of the origin. Thus,

$$\lambda \mathsf{E} \int_0^{T_1} G(\mathbf{M}_0 + t)\, \mathrm{d}t \;=\; \lambda \int_0^{\infty} \int_0^{s} \mathbf{1}\{t > v,\, s - t > w\}\, \mathrm{d}t\, \mathsf{P}(T_1 \in (s, s + \mathrm{d}s))$$

$$=\; \lambda \int_0^{\infty} \int_t^{\infty} \mathbf{1}\{t > v,\, s - t > w\} \mathsf{P}(T_1 \in (s, s + \mathrm{d}s))\, \mathrm{d}t,$$

where the last equality is simply switching the order of integration (Fubini's theorem). Since the integrand is 1 if an only if $t > v$ and $s > t + w$,

$$\lambda \mathsf{E} \int_0^{T_1} G(\mathbf{M}_0 + t)\, \mathrm{d}t \;=\; \lambda \int_v^{\infty} \int_{t+w}^{\infty} \mathsf{P}(T_1 \in (s, s + \mathrm{d}s))\, \mathrm{d}t$$

$$=\; \lambda \int_v^{\infty} \mathsf{P}(T_1 > t + w)\, \mathrm{d}t$$

$$=\; \lambda \int_{v+w}^{\infty} \mathsf{P}(T_1 > \tilde{t})\, \mathrm{d}\tilde{t},$$

where the last equality is just a change of the variable of integration to $\tilde{t} = t + w$.   □

Lemma 3.4.2. T_1 *is exponentially distributed with parameter* λ *if and only if*

$$\mathsf{P}(\tau_1 > w) \ \equiv \ \mathsf{P}(T_1 > w). \tag{3.23}$$

Proof: Applying Palm's theorem with

$$G(\mathbf{M}) \ \equiv \ \mathbf{1}\{\tau_1 > w\}$$

results in the following right-hand side:

$$
\begin{aligned}
\lambda \mathsf{E} \int_0^{T_1} G(\mathbf{M}_0 + t)\,\mathrm{d}t &= \lambda \mathsf{E} \int_0^{T_1} \mathbf{1}\{T_1 - w > t\}\,\mathrm{d}t \\
&= \lambda \int_0^{\infty} \int_0^{s} \mathbf{1}\{s - w > t\}\,\mathrm{d}t\, \mathsf{P}(T_1 \in (s, s + \mathrm{d}s)) \\
&= \lambda \int_0^{\infty} \int_s^{\infty} \mathbf{1}\{s - w > t\}\mathsf{P}(T_1 \in (s, s + \mathrm{d}s))\,\mathrm{d}t \\
&= \lambda \int_0^{\infty} \int_{t+w}^{\infty} \mathsf{P}(T_1 \in (s, s + \mathrm{d}s))\,\mathrm{d}t \\
&= \lambda \int_0^{\infty} \mathsf{P}(T_1 > t + w)\,\mathrm{d}t.
\end{aligned}
$$

Now, since

$$\frac{1}{\lambda} \ = \ \mathsf{E}T_1 \ = \ \int_0^{\infty} \mathsf{P}(T_1 > t)\,\mathrm{d}t$$

(recall Problem 1.11) and since $A \subset B$ implies that $\mathsf{P}(A) = \mathsf{P}(A|B)\mathsf{P}(B)$ (assuming $\mathsf{P}(B) > 0$), then

$$\lambda \mathsf{E} \int_0^{T_1} G(\mathbf{M}_0 + t)\,\mathrm{d}t \ = \ \frac{\int_0^{\infty} \mathsf{P}(T_1 > t + w \mid T_1 > t)\mathsf{P}(T_1 > t)\,\mathrm{d}t}{\int_0^{\infty} \mathsf{P}(T_1 > t)\,\mathrm{d}t}.$$

Therefore,

$$\lambda \mathsf{E} \int_0^{T_1} G(\mathbf{M}_0 + t)\,\mathrm{d}t \ = \ \mathsf{P}(T_1 > w) \ \text{ for all } w \geq 0$$

if and only if

$$\mathsf{P}(T_1 > t + w \mid T_1 > t) \ = \ \mathsf{P}(T_1 > w) \ \text{ for all } w \geq 0,$$

i.e., T_1 is memoryless. Since the exponential is the only memoryless continuous distribution (Problem 2.3 of Chapter 2), the lemma is proved.   □

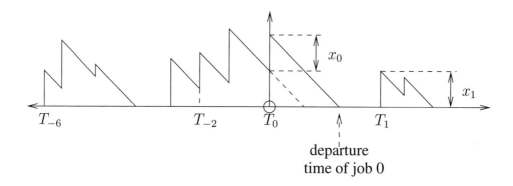

Figure 3.9   Synchronous workload of a single-server, lossless, nonidling queue, $G(\mathbf{M}_0)$.

Now suppose that $\{T_i\}_{i=-\infty}^{\infty}$ is a Poisson process (with mean rate λ), i.e., $\{T_i - T_{i-1}\}_{i=-\infty}^{\infty}$ are IID exponential random variables each with mean $1/\lambda$. Lemma (3.4.2) implies that τ_1 is exponentially distributed with parameter λ. By Lemma 3.4.1,

$$\mathsf{P}(-\tau_0 > v, \tau_1 > w) = e^{-\lambda(v+w)}$$
$$\Rightarrow \; \mathsf{P}(-\tau_0 > v \mid \tau_1 > w)\mathsf{P}(\tau_1 > w) = e^{-\lambda(v+w)}$$
$$\Rightarrow \; \mathsf{P}(-\tau_0 > v \mid \tau_1 > w) = e^{-\lambda v}$$

for all $v, w \geq 0$. Letting $w \to \infty$, we see that τ_0 and τ_1 are independent and $-\tau_0$ is also exponentially distributed with parameter λ. Therefore, if we *insert a point at the origin*, the point process $\{\tau_i\}_{i=-\infty}^{\infty}$ remains a Poisson process! That is, the stationary Poisson point process $\{\tau_i\}_{i=-\infty}^{\infty}$ with a point inserted at the origin is *identical in distribution* to the synchronous Poisson point process $\{T_i\}_{i=-\infty}^{\infty}$.

Now consider the stationary, lossless, FIFO, single-server queue with Poisson arrivals depicted in Figure 3.10. Let τ_j be the arrival time and y_j be the service time, respectively, of the jth job. Recall the statement of (3.17) concerning the stationary workload at time 0:

$$W(0) = \left[\max_{j \leq 0} \left(\sum_{k=j}^{0} y_k \right) + \tau_j \right]^{+} \equiv G(\mathbf{M}).$$

The implication of the previous paragraph is that

$$\mathbf{M}_0 \;\sim\; \mathbf{M} \cup \{0, \tilde{y}\}, \tag{3.24}$$

where $\tilde{y}$ is distributed as the service time of a typical job.[1] Thus,

$$W(0) \;\sim\; \max_{j < 0} \sum_{k=j}^{0} x_k + T_j,$$

---

[1]Equivalently, $\mathbf{M} \sim \mathbf{M}_0 \backslash \{T_0 \equiv 0, x_0\}$, i.e., remove the point at the origin of $\mathbf{M}_0$.

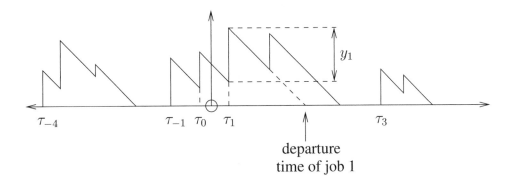

Figure 3.10 Stationary workload of a single-server, lossless, nonidling queue, $W(0) = G(\mathbf{M})$.

where the right-hand side is the workload upon (just before) the *arrival of a typical job*. This is one instance of the rule called Poisson arrivals see time averages (PASTA). By the same argument above, PASTA can be applied to any stationary queue (or queueing system) wherein the "state" (workload, number of jobs, etc.) just prior to time 0 can be written as a function of $\{\tau_j, y_j\}_{j \leq 0}$, i.e., the queue is *causal* or *nonanticipative*.

■ **EXAMPLE 3.3**

Consider the stationary M/M/1 queue with traffic intensity $\rho = \lambda/\mu < 1$; recall the example of Equation (2.44). By PASTA, the distribution of the *number* of jobs in the queue just before the arrival time T of a typical job[2] is geometric with parameter ρ:

$$\mathsf{P}(Q(T-) = i) \quad = \quad (1-\rho)\rho^i \quad \text{for } i \in \mathbb{Z}^+.$$

Note that $Q(T) = Q(T-) + 1 \geq 1$.

The *sojourn time* of an arriving job is the total workload upon its arrival in the queue. To find the distribution of the sojourn time of a typical job, $W(T)$, let $\{\tilde{S}_j\}$ be an IID sequence of random variables that are exponentially distributed with parameter μ. Since the service times are IID and exponentially distributed, the total workload, $W(T)$, is distributed as

$$\left(\sum_{j=1}^{Q(T-)} \tilde{S}_j \right) + R\mathbf{1}\{Q(T) > 0\}, \tag{3.25}$$

[2]$T = T_0 \equiv 0$ in the notation above.

where

$$\sum_{j=1}^{0}(\cdots) \;\equiv\; 0$$

and R is distributed as the residual service time of the job in the server at time T. The memoryless property implies that R is exponentially distributed with parameter μ as well, i.e., simply that

$$W(T) \;\sim\; \sum_{j=1}^{Q(T-)+1} \tilde{S}_j \;=\; \sum_{j=1}^{Q(T)} \tilde{S}_j.$$

Consequently, given $Q(T-) = n$, $W(T)$ (the sojourn time of a typical job) has a gamma (Erlang) distribution with parameters $n + 1$ and μ.

The *mean* sojourn time w can now be obtained using an instance of *Wald's identity* [226]:

$$\mathsf{E}W(T) \;=\; \mathsf{E}Q(T)\mathsf{E}S \tag{3.26}$$

$$= \left(1 + \frac{\rho}{1-\rho}\right)\frac{1}{\mu}$$

$$= \frac{1}{\mu - \lambda}, \tag{3.27}$$

where we used the formula for the mean of the geometrically distributed random variable computed in Section 1.4.2.

Without Poisson arrivals, the implication of PASTA usually does not hold [15]; recall Example 3.2.

3.4.4 Little's result

Campbell's theorem (interpreted as a converse of Palm's theorem 3.4.1) allows us to compute the distribution of $\mathbf{M}$ from that of $\mathbf{M}_0$ for times $t \in \mathbb{R}$:

Theorem 3.4.2. *For any nonnegative function f on $\mathbb{R}^2$,*

$$\lambda\mathsf{E}\int_{-\infty}^{\infty} f(t, x_0)\,\mathrm{d}t \;=\; \mathsf{E}\sum_{i=-\infty}^{\infty} f(\tau_i, y_i).$$

Proof: (Sketch [219].) Consider a small interval of time $(t, t + \mathrm{d}t)$ and the distribution of a typical mark, $\mathsf{P}(x_0 \in (x, x + \mathrm{d}x))$. The quantity $\mathsf{P}(x_0 \in (x, x + \mathrm{d}x))$ would be equal to the fraction of points of the stationary process $\mathbf{M}$ in the interval $(t, t + \mathrm{d}t)$ whose marks

y are in the interval $(x, x + dx)$. Note that the expected number of points in $(t, t + dt)$ is $\lambda \, dt$. The expected number of marks $y \in (x, x + dx)$ in this interval of time is

$$\mathsf{E} \sum_{i=-\infty}^{\infty} \mathbf{1}\{y_i \in (x, x + dx), \ \tau_i \in (t, t + dt)\},$$

where we note that the summand does not depend on t by stationarity. Therefore, by ergodicity,

$$\mathsf{P}(x_0 \in (x, x + dx)) \quad = \quad \frac{1}{\lambda \, dt} \mathsf{E} \sum_{i=-\infty}^{\infty} \mathbf{1}\{y_i \in (x, x + dx), \ \tau_i \in (t, t + dt)\}.$$

Multiplying this equation by $f(t, x)$ and integrating both sides over $\mathbb{R}^2$ gives the desired result. $\qquad\qquad\qquad\qquad\qquad\qquad\qquad\qquad\qquad\qquad\qquad\qquad\qquad\qquad\qquad\quad$ □

A rigorous treatment of Palm and Campbell's theorems is given in [14].

Suppose that the queueing system is lossless and define the mark y_k as the *sojourn time*[3] of the job arriving at time τ_k, i.e., the *departure* time of the kth job is $\tau_k + y_k$ (note that neither Palm nor Campbell's theorem requires any kind of independence among the arrival times or marks of the point process). Also define

$$f(\tau, y) \quad = \quad \mathbf{1}\{\tau \le 0, \ \tau + y > 0\}$$

so that $f(\tau_k, y_k) = 1$ if and only if the kth job is in the queueing system at time 0, the typical time at which the stationary process $\mathbf{M}$ is viewed. Let w be distributed as the mean workload in the queue upon arrival of a typical job and let L be the mean *number* of jobs in the system in steady state. Thus,

$$L \quad = \quad \mathsf{E} \sum_{i=-\infty}^{\infty} \mathbf{1}\{\tau \le 0, \ \tau + y > 0\}$$

and so, by Theorem 3.4.2,

$$L \quad = \quad \lambda \int_{-\infty}^{0} \mathsf{E} \mathbf{1}\{x_0 > -t\} \, dt$$

$$= \quad \lambda \int_{0}^{\infty} \mathsf{P}(x_0 > s) \, ds$$

$$= \quad \lambda \mathsf{E} x_0,$$

where the variable of integration was changed from t to $s = -t$. Finally, note that $w = \mathsf{E} x_0$. Therefore, we have arrived at Little's result:

Theorem 3.4.3.

$$L \quad = \quad \lambda w.$$

---

[3] So, for a lossless, FIFO, single-server queue, $y_k = W(\tau_k)$, which is a function of $\{\tau_i\}_{i \le k}$ and the associated service times.

To reiterate, Little's result relates the average number of jobs in the *stationary* lossless queueing system (i.e., the average number of jobs viewed at a typical time 0) to the mean workload in the queue upon arrival of a typical job (i.e., the mean sojourn time of a job). Theorems 3.4.1, 3.4.2, and 3.4.3 are "conservation" laws of very general applicability.

■ **EXAMPLE 3.4**

By (2.44) and the calculation of the mean of a geometrically distributed random variable in Section 1.4.2, the mean number of jobs in the stationary M/M/1 queue is

$$L = \frac{\rho}{1 - \rho},$$

where we recall that $\rho = \lambda/\mu < 1$ is the traffic intensity.

By Little's result, the mean workload in the M/M/1 queue upon arrival of a typical job (i.e., the mean sojourn time of a job) is

$$w = \frac{L}{\lambda} = \frac{1}{\mu - \lambda},$$

which agrees with (3.27).

Now consider again a lossless, FIFO, single-server queue Q with mean interarrival time of jobs $1/\lambda$ and mean job service time $1/\mu < 1/\lambda$, i.e., mean job arrival rate λ and mean job service rate $\mu > \lambda$. Suppose the queue and arrival process are stationary at time zero. The following result identifies the *traffic intensity* λ/μ with the fraction of time that the stationary queue is busy.

Theorem 3.4.4.

$$P(Q(0) = 0) = 1 - \frac{\lambda}{\mu}. \tag{3.28}$$

Proof: Consider the server separately from the waiting room (as we have not done so far in this book). Assuming that the mean *departure* rate of the waiting room is λ too (see below), Little's result implies that the mean number of jobs in the server is $L = \lambda/\mu$. Finally, since the number of jobs in the server is Bernoulli distributed (with parameter L), the mean corresponds to the probability that the server is occupied (has one job) in steady state. □

We state the following result for future reference.

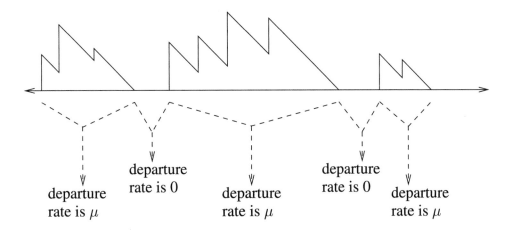

Figure 3.11 Departure rate of a stable ($\lambda < \mu$), lossless, nonidling single-server queue.

Theorem 3.4.5. *For a stable lossless queue, the mean (net) arrival rate equals the mean departure rate in steady state, i.e.,*

$$\lim_{t \to \infty} \frac{A(0,t]}{t} = \lim_{t \to \infty} \frac{D[0,t)}{t}.$$

Proof: The queue is stable implies that $Q(t)/t \to 0$ almost surely as $t \to \infty$. Recall that

$$Q(0) + A(0,t] \quad = \quad Q(t) + D[0,t),$$

where $A(0,t)$ and $D(0,t)$ are the cumulative arrivals and departures over $(0,t)$, respectively. Dividing this equation by t and letting $t \to \infty$ gives the desired result. $\quad\square$

See Figure 3.11, indicating the departure rate corresponding to a queue's sample path. Note that the *mean* departure rate is

$$
\begin{aligned}
\mu \cdot \mathrm{P}(Q > 0) + 0 \cdot \mathrm{P}(Q = 0) \quad &= \quad \mu \cdot \rho \\
&= \quad \lambda,
\end{aligned}
$$

which is consistent with the statements of the previous two theorems.

3.5 ERLANG'S BLOCKING FORMULA FOR THE M/M/K/K QUEUE

In this section, we study another important example whose queue occupancy can be described by a finite birth-death Markov chain. Consider a queue with Poisson arrivals, IID exponential service times, K servers, and no waiting room, i.e., in the notation of Section 3.3, an M/M/K/K queue.[4] As in Section 3.3, let λ be the rate of the Poisson job arrivals and let $1/\mu$ be the mean service time of a job.

Suppose that there are n jobs in the system at time t, i.e., $Q(t) = n$. We can adapt the argument at the end of Section 3.3 to show Q is a birth-death Markov chain and finds its transition rate diagram. Indeed, suppose $Q(t) = n > 0$ and suppose that the past evolution of Q is known (i.e., $\{Q(s) \mid s \leq t\}$ is given). By the memoryless property of the exponential distribution, the *residual* service times of the n jobs are exponentially distributed random variables with mean $1/\mu$. Therefore, by Theorem 2.1.2, Q makes a transition to state $n - 1$ at rate $n\mu$, i.e., for $0 < n \leq K$

$$q_{n,n-1} = n\mu.$$

Now suppose $Q(t) = n < K$. Again by the memoryless property, the *residual* interarrival time is exponential with mean $1/\lambda$. Therefore, Q makes a transition to state $n + 1$ at rate λ, i.e., for $0 \leq n < K$

$$q_{n,n+1} = \lambda.$$

Thus, this is the Markov chain described in the example of Section 2.5.1 with transition rate diagram give in Figure 2.8. The stationary distribution of Q is the truncated Poisson given in Equation (2.43):

$$\sigma_i = \sigma_0 \frac{\rho^i}{i!} \quad \text{for } 1 \leq i \leq K,$$

and

$$\sigma_0 = \left(\sum_{i=0}^{K} \frac{\rho^i}{i!} \right)^{-1}.$$

Now consider a stationary M/M/K/K queue. Suppose we are interested in the probability that an arriving job is *blocked* (dropped) because, upon its arrival, the system is full, i.e., every server is occupied. More formally, we want to find $\mathsf{P}(Q(T_n-) = K)$, where we recall that T_n is the arrival time of the nth job. Since the arrivals are Poisson, we can invoke PASTA to get

$$\mathsf{P}(Q(T_n-) = K) = \sigma_K = \sigma_0 \frac{\rho^K}{K!}, \qquad (3.29)$$

which is called *Erlang's formula*. Note that this result depends on the distribution of the job service times S_i only through the mean $1/\mu$, which not surprising since an exponential service time has only one parameter. For more general service time distributions, it can be shown that (3.29) still holds. Therefore, given the mean service time $1/\mu$, Erlang's result is said to be otherwise "insensitive" to the service time distribution [224, 226].

---

[4]Since the capacity to hold jobs equals the number of servers, there is no waiting room (each server holds one job).

Finally note that, by Little's theorem, the mean number of busy servers in steady state is

$$
\begin{aligned}
L &= \lambda(1 - \sigma_K)\frac{1}{\mu} \\
&= \rho(1 - \sigma_K),
\end{aligned}
$$

where $\lambda(1-\sigma_K)$ is the "net" arrival rate of jobs that *successfully* join the queue (by PASTA). One can easily check that

$$
L = \mathsf{E}Q.
$$

3.6 OVERVIEW OF DISCRETE-TIME QUEUES

Consider now a single-server queue in discrete time $n \in \mathbb{Z}^+$ or $n \in \mathbb{Z}$. Suppose that the server works at a normalized rate of c jobs per unit time and that a_n is the amount of work that arrives at time n. If we assume that, in a given unit of time, service on the queue is performed *prior* to accounting for arrivals (in that same unit of time), then the work to be done at time n is

$$
W(n) = (W(n-1) - c)^+ + a_n, \tag{3.30}
$$

where, again,

$$
(\xi)^+ \equiv \max\{0, \xi\}.
$$

Alternatively, if the arrivals are counted before service in a time slot,

$$
W(n) = (W(n-1) - c + a_n)^+; \tag{3.31}
$$

these dynamics are sometimes called "cut-through" because arrivals to empty queues can depart immediately incurring no queueing delay.

For the dynamics (3.31), the following expression holds:

$$
W(n) = \max_{-\infty < m \leq n} [A(m, n] - c(n - m)], \tag{3.32}
$$

where

$$
A(m, n] \equiv a_{m+1} + a_{m+2} + \cdots + a_n.
$$

For the dynamics (3.30),

$$
W(n) = a_n + \max_{-\infty < m \leq n} [A(m, n) - c(n - m)], \tag{3.33}
$$

where

$$
A(m, n) \equiv a_{m+1} + a_{m+2} + \cdots + a_{n-1}.
$$

One can verify that (3.31) implies (3.32), as (3.30) implies (3.33), by a straightforward induction argument. Conversely, (3.32) and (3.33) can be obtained just as in the continuous-time examples by showing that the time m that achieves the maximum is the start time of the busy period of the queue that contains time n.

■ **EXAMPLE 3.5**

Consider a layer 2 FIFO queue in a communication network receiving fixed-length frames of bytes with a_n frames arriving at time n. If the nonidling server works at rate $c = 1$ frame per unit time, the number of frames in the queue $Q(n) = W(n)$. Discrete-time queues with service rate less than 1 frame per unit time are described in Chapter 2 of [126].

Now consider a FIFO queue with a single nonidling server and infinite waiting room in discrete time. Suppose that the job interarrival times are IID geometrically distributed with mean $1/q$. The service times of the jobs are also IID geometric with mean $1/p$, where $\rho \equiv q/p < 1$. So, the number of jobs in the queue Q is a birth-death Markov chain as depicted in Figure 2.17, i.e., a discrete-time M/M/1 queue. From the invariant distribution $\underline{\sigma}$, the mean number of jobs in the queue is

$$L \;=\; \sum_{k=0}^{\infty} i\sigma_i \;=\; \frac{\rho}{1-\rho}. \tag{3.34}$$

Thus, by Little's formula in discrete time, the mean sojourn time is $1/(p-q)$.

■ **EXAMPLE 3.6**

Consider a TDM wireless downlink of a base station (BS) fed by a single layer 2 FIFO transmission queue of fixed-length frames. Assume that the base station serves a group of N end hosts and that the transmission error events from the BS to the end hosts are IID and occur with probability $1 - p$ in any given time slot. A frame is transmitted by the BS in consecutive time slots until it is received error free. Also assume that the frame arrival process to the downlink transmission queue is a memoryless counting process (Figure 2.14), independent of transmission error events, with "mean rate" $q < p$ frames per time slot. For any arbitrarily selected frame, the probability that a frame belongs to flow i is q_i/q, where

$$\sum_{i=1}^{N} q_i \;=\; q.$$

We want to compute the mean delay of type i frames through this queue.
    First note that, due to transmission errors, the service time of a frame is effectively geometrically distributed with mean

$$1p + 2p(1-p) + 3p(1-p)^2 + \cdots \;=\; \frac{1}{p}. \tag{3.35}$$

So, for the queue to be "stable," we require that

$$\rho \;\equiv\; \frac{q}{p} < 1.$$

By PASTA, the mean sojourn time w_i of type i frames is equal to that of the aggregate flow, w, i.e., $w_i = w$ for all flows i. By Little's formula, the mean number of type i frames in system is

$$L_i = q_i w_i = q_i w = \frac{q_i}{q} L,$$

where L (for the aggregate flow) is given by (3.34). Given (3.35), one may be tempted to claim that $w = L\frac{1}{p}$; to see why this is false (beyond the argument involving Little's formula that was just made), recall the discussion regarding Figure 3.11.

A system of K servers, no waiting room, and geometrically distributed job interarrival and service times is described by a birth-death Markov chain Q as depicted in Figure 2.17 of Section 2.8 with

$$q_i \equiv q \quad \text{and} \quad p_i \equiv ip,$$

i.e., a discrete-time M/M/K/K queue. Therefore, by PASTA in discrete time, the blocking probability is given by Erlang's formula (3.29) with $\rho = q/p$.

Problems

3.1   In Figure 3.12, cumulative arrivals A and departures D of a packet queue are depicted over a period of time in which three packets arrive and depart (both events assumed to occur instantaneously for each packet). For example, the third packet arrives at time 4 ms and is $4 \times 50 = 200$ bytes long.

  (a) What is the delay experienced by the second packet?

  (b) What is the queue occupancy at time 3.5 ms in terms of bytes and number of packets?

3.2   Generalize (3.10) to the case where $Q(0) > 0$.

3.3   Prove (3.4).

3.4   Explain why (3.8) does not hold for *multiple*-server queues.

3.5   Prove (3.17).

3.6   Prove Wald's identity (3.26) for the M/M/1 queue. Also, in the same context, find an expression for $P(W(T) \leq x)$ for $x \geq 0$. Hint: Condition on $Q(T-)$ which, by PASTA, is geometrically distributed with parameter ρ.

3.7   Find a Markov chain describing the number of jobs in an M/M/K/∞ queue.

3.8   Consider a stationary queue handling jobs with IID exponential service times with parameter μ. Consider a Poisson process with parameter $\lambda < \mu/2$. Suppose that at each point of the Poisson process *two* jobs arrive at the queue. This is a simple "batch" Poisson model of the job arrival process.

  (a) Draw the transition rate diagram of the queue occupancy.

  (b) Is it time reversible?

50 bytes

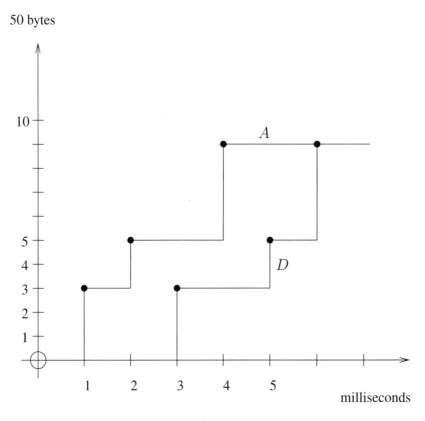

Figure 3.12 Cumulative arrivals and departures from a queue.

(c) Show that the distribution of the workload upon the arrival of a *typical* job is *not* the steady state distribution.

3.9   Consider a FIFO queue with a single work-conserving server, infinite waiting room, batch Poisson arrivals, and mutually independent job service times that are exponentially distributed with mean $1/\mu$. The intensity of Poisson batch arrivals is λ and every batch consists of three jobs.

(a) Draw the transition rate diagram of the queue occupancy (number-of-jobs) process, Q.

(b) State the stability (positive-recurrence) condition for the queue.

(c) Find the probability that the queue is not empty in steady state, i.e., $P(Q > 0)$.

(d) Is Q time reversible? Justify your answer.

Now assume that there are two work-conserving servers instead of just one and at most four jobs in the system at any given time.

(e) Repeat part (a) for this system.

(f) State (but do not try to solve) the balance equation of state 3.

(g) Write an expression for the stationary probability that an arriving job is blocked in terms of $\underline{\sigma}$.

3.10 Consider a queue with *constant* arrival rate of λ. The arrivals have "random phase" θ uniformly distributed over $[0, 1/\lambda]$, i.e., for $i \geq 1$, the ith job arrives at time

$$\theta + \frac{i-1}{\lambda}.$$

The service time of the ith job is S_i, where the S_i are IID, $\mathsf{E}S_i < 1/\lambda$ (i.e., the queue is "stable"), and, to make the queue interesting, $\mathsf{P}(S_i > 1/\lambda) > 0$. Show that

$$\mathsf{E}W(t) \quad = \quad \mathsf{E}(W(a) - U)^+,$$

where t is a typical time (uniformly distributed between two job arrival times), a is a typical job arrival time, and U is a uniform random variable on $[0, 1/\lambda]$ independent of a and W. This is another example where the implications of PASTA fail to hold.

3.11 Show that the cumulative departures D from a lossless, initially empty, FIFO queue with arrival process A and service rate 1 satisfy

$$D(0,t) \quad = \quad \min_{0 \leq s \leq t} \{A(0,s) - s\} + t \quad \text{for all } t \geq 0. \tag{3.36}$$

3.12 Consider a stationary M/M/1 queue.

(a) Find the stationary distribution of the number of jobs and workload in a (stable) M/M/1 queue *but not in the server* (i.e., in the queue proper).

(b) Find the stationary distribution of the number of jobs and the workload in the server of an M/M/1 queue.

(c) Apply Little's formula to both the queue proper and the server.

3.13 Argue that the job *departure* process of an M/M/1 queue is Poisson. This is Burke's theorem (also known as the "output theorem" [219]). Hint: Consider the queue reversed in time and use the fact that the queue occupancy Q is a time-reversible Markov process (Problem 2.13 of Chapter 2). Note that Problem 2.16 is a similar "output theorem" for M/GI/∞ queues.

3.14 Consider a stationary M/M/1/K queue with a maximum capacity to hold $K < \infty$ jobs.

(a) Find the probability that an arriving job is blocked. Hint: The stationary distribution is a truncated geometric.

(b) Find the mean sojourn time of packets that successfully join the queue.

3.15 Consider the M/E$_2$/1 queue in which the IID job service times are Erlang (gamma) distributed with parameters $r = 2$ and μ and the arrival rate is λ. If S is distributed as a job service time, we can write $S = \phi_1 + \phi_2$, where ϕ_1 and ϕ_2 are IID exponential "phases"; recall Example 1.7. Let $X(t)$ be the number of *phases* in the queue at time t.

(a) Argue that X is a Markov process and find its transition rate diagram.

(b) Given the stationary distribution of this Markov process, find an expression for the distribution of the number of jobs in the queue, Q, in steady state.

(c) Similarly find an "underlying" Markov process for an M/E_k/1 queue for $k \in \mathbb{Z}^+$ and relate it to Q.

(d) Repeat part (c) for an E_k/M/1 queue and an E_2/E_2/1 queue.

Note that interarrival times and service times of queues that are described by *phase-type* distributions, composed of Erlang distributions with different "μ" parameters, also lend themselves to Markovian analysis [226].

CHAPTER 4

LOCAL MULTIPLEXING

In this chapter, we begin to consider multiplexing of multiple flows predominantly in the context of a single server (single-bandwidth resource). A preliminary section overviewing the architecture of Internet routers is followed by sections on deterministic traffic shaping and multiplexing of (layer 3) flows of variable-length packets. We conclude with examples of "flow-level" multiplexing, including a description of a generic game-theoretic framework involving usage-based pricing.

4.1 INTERNET ROUTER ARCHITECTURE

Considering the problem of connecting a large number $H \approx 10^9$ end systems/hosts, a network of point-to-point connections would require an enormous number of links, on the order of H^2. The presence of routers (IP layer 3 of the protocol hierarchy) and switches (Ethernet layer 2) in the network dramatically reduces the number of required links resulting in a topology that is *scalable* with the number of end systems.

We now give an overview of the architecture of Internet routers. High-end Internet routers are extremely large, fast, and complex systems presently having the ability to forward at aggregate packet rates in the terabits-per-second range. In Chapter 3, we studied queues handling "jobs," where a job can be interpreted as a packet transmission task. We will see how packet queues reside in the packet memories of the ingress and egress linecards of a router.

4.1.1 Big picture of an IP (layer 3) router

In Figure 4.1, a 3×3 router R is shown in two equivalent ways. The depiction at the bottom using unidirectional links is more convenient for the following discussion of the generic architecture of an Internet router. Large modern routers can have on the order of 128 ports (i.e., are 128×128) with each port operating at optical carrier (OC) 192 (about 10 Gbps) giving a total peak throughput of the router on the order of 128×10 Gbps or about a terabit per second. The linecard and fabric organization of a router are indicated in Figure 4.2. In practice, the ingress and egress linecards of the same interface are on a single board and share a local host central processing unit (CPU). The local host CPUs are connected to a master CPU (large work station) for the entire router.

4.1.2 Ingress linecard

Components of an ingress linecard and switch fabric will now be discussed; see Figure 4.3. The IP packets are extracted from the Synchronous Optical Network (SONET) or Ethernet frames arriving to an ingress linecard by the deframer device. The *headers* of the packets are then examined by a complex network processor (NP) device. On the fly, the NP will:

- decide how to forward the packet,

- update statistics of the aggregate flow of the ingress linecard or of the particular flow (session) to which the packet may belong [200],

- enforce any traffic parameters of the flow (e.g., using a token bucket; see Section 4.2 below),

- decrement the time-to-live (TTL) field of the packet, and

- possibly apply a firewall filter.

Application of a firewall, TTL decrementer, or token bucket policer may result in the packet being immediately discarded. A primary function of an ingress NP is to make the local forwarding decision of the packet, which simply amounts to deciding to which output port the packet will be transmitted. The forwarding decisions are based on the router's participation in the Internet's packet-routing protocols; see Chapter 6. A label carrying the decisions made by the NP is appended to the forwarded packet to inform the other devices in the router that will handle it; this label is stripped from the packet prior to its transmission out of the router.

After the network processor, the packet is stored in a packet memory [137] controlled by the ingress traffic management (iTM) device. The enqueue operation of the iTM will separately queue packets according to their output port destinations; see the packet flow demultiplexer (demux) of Figure 4.4. This *virtual output queueing* (VOQ) prevents head-of-line blocking [120].

In ingress packet memory, packets can be further grouped (and separately queued) according to other attributes as identified by the NP and stored in the packet's label. For

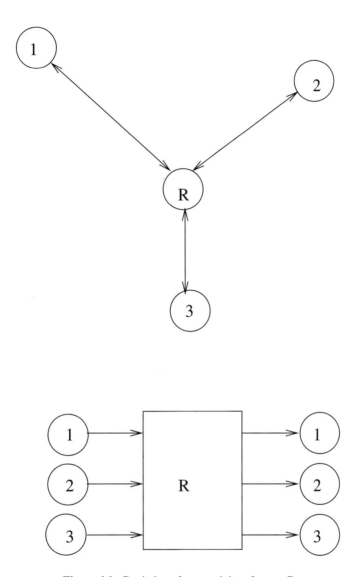

Figure 4.1   Depiction of connectivity of router R.

example, we could partition all the packets flowing to a given output port according to their IP port numbers or transport layer protocol: Transmission Control Protocol (TCP) or User Datagram Protocol (UDP). For the latter case, a three-queue system per output port could be used for TCP control packets (SYN, SYN-ACK, etc.), TCP data packets, and UDP packets; see Figure 4.5. There are proposals for frameworks requiring a system of queues corresponding to different *network*-layer classes of service (the "diffserv" framework [24]) or bandwidth-provisioned label-switched paths [12, 188].

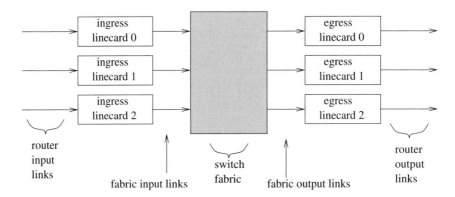

Figure 4.2 Linecards and fabric of 3×3 router.

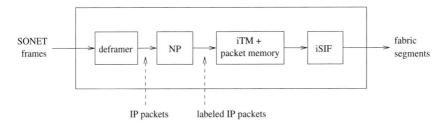

Figure 4.3 Ingress linecard (input port processor).

Thus, a two-level hierarchical dequeue (scheduler) would be required: *quality-of-service* (QoS) scheduling among the queues per output port (at least to ensure a minimal amount of bandwidth per queue) and scheduling among the output ports; see Figures 4.4 and 4.5. Scheduling at the VOQ level of the iTM is typically coupled with switch fabric arbitration to evacuate packets to their destined output ports as rapidly as possible. Note that, for each identified flow (QoS queue), in-order forwarding of packets is expected of the router. Also note that all individual queues are implemented as singly linked lists permitting operations only at their head (dequeue) and tail (enqueue) [137]. Operations involving insertion or deletion of packets in the interior of a queue or search of the queue's contents (requiring implementation with a doubly linked list) are simply impractical at high data rates.

Switch fabrics are best designed to operate on fixed-length data segments. The ingress switch interface device (iSIF) forms such segments from variable-length IP packets destined for the same output port. Indeed, the iSIF may have a small *segment* queue for each output port. A packet may be entirely contained within a segment (depending on the packet's size) or it may be divided among multiple segments.

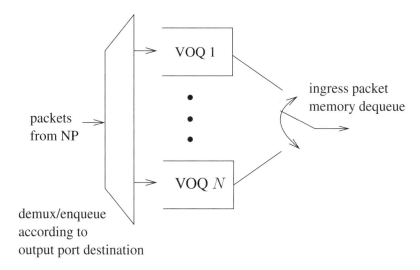

Figure 4.4   Virtual output queues of an ingress packet memory.

4.1.3 Switch fabric

An $N \times N$ switch fabric simultaneously transmits (switches) N segments from the input ports to the output ports. To do this and avoid high memory bandwidth requirements (N times that of the ingress packet memory), no two segments being switched at a given time should be destined to the same output port. This requirement is eased for switches that are not based on memoryless crossbar fabrics (e.g., shared memory, multistage fabrics [100]) at the expense of additional latency. Large, distributed crossbar fabrics may have a bank of virtual *input* queues (VIQs) at the interface to each output port in order to deal with certain timing-related memory-bandwidth issues.

   A recent reference for interconnection networks, such as switch fabrics, is [56]. The process by which segments are selected for transmission into the fabric is called arbitration. Packet-level arbitration [154] works on a shorter time scale than flow/connection-level arbitration. Significantly complex computations for flow-level arbitration, such as that based on Slepian-Duguid [100] or Birkoff-von Neumann decompositions (two-stage switches) [37, 38], can be amortized over a longer time scale. More specifically, flows can be taken to join and leave the router on a millisecond time scale compared to the sub-microsecond time scale of the transmission time of a packet. Packet-level arbitration can be used to more dynamically "fill in the gaps" left by flow-level arbitration.

   The switch fabric is also expected to have a multicasting function, i.e., it can simultaneously switch multiple copies of a multicast packet to its (multiple) destined output ports. Such *local* multicasting functions can be composed to create multicast trees that span the entire network [139]. Because of the additional constraints of multicasting and their rela-

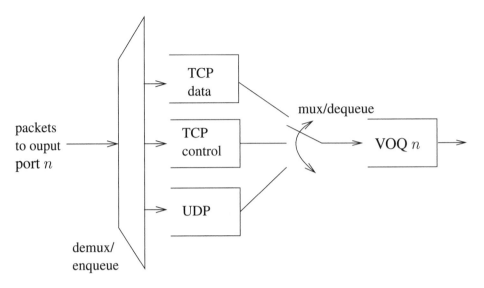

Figure 4.5   Three tributary queues of a transmission VOQ.

tively limited numbers compared to unicast packets, multicast packets typically have some measure of priority over unicast in the fabric arbitration process. We now discuss a heuristic for arbitration of provisioned time-division multiplexed (TDM) multicast flows given in [230].

Suppose that there N linecards, i.e., an $N \times N$ switch fabric. Assume that the N linecards have data paths of R packet-segments per second. Thus, a time slot of the switch fabric has duration R^{-1} seconds. Consider a multicast connection j across the fabric that has bandwidth allocation that is a multiple of R, $n_j R$. In the following, connection j will generate n_j identical vectors v each indicating which (single) ingress source port and which egress destination ports constitute the multicast connection under consideration. Let A be the set of all such vectors (including identical instances of the same connection) of such multicast connections. Define T as the least common multiple of n_j. Our objective is to schedule all vectors v in A at least once every T time slots.

Definition 4.1.1. *Two vectors in A are said to be* compatible *if they are disjoint, i.e., if they have no common input or output ports; otherwise they are said to contend.*

Packet segments from two multicast connections with compatible vectors can be transmitted in the same time slot through the switch fabric. A multicast time slot assignment problem can now be defined: Assuming that there is no overbooking of bandwidth on any input or output link, find a schedule that allocates a time slot to each vector $v \in A$ once every T time slots.

Theorem 4.1.1. *A feasible multicast time slot assignment problem is NP hard.*

Proof: Construct a graph whose vertices (nodes) correspond to elements (vectors) in A. Links connect all pairs of nodes that are compatible with each other. Consider N different colors, where we note that N is an obvious upper bound on the number vectors that can be scheduled in the same time slot. Consider a set of vectors that are scheduled in the same time slot and suppose that a different color is assigned each such vector. Clearly, the multicast time slot assignment problem is equivalent to the vertex N-colorability problem [79]: With N different colors, assign colors to the graph so that no two vertices connected by a link are assigned the same color. □

Basically, CBO is a greedy algorithm. The most contentious connection (i.e., the connection that contends with the greatest number of other connections) is scheduled in the first time slot of the frame. The next most contentious connection that is compatible with the first one scheduled is then scheduled for the same time slot and so on until no further connections can be scheduled in the first time slot. At this point, the degree of contentiousness of the unscheduled flows is recomputed (decremented) to account for those connections that were scheduled in the first time slot and the scheduling process is conducted for the second time slot of the frame as it was for the first. Other criteria of the connections or the port indexes (e.g., out-degree of the connection or residual demand for the switch port) could be used to break ties when scheduling the first connection of a time slot.

■ **EXAMPLE 4.1**

Suppose a 5×5 fabric needs to schedule the following nine connections:

Connection Index	Input Port Index	Output Port Index
A	0	$1, 2, 3$
B	0	$2, 3, 4$
C	1	4
D	1	4
E	1	3
F	2	$0, 4$
G	3	2
H	4	$0, 2, 3$
I	4	2

That is, packets from multicast connection H arrive on input port 4 and are (simultaneously) multicast onto output ports 0, 2, and 3. Note that connections C, D, E, G, and I are unicast and that C and D could represent a connection that is allocated twice the bandwidth of the rest. Also note that five different connections request output port 2. Thus, the fabric's scheduling frame is at least five time slots long.

The degrees of contention of the connections are given in the following table. The contention values immediately prior to each time slot (row) is recorded in each row.

An "x" indicates that the connection has been previously scheduled. The number in bold indicates that the corresponding connection is being scheduled in that time slot. The largest (residual contention) number in bold for a time slot corresponds to the first connection scheduled under CBO.

Time Slot\Connection Index	A	B	C	D	E	F	G	H	I
0	5	**8**	4	4	5	4	4	6	4
1	4	x	**3**	3	4	3	3	**5**	3
2	**3**	x	x	**2**	2	1	2	x	2
3	x	x	x	x	**0**	**0**	**1**	x	1
4	x	x	x	x	x	x	x	x	**0**

That is, connection B contends with all of the other eight connections. So, B is scheduled first in the first time slot. In the second time slot, connection H is scheduled first and then C, which is compatible with H, is also scheduled. No other remaining connections are compatible with *both* H and C so we go on to the next time slot. Note that in the third time slot D is chosen after A as it has highest contention (two), even though F is multicast and D is unicast. In Figure 4.6, the fabric configurations of each time slot are depicted. Again, the fabric cycles through these five configurations in sequence and each connection therefore receives at most one-fifth of a link's bandwidth R through the fabric.

4.1.4 Egress linecard

The egress SIF (eSIF) device of an egress linecard (see Figure 4.7) is for packet *reassembly*, including simple extraction, from the fabric segments. Reassembly is sometimes handled by the egress traffic management (eTM). In some routers, there is an egress network processor (eNP) to reclassify packets for the purposes of the egress packet memory and output link, i.e., in the context of the flows being multiplexed on the output link. The egress packet memory, controlled by the eTM device, stores variable-length IP packets. Upon dequeuing from the egress packet memory, the framer device forms SONET or Ethernet frames for the purposes of transmission onto the output link.

The egress packet memory may have an organization similar to that depicted in Figure 4.5 for the ingress linecard with the VOQs replaced by queues feeding separate bandwidth-provisioned "channels" partitioning the output link (such channelization is common at links crossing boundaries of networks owned by separate entities). So, bandwidth scheduling occurs among the channel queues. Scheduling among the *class-of-service* (CoS) queues feeding into a channel could be a hybrid of bandwidth and priority.

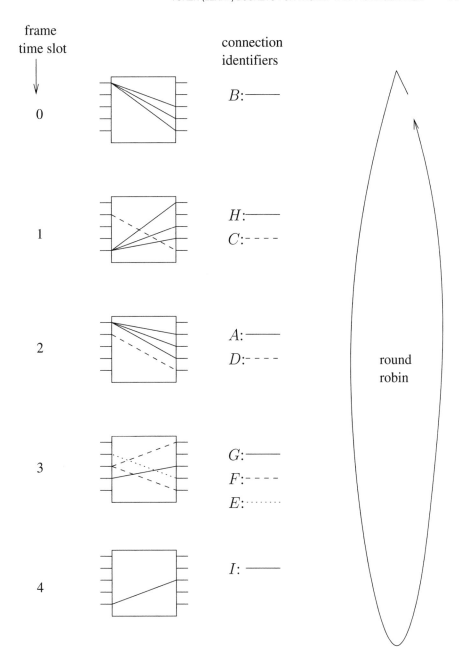

Figure 4.6 Example schedule of fabric configurations.

4.2 TOKEN (LEAKY) BUCKETS FOR PACKET TRAFFIC REGULATION

Suppose that one network provider wishes another to carry a certain flow of packets. The network providers strike a *service-level agreement* (SLA) wherein the transmitting network

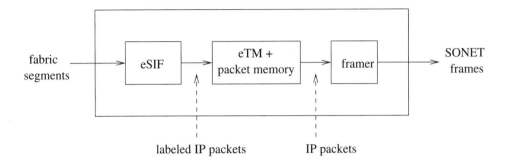

Figure 4.7 Egress linecard (output port processor).

agrees that his or her packet flow will conform to certain parameters. A preferable choice of flow parameters would be those that are:

- significant from a queueing perspective, simply to ensure conformity by the sending network, and

- simple to police by the receiving network.

We have seen how useful the mean arrival rate (typically denoted by λ) is in terms of predicting queueing behavior. The mean arrival rate is, however, difficult to police as it is only known after the flow has terminated. Instead of the mean arrival rate, we consider flow parameters that are policeable on a packet-by-packet basis. Suppose that when the flow of packets arrives to a dedicated FIFO queue with a constant service rate of ρ bytes per second (Bps), the backlog of the queue never exceeds σ bytes. One can define σ as the *burstiness* of a flow of packets as a function of the rate ρ used to service it. Such a definition for burstiness informs a node so that it can allocate both memory and bandwidth resources in order to accommodate such a regulated flow. Moreover, by limiting the burstiness of a flow, one also limits the degree to which it can affect other flows with which it shares network resources. Indeed, such regulation was standardized by the ATM Forum and adopted by the Internet Engineering Task Force (IETF) [94, 95].

Suppose that at some location there is a *flow of packets* A specified by the sequence of pairs (T_i, l_i), where T_i is the arrival time of the ith packet in seconds ($T_{i+1} > T_i$) and l_i is the length of that packet in bytes. More precisely, if c Bps is the peak rate of the medium of communication and T_i is the arrival time of the leading edge of the ith packet, then we require that $T_{i+1} > T_i + l_i/c$, where $T_i + l_i/c$ is the time at which the ith packet has *completely* arrived. The total number of bytes that arrives over an interval of time $(s, t]$ is

$$A(s, t] = \sum_i \min\{l_i, (t - T_i)c\}\mathbf{1}\{s < T_i \le t\}.$$

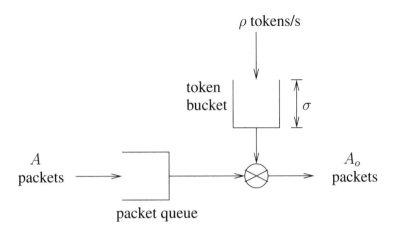

Figure 4.8 A token bucket traffic shaper.

In the following, we will assume $c = \infty$ for simplicity. This gives

$$A(s,t] \;=\; \sum_i l_i \mathbf{1}\{s < T_i \le t\}.$$

Assume that this packet flow arrives to a token bucket mechanism as depicted in Figure 4.8. A token represents a byte and tokens arrive at a *constant* rate of ρ tokens per second to the token bucket which has a limited capacity of σ tokens. A (head-of-line) packet i leaves the packet FIFO queue when l_i tokens are present in the token bucket; when the packet leaves, it consumes l_i tokens, i.e., they are removed from the bucket. Note that this mechanism requires that σ be larger than the largest packet length (again, in bytes) of the flow.

Let $A_o(s,t]$ be the total number of bytes *departing* from the packet queue over the interval of time $(s,t]$. The following result follows directly by consideration of the maximal amount of tokens that can be consumed over an interval of time. It holds for all arrival processes A to the packet queue.

Theorem 4.2.1. *For all times $s \le t$,*

$$A_o(s,t] \;\le\; \sigma + \rho(t-s).$$

Any flow A that satisfies the statement of Theorem 4.2.1 is said to satisfy a (σ, ρ) *constraint* [50]. In the jargon of [94, 95], ρ could be a *sustained information rate* (SIR) and σ a *maximum burst size* (MBS). Alternatively, ρ could be a peak information rate (PIR), in which case σ would usually be taken to be the number of bytes in a maximally sized packet.

Let $Q(t)$ be backlog at time t of a queue with arrival flow A and a dedicated server with constant rate ρ.

Theorem 4.2.2. *The flow A is (σ, ρ) constrained if and only if $Q(t) \leq \sigma$ for all time t.*

Proof: The proof follows from the fact that the maximum queue size is

$$\max_{t} Q(t) \;=\; \max_{t}\; \max_{s:\, s\leq t} \{A(s,t] - \rho(t-s)\}.$$

Substituting the inequality in Theorem 4.2.1 gives the result.   □

We have shown how the token bucket of Figure 4.8 can delay packets of the arrival flow A so that the departure flow A_o is (σ, ρ) constrained. This is known as traffic *shaping*. The receiving network of the exchange of flows described above may wish to:

- shape the flow using a (σ, ρ) token bucket, or

- simply identify (mark) any packets that are deemed out of the (σ, ρ) *profile* of the flow, or

- drop any out of profile packets.

The last two actions are known as traffic *policing*. There are two main devices used for traffic policing. The first is a token bucket device like that of Figure 4.8 but without the packet queue. A packet is dropped or marked out of profile if and only if there are not sufficient tokens (according to its length) in the token bucket upon its arrival.

Alternatively, by Theorem 4.2.2, one can use a policer as depicted in Figure 4.9. A packet is dropped or marked out-of-profile if and only its arrival and inclusion in the *virtual queue* would cause its backlog Q to become larger than σ; when this happens, the arriving packet is not included in the virtual queue. Note that the virtual queue can be maintained by simply keeping track of two state variables: the queue length, Q, upon arrival of the previous packet and the arrival time, a, of the previous packet. Thus if a packet of length l bytes arrives at time T and is admitted into the virtual queue, then

$$Q \;\leftarrow\; \max\{Q - \rho(T-a), 0\} + l$$

and

$$a \;\leftarrow\; T.$$

This (event-driven) operation requires one multiplication operation per packet. Alternatively, one could maintain the departure time d of the most recently admitted packet instead of the queue occupancy Q; see Problem 4.3 at the end of the chapter.

4.3 MULTIPLEXING FLOWS OF VARIABLE-LENGTH PACKETS

Suppose that at some location N flows are to be multiplexed (scheduled) into a single flow. The flows are indexed by $n \in \{0, 1, ..., N-1\}$. Suppose each flow is assigned its

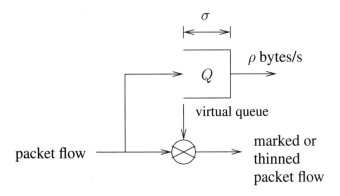

Figure 4.9 A (σ, ρ) constraint policer.

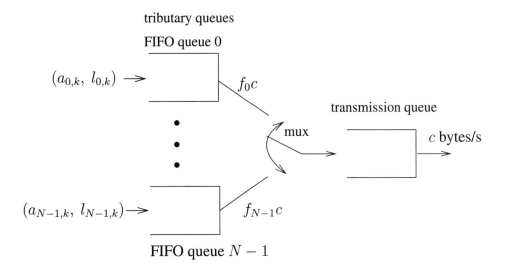

Figure 4.10 Multiplexing N packet flows.

own tributary queue and the output flows of the tributary queues are multiplexed into the transmission queue; see Figure 4.10. How the multiplexing occurs depends on the kinds of relative priorities the flows possess.

4.3.1 Multiplexing with a single FIFO queue

In this case, the method of multiplexing the queues would be based only on the arrival time of the packets to the head of their tributary queue: Packets that arrive earlier are served first by the scheduler. Here and in the following, ties are broken arbitrarily.

In the TCP/UDP context of Figure 4.5, this method has at least one serious problem. During periods of congestion, the TCP data flows will back off (congestion avoidance phase), leaving the bandwidth resources to the remaining unresponsive (to congestion) sessions, which is "unfair" to the responsive TCP sessions [151].

4.3.2 Strict priority

In strict priority multiplexing, flows are ranked according to priority. A flow is served by the scheduler only if no packets of any higher priority flows are queued. Even when the volume of high priority traffic is limited, there remains the potential problem of long-term starvation of bandwidth to lower priority flows.

The problems with both priority and single FIFO multiplexing can be solved by using a scheduler that can allocate a minimal amount of *bandwidth* to a flow in order to prevent long-term starvation of bandwidth to that flow. Bandwidth may also be allocated to flows without clear priority designations (as in Figure 4.5) or to flows that are explicitly provisioned by, e.g., using a provisioned label-switched path (LSP) under Multiprotocol Label Switching (MPLS). Also, it may be desirable to share excess capacity (reserved-but-unused plus unreserved capacity) according to certain priority rules, e.g., sharing in proportion to allocated bandwidth (*rate proportionally fair* sharing) [84, 166].

4.3.3 Deficit round-robin

Under *round-robin* multiplexing (scheduling), time is divided into successive *rounds*, each not necessarily of the same time duration. Suppose that in each round there is a rule allowing for at most one packet per tributary queue to be transmitted into the transmission queue. A problem here is that flows with large-sized packets (e.g., large file transfers using TCP) will monopolize the bandwidth and starve out flows of small-sized packets (e.g., those of streaming media). Thus, one might want to regulate the total number of *bytes* that can be extracted from any given tributary queue in a round. This leads to the notion of deficit round-robin (DRR) scheduling [215].

To describe a DRR mechanism, we need the following definitions. Let $L_{\max}$ be the size, in bytes, of the largest packet and $L_{\min}$ the size of the smallest. Here, the priority of a flow has to do with the fraction f_n of the total link bandwidth c bytes per second assigned to it, where we do not *overbook*, i.e.,

$$\sum_{n=1}^{N} f_n \leq 1.$$

Each flow is assigned its own FIFO queue by the multiplexer. Finally, let

$$f_{\min} = \min_{n} f_n,$$

i.e., the minimal allotment of bandwidth to a queue.

Under DRR, at the beginning of each round, each *nonempty* FIFO queue is allocated a certain number of tokens. Packets departing a queue consume their byte length in tokens from the queue's allotment. Queues are serviced in a round until their token allotment becomes insufficient to transmit their head-of-line packet. For example, if a queue is allocated 8000 tokens at the start of a round and has six packets queued each of length 1500 bytes, then the first five of those packets are served leaving the trailing sixth packet in the queue and $8000 - 5 \times 1500 = 500$ tokens unused.

The nth queue is allocated

$$\frac{f_n}{f_{\min}} L_{\max}$$

tokens at the start of a round (again, if it is not empty), thereby ensuring that at least one packet from this queue will be transmitted in the round irrespective of the packet's size. If a queue has no packets at the end of a round, its token allotment may be reset to zero.

Note that the token allotments per round can be precomputed given the allotments f_n, which change at a much slower "connection-level" time scale than that of the transmission time required for a single packet ($L_{\max}/c$). One could replace $f_{\min}$ in the token allocation rule by the minimum bandwidth allocation among *nonempty* queues at the start of a round, but the result would be a significant amount of computation *per round* possibly precluding a high-speed implementation.

The following theorem demonstrates that DRR scheduling indeed allocates bandwidth consistent with the parameters f_n.

Theorem 4.3.1. *If the nth queue is not empty at the beginning of each of k consecutive rounds, then the total number of bytes $D_n(k)$ transmitted from this queue during these rounds satisfies*

$$(k-1)\frac{f_n}{f_{\min}} L_{\max} + L_{\min} \ \leq \ D_n(k) \leq \ \frac{f_n}{f_{\min}} L_{\max} - L_{\min} + k\frac{f_n}{f_{\min}} L_{\max}.$$

Proof: The upper bound is obtained assuming that all allocated tokens are consumed in addition to a maximal amount of carryover tokens from the round prior to the k consecutive ones under consideration. The lower bound is obtained by assuming no carryover tokens from a previous round combined with a maximal number of unused tokens in the last round. □

If two queues n and m are nonempty at the start of each of k consecutive rounds, this theorem can be directly used to show

$$\lim_{k \to \infty} \frac{D_n(k)}{D_m(k)} \ = \ \frac{f_n}{f_m};$$

see Problem 4.4. That is, DRR is rate proportionally fair.

The general advantage of round-robin schedulers is that they require a minimal amount of computation *per packet* to be implemented.

4.3.4 Shaped VirtualClock

We will now describe a scheduler that employs timestamps to give packets service priority over others [238] but restricts consideration only to packets that meet an eligibility criterion [102, 209, 214, 236] to limit the jitter of the individual output flows. This trait, which is lacking in DRR, is important for link channelization (partitioning a link into smaller channels) at network boundaries where SLAs are struck and policed.

For all i and n, (n, i) denotes the ith packet of the nth flow. Packet (n, i) is assigned a service deadline $d_{n,i}$ and a service eligibility time $\varepsilon_{n,i}$. A packet is said to be eligible for service at time t if $\varepsilon \leq t$. As with DRR, once a packet is "scheduled" by the multiplexer (begins service), its service is not interrupted. Upon service completion of a packet, the next packet selected for service will be the one with the smallest deadline among all eligible packets. Assuming the queues are FIFO, only head-of-queue packets need to be considered by the multiplexing (scheduling) algorithm. Each packet (n, i) has two other important attributes: its arrival time $a_{n,i}$ to the multiplexer and its size in bytes, l_i. Under what we will hereafter call shaped VirtualClock (SVC) scheduling,

$$\varepsilon_{n,i} = \max\{d_{n,i-1}, a_{n,i}\}, \tag{4.1}$$

$$d_{n,i} = \varepsilon_{n,i} + \frac{l_i}{f_n c}. \tag{4.2}$$

Note that if the nth flow were instead to arrive to a queue with a *dedicated* server of constant rate $f_n c$ bytes per second, then packet (n, i) would:

- reach the head of the queue (and begin service) at its eligibility time $\varepsilon_{n,i}$ and

- *completely* depart the server at its service deadline $d_{n,i}$.

In the following, this queue will be called the nth *isolated queue* (with dedicated server of rate $f_n c$ and arrivals coupled to those of the nth multiplexed queue).

Lemma 4.3.1. *Just prior to the start time of a busy period of the multiplexer, the aggregate eligible work to be done of all N isolated queues is zero.*

Proof: Note that the departures from the isolated queues represent the *only* packets eligible for service among the queues served by the scheduler. Thus, one can conceive of the sum of the byte departures from isolated queues creating "work to be done" for the multiplexer. The departure rate at some time t, $r_n(t)$ from the nth isolated queue is either $f_n c$ bytes per second or zero depending on whether the queue is empty. Thus,

$$\sum_{n=1}^{N} r_n(t) \leq c. \tag{4.3}$$

That is, the multiplexer is working at least as fast as the servers of the isolated queues at any given time. The eligible work to be done by the multiplexer is always less than the aggregate of that of the servers of the coupled isolated queues.   □

Now recall $L_{\max}$ is the maximum size of a packet (in bytes), a quantity that is typically about 1500 in the Internet. The following theorem demonstrates that SVC schedules bandwidth appropriately in our time-division multiplexing context:

Theorem 4.3.2. *For all n and i, the time at which packet (n, i) completely departs from the multiplexer of the ith packet of the nth flow is not more than*

$$d_{n,i} + \frac{L_{\max}}{c}.$$

Proof: Let β be the start time of the multiplexer (mux) busy period in which packet (n, i) (chosen arbitrarily) is served. The previous lemma implies that $\varepsilon_{n,i} \geq \beta$ (otherwise eligible work would be available to the mux at time $\beta-$ and, therefore, a mux busy period would not start at β).

Case 1: First suppose that, during this busy period, no packet having deadline $> d_{n,i}$ is scheduled by the mux prior to packet (n, i). The maximum amount of eligible packets with service deadlines $\leq d_{n,i}$ that can be generated by the N queues (flows) over the interval $[\beta, d_{n,i}]$ is less than or equal to

$$\sum_{n=1}^{N} f_n c[d_{n,i} - \beta] \quad \leq \quad c[d_{n,i} - \beta] \text{ bytes,}$$

where this upper bound is the work performed by the mux over the same time interval. This work includes packet (n, i) itself, i.e., the packet departs the mux by its deadline. Note that the busy period of the mux may in fact end prior $d_{n,i}$ in this case.

Case 2: Alternatively, suppose that at least one packet, say (m, j) of flow $m \neq n$, is scheduled prior to packet (n, i) with service deadline $d_{m,j} > d_{n,i}$. For this to be possible, $\varepsilon_{m,j} < \varepsilon_{n,i}$. Consider the *largest* eligibility time ε^* among all such packets (m, j). Note that the time t^* at which this packet completes service satisfies

$$t^* = \varepsilon^* + \frac{L_{\max}}{c} \quad \leq \quad \varepsilon_{n,i} + \frac{L_{\max}}{c}.$$

So, at time t^*, all eligible packets with service deadlines $\leq d_{n,i}$ are considered by the mux. By Case 1 above, the departure time of packet (n, i) will be

$$\leq t^* + \frac{l_{n,i}}{f_n c} \quad \leq \quad \varepsilon_{n,i} + \frac{L_{\max}}{c} + \frac{l_{n,i}}{f_n c} \quad = \quad d_{n,i} + \frac{L_{\max}}{c}$$

as desired. $\square$

Theorem 4.3.2 is a kind of *guaranteed-rate* result [126] for the SVC multiplexer. The SVC multiplexer also has an appealing property of bounding the jitter of every output flow. Consider any flow/queue n and note that the ith packet of this flow will have *completely departed the multiplexer* between times $\varepsilon_{n,i} + l_{n,i}/c$ and $d_{n,i} + L_{\max}/c$, where $l_{n,i}/c$ is the total transmission time of the packet. We can use this fact and the fact that, by definition,

$$d_{n,i} \quad \leq \quad \varepsilon_{n,i+1}$$

to show:

Theorem 4.3.3. *The cumulative* departures *from the nth queue of the multiplexer over an interval of time* $[s, t]$ *is less than or equal to* $f_n c(t - s) + 2L_{\max}$ *bytes.*

The proof is left as an exercise. There is a significant base of literature on scheduling, see, e.g., [51, 80, 126, 166, 176, 184, 209, 214, 236]. In particular, a hybrid of weighted round robin and SVC, amortizing the scheduling computation of SVC over a connection-level time scale, leads to a joint shaping and (deficit round-robin) scheduling mechanism for flows of variable-length packets [111].

4.4 SERVICE CURVES

An alternative formulation of guaranteed service to that of Theorem 4.3.2 is given by the *service curve* concept on which a kind of network "calculus" is based for determining delay and jitter bounds for a packet flow as it traverses a series of multiplexed FIFO queues, each of which may be shared with other flows.

Consider a queue occupancy process Q with cumulative arrivals A. Assume that the queue receives a service rate of exactly ρ bytes per second. In [232], it was said that A has *generalized stochastically bounded burstiness (gSSB) with bound f at ρ* if, for all time $t \geq 0$,

$$\mathsf{P}(Q(t) \geq \sigma) \leq f(\sigma), \qquad (4.4)$$

where $f \geq 0$ is a nonincreasing function with $f(0) = 1$ and, as before, $Q(0) = 0$ and, for $t > 0$,

$$Q(t) = \max_{0 \leq s \leq t} A(s, t] - \rho(t - s).$$

We denote $A \ll (\rho, f)$ if A has gSSB with bound f at ρ. Note that this definition reduces to the (σ, ρ) constraint when $f(\sigma) \equiv 0$ and recall that, unlike the gSBB, the (σ, ρ) constraint is policeable on a packet-by-packet basis.

Now consider a scheduler acting on a queue with cumulative arrivals A so that the cumulative departures D from that queue satisfy

$$\begin{aligned} D[0, t] &\geq \min_{0 \leq s \leq t} A[0, s] + \beta(t - s) \\ &= \min_{0 \leq s \leq t} A[0, t - s] + \beta(s) \end{aligned} \qquad (4.5)$$

for all time $t \geq 0$ and all arrivals A such that the queue is always backlogged over the interval $[0, t]$. In this case, the scheduler is said to offer a *service curve* β [52] to the flow, where β is a nondecreasing function such that $\beta(0) = 0$. With regard to (4.5), recall the expression for cumulative departures of a FIFO queue in Equation (3.36). The following theorem shows how the gSBB of a flow changes as it passes through a queue with a service curve.

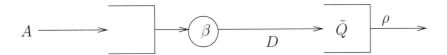

Figure 4.11 Output gSSB of a service-curve scheduler.

Theorem 4.4.1. *For a queue with service curve* β, *if* $A \ll (\rho, f)$, *then* $D \ll (\rho, g)$, *where*

$$g(x) \;\equiv\; f\left(x + \min_{s \geq 0}\{\beta(s) + \rho t\}\right).$$

Proof: Consider the backlog of a queue $\tilde{Q}$ whose *arrivals* are D. That is, consider Figure 4.11, in which the first queue is the scheduler giving a service curve β.

By (3.15), the queue occupancy

$$
\begin{aligned}
\tilde{Q}(t) \;&=\; \max_{0 \leq s \leq t} D[0,t] - D[0,s] - (t-s)\rho \\
&\leq\; \max_{0 \leq s \leq t} A[0,t] - \left(\min_{0 \leq u \leq s} A[0,u] + \beta(s-u)\right) - (t-s)\rho \\
&=\; \max_{0 \leq s \leq t} \max_{0 \leq u \leq s} A[0, t-s+u] - \rho(t-s+u) + \rho u - \beta(u) \\
&\leq\; Q(t) + \max_u \rho(u) - \beta(u).
\end{aligned}
$$

Applying this inequality to the definition of gSSB (4.4) proves the theorem. □

The scheduler SCED+ [51] was designed to achieve output service curves. Also, suppose a scheduler has guaranteed-rate property parameter μ (SVC has $\mu = L_{\max}/c$ by Theorem 4.3.2) for a queue with bandwidth allocation ρ. It is straightforward to show the scheduler has service curve

$$\beta(t) \;=\; \max\{\rho t - \rho\mu, 0\}. \tag{4.6}$$

The proof of this statement is left as an exercise.

4.5 CONNECTION MULTIPLEXING ON A SINGLE TRUNK

In this section we consider circuit switching involving a single link with capacity c circuits and N users. The nth user has connection setup requests according to a Poisson process with intensity λ_n and exponentially distributed connection holding times with mean $1/\mu_n$ and each connection requires k_n circuits. This is the simplest example of a *multiservice loss network*; see Chapter 5.

Theorem 4.5.1. *The connection blocking probability of the nth user in steady state is*

$$1 - \frac{G(c - k_n)}{G(c)},$$

where

$$\rho_n \equiv \frac{\lambda_n}{\mu_n},$$

and the partition function G is defined as

$$G(c) = \sum_{\underline{x} \in S(c)} \prod_{n=1}^{N} \frac{\rho_n^{x_n}}{x_n!}$$

with state space

$$S(c) = \left\{ \underline{x} \in (\mathbb{Z}^+)^N \mid \sum_{n=1}^{N} k_n x_n \le c \right\}.$$

Proof: One can first prove by detailed balance that the invariant distribution of the system is

$$\sigma(\underline{x}) = \frac{1}{G(c)} \prod_{n=1}^{N} \frac{\rho_n^{x_n}}{x_n!};$$

see Section 5.1. Note that the numerator in the claimed blocking probability is $G(c) - G(c - k_n)$ which involves summation over state-space

$$S(c) \backslash S(c - k_n) = \left\{ \underline{x} \in (\mathbb{Z}^+)^N \mid c - k_n < \sum_{n=1}^{N} k_n x_n \le c \right\},$$

i.e., the claimed blocking probability sums over all system "blocking" states $\underline{x}$ for the nth user (states which do *not* involve k_n unoccupied circuits). The theorem then follows by PASTA.   □

This blocking probability lends itself to efficient calculation via the Kaufman-Roberts iteration; see [45, 189] and Chapter 18 of [186].

■ **EXAMPLE 4.2**

In Figure 4.12, the state spaces $S(c)$ and $S(c) \backslash S(c - k_n)$ are depicted for $N = 2$ classes, i.e., $n \in \{1, 2\}$, with $k_1 = 1$ and $k_2 = 2$.

Multiprotocol label switching [188] enables the establishment of *bandwidth-provisioned* label-switched paths (LSPs) between routers in the Internet. A unidirectional LSP is set

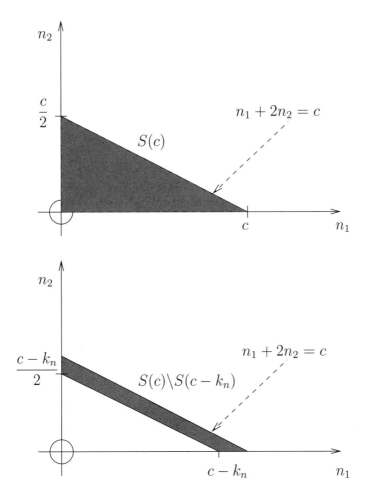

Figure 4.12 State spaces for a two-class trunk.

up from an ingress label-edge router (LER) to an egress LER through a number of label-switched routers (LSRs). RSVP-TE [12] or CR-LDP can be used in the setup of bandwidth-provisioned LSPs. Once an LSP is set up, specified flows of packets, collectively called the forward equivalence class (FEC) of the LSP, are identified by the ingress LER and labeled prior to transmission to the next LSR on the LSP. Instead of OSPF or BGP, local forwarding (destination output port) decisions by LSRs for such packets are quickly made by inputing the labels carried in their headers to MPLS forwarding tables. In the process, the labels of the packets are changed ("switched") for the benefit of the next LSR handling the packets on their LSP. Thus, the MPLS forwarding tables in the LSRs collectively define the routes of the LSPs [188]. The LSR that is the egress LER of the LSP forwards exiting packets according to the native routing protocols in the Internet (OSPF and BGP). MPLS is discussed further in Section 6.1.2.

4.6 A GAME-THEORETIC FRAMEWORK FOR MULTIPLEXING PACKET FLOWS

In this section, we begin to explore how resource pricing may be used to control user demand. In our context, the commodity is bandwidth and, by dynamically modifying (increasing) prices for bandwidth, one can control congestion (excessive demand). The introduction of such mechanisms faces many obstacles, including the deployment of corresponding *billing* technology and unclear commercial advantages over the present system of largely flat-rate (unlimited-use) charging for end-user access [162]. However, the *future* commercial and security advantages of resource overprovisioning strategies together with flat-rate pricing are not clear either. Moreover, many protocols for resource sharing are very vulnerable to misuse by selfish users; pricing mechanisms have been proposed to create the right kind of incentives for conformant user behavior [202]. So, the use of price controls is currently receiving a great deal of attention both in the literature by researchers and among service providers.

We now study the existence of equilibrium behavior of a population of N users competing for resource units (bandwidth) which are offered for sale by a network. We formulate a generic noncooperative game that can be applied to several local area networking situations. In the following, no explicit negotiation between the users and network are assumed. The users are informed of the network's current pricing, infer their received qualities of service, and take action based on their needs and willingness to pay. The network infers total user demand (by, say, monitoring queue backlogs) and adjusts its prices accordingly.

Suppose that each user n has a control (or "access" or "input") parameter λ_n and receives a certain QoS $\theta_n(\underline{\lambda})$, where

$$\underline{\lambda} \equiv (\lambda_1, \lambda_2, ..., \lambda_N),$$

i.e., the nth user's QoS depends on the action taken by other users. The QoS may involve transmission latency, packet loss rate, throughput, or may simply be defined as an amount of bandwidth allocated to the user by the network. We assume that the network charges a fixed amount M per unit resource consumed. Each user n seeks to maximize his or her net utility or net benefit, in this case

$$U_n(\theta_n) - M\theta_n,$$

where U_n is the utility function for the nth user.

Assume the following:

(a) $\lambda_n \in [0, \lambda_n^{\max}]$ for some fixed finite $\lambda_n^{\max} > 0$,

(b) $\theta_n(\underline{\lambda})$ is an increasing and differentiable function of λ_n,

(c) $\theta_n(\cdot)$ is continuous in $\prod_{n=1}^{N}[0, \lambda_n^{\max}]$,

(d) $\theta_n(\underline{\lambda}) = 0$ for all $\underline{\lambda}$ such that $\lambda_n = 0$,

(e) U_n is increasing and $U_n(0) = 0$, and

(f) U_n' is decreasing, i.e., U_n is concave.

Examples of simple functions θ representing network dynamics are the subject of the following example and Problem 4.11 at the end of this chapter.

■ **EXAMPLE 4.3**

Suppose that the user under consideration is *willing to pay* m dollars for each successfully transmitted byte (of a particular application) interpreted in the following way: When $M = m$, the user will desire only a throughput of Θ. When $M > m$, the user's desired throughput, $y^*(M) = 0$. Over the interval $0 \leq M \leq m$, $y^*(M)$ is decreasing and $y^*(0) = \pi$, where π is the maximum possible throughput requirement of the associated application. The following is an example formula for a user's desired throughput consistent with the previous discussion and parameterized by m, Θ, π:

$$y^*(M) \;=\; \begin{cases} 0 & \text{if } M > m, \\ \min\{m\Theta/M, \; \pi\} & \text{if } 0 \leq M \leq m \end{cases} \tag{4.7}$$

(clearly, demand y^* can decrease with increasing price M in other ways). In practice, the user will try to choose his or her throughput θ so as to maximize his or her net benefit $U(\theta) - M\theta$ (utility minus cost). The maximizing value of θ is $(U')^{-1}(M)$. Equating with (4.7) gives

$$y^*(M) \;=\; (U')^{-1}(M) \;=\; \begin{cases} 0 & \text{if } M > m, \\ \min\{m\Theta/M, \; \pi\} & \text{if } 0 \leq M \leq m. \end{cases}$$

Therefore, (4.7) corresponds to the utility function

$$U(\theta) \;=\; \begin{cases} m\theta & \text{if } 0 \leq \theta \leq \Theta, \\ m\Theta(\log(\theta/\Theta) + 1) & \text{if } \Theta < \theta \leq \pi, \\ m\Theta(\log(\pi/\Theta) + 1) & \text{if } \pi < \theta. \end{cases} \tag{4.8}$$

This utility U is concave and nondecreasing. Also, U is strictly increasing on $[0, \infty)$ only when $\pi = \infty$. Moreover, U is strictly concave on $[0, \infty)$ only when $\Theta = 0$ and $\pi = \infty$, which is the case where the user's QoS requirements are "elastic" [124, 201], i.e., the utility gradually increases but sublinearly as a "law of diminishing returns." See Figure 4.13.

Assumption (f) implies $\arg\max_\theta\{U_n(\theta) - M\theta\}$ is unique; therefore, let

$$y_n \;\equiv\; (U'_n)^{-1}(M)$$

and assume that $y_n > 0$. The nth user sequentially adjusts his or her control parameter λ_n in an attempt to make the received QoS, $\theta_n(\underline{\lambda})$, equal to y_n. The following theorem is an immediate consequence of Brouwer's fixed-point theorem [27, 205].

Theorem 4.6.1. *If a jointly continuous function G satisfies the property*

$$G(y, \theta, \lambda) \begin{cases} \equiv \lambda & \text{if } y = \theta, \\ > \lambda & \text{if } y > \theta, \\ < \lambda & \text{if } y < \theta, \end{cases} \tag{4.9}$$

then the iteration in j

$$\lambda_n^{j+1} = \min\left\{G(y_n, \theta_n(\underline{\lambda}^j), \lambda_n^j), \; \lambda_n^{\max}\right\}, \; n \in \{1, 2, ..., N\}, \tag{4.10}$$

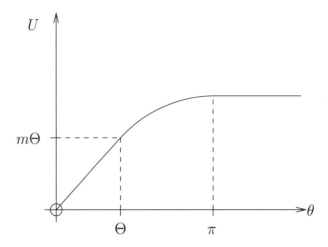

Figure 4.13 Example of user utility function.

has a fixed point.

The function G represents the end user's rate control strategy of the *game* (4.10). Examples include multiplicative increase and multiplicative decrease, i.e.,

$$G(y, \theta, \lambda) = \frac{y}{\theta}\lambda, \qquad (4.11)$$

and additive increase and multiplicative decrease (as with TCP). Note that we are implicitly assuming that every user does *not* divulge his or her utility function and, in particular, does not divulge their demand y_n for a given price M. This fixed-point iteration requires *only* that at each step j the *users ascertain (estimate/assess) their own received QoS*, θ, which results from their choice of control parameter, λ. Thus, we assume that the "network" dynamics for fixed control parameters are fast compared to the slow time scale of the iteration (4.10) allowing the users to observe the steady-state results of their actions. Were the network to adjust its price(s) M (up or down according to the measured level of user-demand (congestion)), it would, in turn, do so on a slower time-scale than that of the user iteration (4.10).

Definition 4.6.1. *A fixed point* $\underline{\lambda}^*$ *is said to be a* Nash equilibrium point (NEP) *if, for all users* n, *the net utility*

$$U_n(\theta_n(\underline{\lambda})) - M\theta_n(\underline{\lambda})$$

is maximized at $\lambda_n = \lambda_n^*$ *assuming* $\lambda_j = \lambda_j^*$ *for all* $j \neq n$, *i.e., for all* n,

$$\lambda_n^* = \arg\max_{0 \leq \lambda \leq \lambda_n^{\max}} U_n(\theta(\lambda; \underline{\lambda}_{-n}^*)) - M\theta(\lambda; \underline{\lambda}_{-n}^*),$$

where $(\lambda; \underline{\lambda}^*_{-n})$ is the N-vector whose kth component is λ^*_k for all $k \neq n$ and whose nth component is λ.

Note that at a NEP there is no incentive for a user to unilaterally change his or her action while the others' actions remain fixed. The following simple theorem concerns the fixed points $\underline{\lambda}^*$ of the generic iteration (4.10).

Theorem 4.6.2. *For the game (4.10) of Theorem 4.6.1:*

(a) If $\lambda^*_n < \lambda^{\max}_n$, $\theta_n(\underline{\lambda}^*) = y_n$.

(b) $\theta_n(\underline{\lambda}^*) \leq y_n$.

(c) Each such fixed point is a NEP.

Proof: (a) and (b): From (4.10), λ^*_n equals either $\lambda^{\max}_n$ or $G(y_n, \theta_n(\underline{\lambda}^*), \lambda^*_n)$, which is smaller than $\lambda^{\max}_n$. If

$$\lambda^*_n = G(y_n, \theta_n(\underline{\lambda}^*), \lambda^*_n) < \lambda^{\max}_n,$$

then (a) follows from the definition of G. If $\lambda^*_n = \lambda^{\max}_n$, then

$$G(y_n, \theta_n(\underline{\lambda}^*), \lambda^*_n) \geq \lambda^{\max}_n.$$

Hence, $\theta_n(\underline{\lambda}^*) \leq y_n$ holds.

(c): Given the continuity assumption of each θ_n and the definition of y_n, it is clear that all fixed points in the interior of $\prod^N_{n=1}[0, \lambda^{\max}_n]$ are NEPs. By (a) and (b), to show that a fixed point $\underline{\lambda}^*$ on the boundary of $\prod^N_{n=1}[0, \lambda^{\max}_n]$ (i.e., some of whose components are $\lambda^{\max}_n$ for some n) is a NEP, we will show that if

$$\lambda^*_n = \lambda^{\max}_n, \tag{4.12}$$

then

$$\lambda^{\max}_n = \arg \max_{0 \leq \lambda \leq \lambda^{\max}_n} f(\lambda),$$

where

$$f(\lambda) \equiv U_n(\theta_n(\lambda; \underline{\lambda}^*_{-n})) - M\theta_n(\lambda; \underline{\lambda}^*_{-n}).$$

This statement clearly follows if $f' \geq 0$ (f is nondecreasing) over the *whole* interval $[0, \lambda^{\max}_n]$. By direct differentiation,

$$f'(\lambda) = \left(U'_n(\theta_n(\lambda; \underline{\lambda}^*_{-n})) - M\right) \frac{\partial \theta_n(\lambda; \underline{\lambda}^*_{-n})}{\partial \lambda_n}.$$

First note that $\partial \theta_n(\lambda; \underline{\lambda}^*_{-n})/\partial \lambda_n \geq 0$ by assumption. By statement (b),

$$\theta_n(\underline{\lambda}^*) \leq y_n \equiv (U'_n)^{-1}(M);$$

therefore, because U'_n is nonincreasing by assumption,

$$U'_n(\theta_n(\underline{\lambda}^*)) = U'_n(\theta_n(\lambda_n^{\max}; \underline{\lambda}^*_{-n})) \quad \geq \quad M.$$

Again, because U'_n is nonincreasing and because θ_n is nondecreasing in λ_n (also by assumption), the previous inequality implies

$$U'_n(\theta_n(\lambda; \underline{\lambda}^*_{-n})) \quad \geq \quad M$$

for all $\lambda \leq \lambda_n^{\max}$ as desired. □

■ EXAMPLE 4.4

Recall the ALOHA wireless random multiple access system in Problem 1.22 of Chapter 1. Now assume that the users adjust their retransmission parameters λ_n (i.e., they are not all the same fixed value p) and that the QoS of a user is their average throughput i.e.,

$$\theta_n(\underline{\lambda}) \quad = \quad \lambda_n \prod_{i \neq n} (1 - \lambda_i).$$

Consider the game (4.10) with update function (4.11) for this ALOHA context with

$$\lambda_n^{\max} \quad = \quad 1$$

for all n, and consider a NEP $\underline{\lambda}^*$.

First, if $\underline{\lambda}^*$ solves

$$\lambda_n \quad = \quad \frac{y_n}{\prod_{i \neq n}(1 - \lambda_i)} \quad \text{for all } 1 \leq n \leq N \tag{4.13}$$

and $0 < \lambda_n^* < 1$ (i.e., $\lambda_i^* \in (0, 1)$) for *some* n, then $0 < \lambda_i^* < 1$ for all $i \neq n$ as well. Second, if, for some n, the polynomial in λ_n

$$\lambda_n(1 - \lambda_n)^{N-1} - y_n \prod_{i \neq n} \left(1 + \left(\frac{y_i}{y_n} - 1 \right) \lambda_n \right) \tag{4.14}$$

has a real root $\lambda_n^* \in (0, 1)$, then (4.13) has a real solution $\underline{\lambda}^*$ in $(0, 1)^N$.

Lyapunov stability methods were applied to study the limiting behavior of the generic fixed-point iteration for ALOHA [109] and single-trunk Erlang loss systems [110]. A Markov chain describing an ALOHA system on a graph (spatially interfering access points) was studied in [26]. Several authors have also studied *dynamic* pricing mechanisms in a networking context; see Chapter 6. Increasing but *non*concave utility functions (i.e., S-shaped functions approximating a discontinuous step) are indicative of users with *in*elastic QoS requirements; see [140]. Note that in our problem formulation above, $U(\theta(\cdot))$ may be a nonconcave function.

4.7 DISCUSSION: LOCAL MEDIUM ACCESS CONTROL OF A SINGLE WIRELESS CHANNEL

Carrier sense multiple access with collision avoidance (CSMA/CA) [22, 33] systems reduce collisions (interfering packet transmissions) via channel monitoring and interframe spacing rules, and also use windowing-based backoff random access in response to collisions [139]. Hybrids of random-access and round-robin scheduling have also been proposed for time-division multiple access (TDMA) of a wireless channel. A vast literature exists for non-TDMA "spread-spectrum" methods, including those based on code-division multiple access (CDMA) and pseudorandom frequency hopping (as in Bluetooth); see Problem 4.12 below.

Problems

4.1   Start with the expression (3.3) from Chapter 3 and assume (σ, ρ) constrained arrivals to obtain a bound on EQ and, thereby, on $P(Q \geq M)$.

4.2   Suppose a flow is both (σ, ρ) and (L, π) constrained with $\rho < \pi$ bytes per second and $\sigma > L$ bytes. Such a constraint can be achieved by a dual leaky bucket (two leaky buckets in series) [4, 5].

 (a) Find a tight upper bound on the cumulative transmission (in bytes) of the flow over an interval of time of length t [95].

 (b) Find the smallest b such that the flow is (b, c) constrained for a given c such that $\rho < c < \pi$. Hint: Plot the line ct with the answer to part (a).

The queueing behavior of such dually constrained flows was studied further in [128].

4.3   Consider the policer of Figure 4.9.

 (a) How would it function if it were to maintain the departure time of the most recently admitted packet d instead of the queue length Q. Is the state variable a required?

 (b) Look up the packet markers defined in [94, 95] and determine whether they are implemented using the mechanism in Figure 4.8 (without the packet queue) or Figure 4.9 and what state variables are maintained.

4.4   Under DRR, suppose two queues n and m are nonempty at the start of each of k consecutive rounds. Find expressions for upper and lower bounds on the ratio $D_n(k)/D_m(k)$ and show that this ratio converges to f_n/f_m as $k \to \infty$.

4.5   Prove Theorem 4.3.3.

4.6   Show that, under SVC, the service curve D of a queue with bandwidth share f is

$$D_f(t) \quad = \quad \max\{fct - L_{\max}, \ 0\}.$$

4.7   Prove the statement of (4.6). Hint: Suppose the service deadlines of an arrival process $\{A, a\}$ are d for a bandwidth allocation ρ, i.e., definition (4.2). Let $\tilde{d}$ be the departure times from the scheduled queue under consideration so that the cumulative departures from the queue are

$$\tilde{D}[0, t] \quad = \quad \sum_n \mathbf{1}\{\tilde{d}_n \leq t\} \geq \sum_n \mathbf{1}\{d_n + \mu \leq t\},$$

where the last inequality is the assumed guaranteed rate property.

4.8   Prove a guaranteed rate property like that of Theorem 4.3.2 but for the basic VirtualClock scheduler that does not use eligibility times, i.e., the eligibility time of a packet is simply its arrival time. Note that VirtualClock does not possess the same per-flow output jitter bounds of SVC.

4.9   A concave cost *function* $M(\theta)$ could be used instead of a proportional cost $M\theta$ to encourage additional user consumption with volume discounts. If $U'_n(\theta) - M'(\theta)$ is a decreasing function of θ, then we have a unique maximizing value of $U_n - M$:

$$\hat{y}_n \equiv \arg\max_\theta \{U_n(\theta) - M(\theta)\}.$$

If $M(\theta)$ is a concave differentiable function of θ with $M(0) = 0$, $U'_n(0) > M'(0)$, and $U'_n - M'$ decreasing, determine whether Theorem 4.6.2 continues to hold with y_n replaced by $\hat{y}_n$ for all n.

4.10   Prove the statements of Equations (4.13) and (4.14).

4.11   Find an expression for the QoS $\theta_n(\underline{\lambda})$ used in the generic game (4.10), where the users share a single trunk of C circuits, assuming each user controls the intensity λ_n of their connection setup request process submitted to the network, the average holding time of a connection of the nth user is $1/\mu_n$, and the QoS of a user is the steady-state number of active connections they hold.

4.12   Suppose that there are K channels and $N \leq K$ nodes. The nodes are synchronized and time is slotted. In each time slot, each node selects a channel at random and attempts to transmit a single packet, i.e., a frequency-hopping spread-spectrum system. Find an expression for the probability that one or more transmission collisions occur in a time slot.

4.13   This problem explores a simple power control iteration for the uplink of a wireless cellular network. Consider an end system j whose base station is denoted b_j. Let $h_{b_j k}$ be the *path gain* from node k and p_k^i be the transmission power of node k after i iterations of the following algorithm. Let R_k be the desired transmitted data rate of node k, W be the channel bandwidth, and σ^2 be the background Gaussian noise power. The throughput of node j's uplink (from node j to b_j) is

$$\gamma_j W \frac{h_{b_j j} p_j^i}{\sigma^2 + \sum_{k \neq j} h_{b_j k} p_k^i},$$

where γ_j is a parameter that weakly depends on j [197]; note the signal-to-interference-and-noise ratio in this expression. Assume end-system mobility is negligible (and hence the $h_{b_j k}$ terms are constant) during the iteration

$$p_j^{i+1} = \gamma_j R_j \frac{\sigma^2 + \sum_{k \neq j} h_{b_j k} p_k^i}{W h_{b_j j}}.$$

(a) Show that the iteration can be written, in vector form, as

$$\underline{p}^{i+1} = A\underline{p}^i + \underline{s},$$

i.e., find the square matrix A and vector s.

(b) Find a condition on A so that a unique fixed point $\underline{p}^*$ exists.

(c) Find a condition on A so that $\underline{p}$ converges to $\underline{p}^*$.

CHAPTER 5

QUEUEING NETWORKS WITH STATIC ROUTING

In this chapter, we introduce two classical stochastic queueing models: "loss" networks modeling circuit-switched networks and Jackson networks that can be used to model packet-switched networks and packet-level processors. Static routing is considered in the former and purely randomized routing with static routing probabilities is considered in the latter. Dynamic routing is the subject of Chapter 6.

5.1 LOSS NETWORKS

In this section, we consider circuit-switched loss networks for which the basic references are [123, 189]. The traditional telephone system is circuit switched. Also, there is significant MPLS deployment in the Internet today allowing LSPs (similar to ATM "virtual" circuits) to connect different access points of an Internet service provider (ISP). Circuit-switched frame relay continues to handle a substantial amount of virtual private network (VPN) and leased-line service.

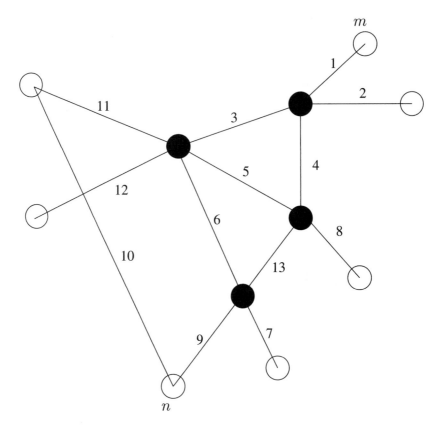

Figure 5.1   An example loss network.

■ **EXAMPLE 5.1**

Consider Figure 5.1 depicting a network with 13 enumerated links. Note that the cycle-free routes connecting nodes (end systems) m and n are

$$
\begin{aligned}
r_1 &= \{1, 3, 6, 9\}, \\
r_2 &= \{1, 4, 13, 9\}, \\
r_3 &= \{1, 4, 5, 6, 9\}, \\
r_4 &= \{1, 3, 5, 13, 9\},
\end{aligned}
$$

where we have described each route by its link membership as above. We will return to this example in the following.

Consider a network connecting together N end systems/users. Bandwidth in the network is divided into fixed-size amounts called *circuits*, e.g., a circuit could be a 64 kbps channel (voice line) or a T1 line of 1.544 Mbps. Let L be the number of network links and let c_l circuits be the fixed capacity of network link l. Let R be the number of distinct bidirectional routes in the network, where a route r is defined by a group of links $l \in r$. Let $\mathcal{R}$ be the set of distinct routes so that $R = |\mathcal{R}|$. Finally, define the $L \times R$ matrix $\mathbf{A}$ with Boolean entries $a_{l,r}$ in the lth row and rth column, where

$$a_{l,r} = \begin{cases} 1 & \text{if } l \in r, \\ 0 & \text{if } l \notin r. \end{cases}$$

That is, each column of $\mathbf{A}$ corresponds to a route and each row of $\mathbf{A}$ corresponds to a link.

■ **EXAMPLE 5.2**

The four routes r_1 to r_4 for the network of 13 links given in Example 5.1 are described by the 13×4 matrix

$$\mathbf{A} = \begin{bmatrix} 1 & 1 & 1 & 1 \\ 0 & 0 & 0 & 0 \\ 1 & 0 & 0 & 1 \\ 0 & 1 & 1 & 0 \\ 0 & 0 & 1 & 1 \\ 1 & 0 & 1 & 0 \\ 0 & 0 & 0 & 0 \\ 0 & 0 & 0 & 0 \\ 1 & 1 & 1 & 1 \\ 0 & 0 & 0 & 0 \\ 0 & 0 & 0 & 0 \\ 0 & 0 & 0 & 0 \\ 0 & 1 & 0 & 1 \end{bmatrix}.$$

5.1.1 Fixed-route arrival rates

In this section, we assume that each *route* has an independent associated Poisson connection arrival (circuit setup) process with with intensity λ_r. This situation arises if, for each pair of end nodes π, there is an independent Poisson connection arrival process with rate Λ_π that is randomly thinned among the routes $\mathcal{R}_\pi$ connecting π so that there are independent Poisson arrivals to each route $r \in \mathcal{R}_\pi$ with rate $p_{\pi,r} \geq 0$, where these fixed "routing" parameters satisfy

$$\sum_{r \in \mathcal{R}_\pi} p_{\pi,r} = 1.$$

Define $X_r(t)$ as the number of occupied circuits on route r at time t and define the corresponding random vector $\underline{X}(t)$. Let

$$\underline{e}_r \qquad\qquad\qquad (5.1)$$

be the R-vector with zeros in every entry except for the rth row whose entry is 1. If an existing connection on route r terminates at time t,

$$\underline{X}(t) = \underline{X}(t-) - \underline{e}_r.$$

Similarly, if a connection on route r is admitted into the network at time t,

$$\underline{X}(t) \;=\; \underline{X}(t-) + \underline{e}_r.$$

Clearly, a connection cannot be admitted (i.e., is *blocked*) along route r^* at time t if *any* associated link capacity constraint is violated, i.e., if, for some $l \in r^*$,

$$\sum_{r \mid l \in r} X_r(t-) = c_l.$$

An R-vector $\underline{x}$ is said to be *feasible* if it satisfies all link capacity constraints, i.e., for all links l,

$$(\mathbf{A}\underline{x})_l = \sum_{r \mid l \in r} x_r \in \{0, 1, 2, \; ..., \; c_l\}.$$

Thus, the state space of the stochastic process $\underline{X}$ is

$$S(\underline{c}) \;\equiv\; \{\underline{x} \in (\mathbb{Z}^+)^R \mid \mathbf{A}\underline{x} \le \underline{c}\}.$$

■ **EXAMPLE 5.3**

For the network of Figure 5.1, note that link 1 is common to all routes of Example 5.1. Thus,

$$\underline{x} \;=\; \begin{bmatrix} 1 \\ 1 \\ 1 \\ 1 \end{bmatrix}$$

is feasible if the capacities $c_l = 4$ for all links l but is *not* feasible if $c_1 < 4$ because

$$(\mathbf{A}\underline{x})_1 = 4,$$

where $\mathbf{A}$ is given in Example 5.2.

In this section, we also assume that for each route r the connection lifetimes are independent and exponentially distributed with mean $1/\mu_r$. Under this assumption, it is easily seen that the stochastic process $\underline{X}$ is a Markov chain wherein the state transition $\underline{x} \to \underline{x} + \underline{e}_r \in S(\underline{c})$ occurs with rate λ_r and the the state transition $\underline{x} \to \underline{x} - \underline{e}_r \in S(\underline{c})$ occurs with rate $x_r \mu_r$.

Theorem 5.1.1. *The loss network $\underline{X}$ is time reversible with stationary distribution on $S(\underline{c})$ given by the product form*

$$\sigma(\underline{x}) \;=\; \frac{1}{G(\underline{c})} \prod_{r \in \mathcal{R}} \frac{\rho_r^{x_r}}{x_r!}, \tag{5.2}$$

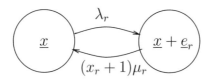

Figure 5.2 Part of the TRD of a loss network.

where

$$\rho_r \;=\; \frac{\lambda_r}{\mu_r},$$

$\underline{c}$ is the L-vector of link capacities, and

$$G(\underline{c}) \;=\; \sum_{\underline{x}\in S(\underline{c})} \prod_{r\in\mathcal{R}} \frac{\rho_r^{x_r}}{x_r!} \tag{5.3}$$

is the normalizing term (partition function) chosen so that $\sum_{\underline{x}\in S(\underline{c})}\sigma(\underline{x}) = 1$.

Proof: Assuming $\underline{x}, \underline{x}+\underline{e}_r \in S(\underline{c})$ for some $r \in \mathcal{R}$, a generic detailed balance equation is

$$\lambda_r\sigma(\underline{x}) \;=\; (x_r+1)\mu_r\sigma(\underline{x}+\underline{e}_r);$$

see Figure 5.2. The theorem statement therefore follows if σ given by (5.2) satisfies this equation. So, substituting the expression (5.2) for σ and canceling from both sides the normalizing term $G(\underline{c})$ and all terms pertaining to routes other than r give

$$\lambda_r\frac{\rho_r^{x_r}}{x_r!} \;=\; (x_r+1)\mu_r\frac{\rho_r^{x_r+1}}{(x_r+1)!}.$$

This equation is clearly seen to be true after canceling $x_r + 1$ on the right-hand side, then canceling $\rho^{x_r}/x_r!$ from both sides, and finally recalling $\rho_r \equiv \lambda_r/\mu_r$.   □

Note how G depends on $\underline{c}$ through the state space $S(\underline{c})$ and compare with the definition of the partition function in Theorem 4.5.1 for a single link with multiclass connections. This result can be generalized to multiclass networks [122, 189] and holds for different job service time distributions [224] (i.e., the theorem statement is "insensitive" to service time distribution).

5.1.2 Exact expression for connection blocking

A connection is admitted on route r at time t only if a circuit is available, i.e., only if $(\mathbf{A}\underline{X}(t-))_l \leq c_l - 1$ *for all* $l \in r$, where $(\mathbf{A}\underline{x})_l$ represents the lth component of the

L-vector $\mathbf{A}\underline{x}$. Consider the L-vector $\mathbf{A}\underline{e}_r$, i.e., the rth column of $\mathbf{A}$ whose lth entry is

$$(\mathbf{A}\underline{e}_r)_l \;=\; \begin{cases} 1 & \text{if } l \in r, \\ 0 & \text{if } l \notin r. \end{cases}$$

Thus, the L-vector $\underline{c} - \mathbf{A}\underline{e}_r$ has lth entry

$$c_l - (\mathbf{A}\underline{e}_r)_l \;=\; \begin{cases} c_l - 1 & \text{if } l \in r, \\ c_l & \text{if } l \notin r. \end{cases}$$

Theorem 5.1.2. *The steady-state probability that a connection is blocked on route r is*

$$B_r \;=\; 1 - \frac{G(\underline{c} - \mathbf{A}\underline{e}_r)}{G(\underline{c})}. \tag{5.4}$$

Proof: First note that B_r is 1 minus the probability that the connection is admitted (on every link $l \in r$). Therefore, by PASTA,

$$B_r \;=\; 1 - \sum_{\mathbf{A}\underline{x} \leq \underline{c} - \mathbf{A}\underline{e}_r} \sigma(\underline{x})$$

$$=\; 1 - \frac{1}{G(\underline{c})} \sum_{\underline{x} \in S(\underline{c} - \mathbf{A}\underline{e}_r)} \frac{\rho_r^{x_r}}{x_r!},$$

from which (5.4) directly follows by definition of the normalizing term G. $\qquad \square$

5.1.3 Fixed-point iteration for approximate connection blocking

The computational complexity of the partition function G grows rapidly as the network dimensions (L, R, N, etc.) grow [189]. In this section, we formulate an iterative method for determining approximate blocking probabilities under the assumption that the individual links *block* connections independently. Consider a single link l^* and let b_{l^*} be its unknown blocking probability. For the moment, assume that the link blocking probabilities b_l of all other links $l \neq l^*$ are known. Consider a route r containing link l^*. By the independent blocking assumption, the incident load (traffic intensity) of l^* from this route, after blocking by all of the route's other links has been taken into account, is

$$\rho_r \prod_{l \in r \,|\, l \neq l^*} (1 - b_l).$$

Thus, the total load of link l^* is reduced[1] by blocking to

$$\sum_{r \,|\, l^* \in r} \rho_r \prod_{l \in r \,|\, l \neq l^*} (1 - b_l) \;\equiv\; \hat{\rho}_{l^*}(\underline{b}_{-l^*}),$$

---

[1]Or "thinned"; see Problem 2.12 of Chapter 2.

where $\underline{b}_{-l}$ is the $(L-1)$-vector of link blocking probabilities *not* including that of link l. By the independent blocking assumption, the blocking probability of link l^* must therefore be

$$b_{l^*} \;=\; \mathcal{E}(\hat{\rho}_{l^*}(\underline{b}_{-l^*}),\, c_{l^*}), \tag{5.5}$$

where $\mathcal{E}$ is Erlang's blocking formula (3.29):

$$\mathcal{E}(\rho, c) \;\equiv\; \mathcal{E}_c(\rho) \;\equiv\; \frac{\rho^c/c!}{\sum_{j=0}^{c} \rho^j/j!}.$$

System (5.5) is known as a *reduced-load approximation*.

Clearly, the link blocking probabilities $\underline{b}$ must *simultaneously* satisfy Equation (5.5) for all links l^*, i.e., (5.5) is a system of L equations in L unknowns. Approaches to numerically finding such an L-vector $\underline{b}$ include Newton's method and the following *fixed-point iteration* (method of successive approximations). Beginning from an arbitrary initial $\underline{b}^0$, after j iterations set

$$b_l^j \;=\; \mathcal{E}(\hat{\rho}_l(\underline{b}_{-l}^{j-1}), c_l) \text{ for all links } l. \tag{5.6}$$

Brouwer's fixed-point theorem gives that a solution $\underline{b} \in [0,1]^L$ to (5.6) exists [27]. Uniqueness of the solution follows from the fact that a solution to (5.5) is the minimum of a convex function [123, 189].

Given the link blocking probabilities $\underline{b}$, under the independence assumption, the *route* blocking probabilities are

$$B_r \;=\; 1 - \prod_{l \in r}(1 - b_l)$$

$$=\; \sum_{l \in r} b_l + \mathrm{o}\left(\sum_{l \in r} b_l\right),$$

i.e., if $\sum_{l \in r} b_l \ll 1$, then

$$B_r \;\approx\; \sum_{l \in r} b_l.$$

That is, the blocking probability is approximately *additive*.

5.2 STABLE OPEN NETWORKS OF QUEUES

In the previous section, an idealized circuit-switched network was considered in which a "job" (connection or call) occupied a circuit on every link of a route and there was no waiting room for jobs. The arrival rates to the routes r are fixed λ_r. In this section, we will consider an idealized packet-switched network where the routing decisions, made at each node forwarding the packets (jobs), are random. Also, the service times at the nodes that a given packet visits are random and independent with distribution depending on the forwarding node. If the network is modeling packets flowing through Internet routers, then this too is somewhat of an idealization considering that all of a given packet's service times would be proportional to its length. A histogram of packet length distributions in the Internet is given in [2]. The mean packet service times could be determined from such a histogram and the (constant) service rate of the associated node/router. The material in this section has applications beyond a Markovian model of a packet-switched network; for example, the flow balance equations of Section 5.2.1 below can also be used to model the interworkings of the various "engines" within a network processor.

Consider a group of $N \geq 2$ lossless, single-server, work-conserving queueing stations. Packets at the nth station have a mean required service time of $1/\mu_n$ for all $n \in \{1, 2, ..., N\}$. The packet arrival process to the nth station is a superposition of $N + 1$ component arrival processes. Packets *departing* the mth station are *routed* to and immediately arrive at the nth station with probability $r_{m,n}$. Also, with probability $r_{m,0}$, a packet departing station m leaves the queueing network forever; here we use station index 0 to denote the world outside the network. Clearly, for all m,

$$\sum_{n=0}^{N} r_{m,n} = 1.$$

Arrivals from the outside world arrive to the nth station at rate Λ_n. It is these interactions with the outside world that make the network *open*.

5.2.1   Flow balance equations

Let λ_n be the total arrival rate to the nth station. These quantities can be found by solving the so-called *flow balance equations* which are based on the notion of conservation of flow and require that all queues are *stable*, i.e., $\mu_n > \lambda_n$ for all n. By Theorem 3.4.5, the flow balance equations are, for all $n \in \{1, 2, ..., N\}$,

$$\lambda_n = \Lambda_n + \sum_{m=1}^{N} \lambda_m r_{m,n}. \tag{5.7}$$

Note that the flow balance equations can be written in matrix form:

$$\underline{\lambda}^{\mathrm{T}}(\mathbf{I} - \mathbf{R}) = \underline{\Lambda}^{\mathrm{T}},$$

where the $N \times N$ matrix $\mathbf{R}$ has entry $r_{m,n}$ in the mth row and nth column. Thus, the flow balance equations can be uniquely solved if $\det(\mathbf{I} - \mathbf{R}) \neq 0$, i.e., $\mathbf{I} - \mathbf{R}$ is invertible so that

$$\underline{\lambda}^{\mathrm{T}} = \underline{\Lambda}^{\mathrm{T}}(\mathbf{I} - \mathbf{R})^{-1}.$$

Again, we are assuming that $\underline{\lambda} < \underline{\mu}$. This also requires that $r_{m,0} > 0$ for some station m (i.e., packets can exit the network). Otherwise, $\mathbf{R}$ would be a *stochastic* matrix (all entries nonnegative and all rows sum to 1) so that 1 is an eigenvalue of $\mathbf{R}$ and, therefore, 0 is an eigenvalue of $\mathbf{I} - \mathbf{R}$, i.e., $\mathbf{I} - \mathbf{R}$ is not invertible [99].

We can also write a flow balance equation between the outside world and the queueing network as a whole by summing (5.7) over $n \in \{1, ..., N\}$:

$$\sum_{n=1}^{N} \Lambda_n = \sum_{n=1}^{N} \lambda_n r_{n,0}, \tag{5.8}$$

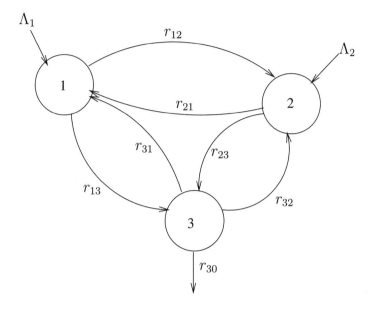

Figure 5.3 An example packet network.

i.e., the total flow into the network equals the total flow out of the network.

The flow balance equations hold in great generality. In the following, we will apply them to derive the stationary distribution of a special network with Markovian dynamics.

■ EXAMPLE 5.4

For the example network of Figure 5.3 with three lossless FIFO queues, queues 1 and 2 respectively have exogenous arrival rate Λ_1 and Λ_2 packets per second. The mean service time at queue k is $1/\mu_k$. The nonzero packet routing probabilities are

$$
\begin{aligned}
r_{12} &= r_{13} = \tfrac{1}{2} \\
r_{21} &= r_{23} = \tfrac{1}{2}, \\
r_{31} &= r_{32} = r_{30} = \tfrac{1}{3},
\end{aligned}
$$

where the subscript 0 represents the outside world.

Assuming that the queues are all stable, the flow balance equations are

$$
\begin{aligned}
\lambda_1 &= \Lambda_1 + \tfrac{1}{2}\lambda_2 + \tfrac{1}{3}\lambda_3, \\
\lambda_2 &= \Lambda_2 + \tfrac{1}{2}\lambda_1 + \tfrac{1}{3}\lambda_3, \\
\lambda_3 &= \tfrac{1}{2}\lambda_1 + \tfrac{1}{2}\lambda_2.
\end{aligned}
$$

Thus, in matrix form,

$$
\begin{bmatrix} 1 & -\frac{1}{2} & -\frac{1}{3} \\ -\frac{1}{2} & 1 & -\frac{1}{3} \\ -\frac{1}{2} & -\frac{1}{2} & 1 \end{bmatrix} \underline{\lambda} = \begin{bmatrix} \Lambda_1 \\ \Lambda_2 \\ 0 \end{bmatrix},
$$

which implies

$$
\underline{\lambda} = \begin{bmatrix} 1 & -\frac{1}{2} & -\frac{1}{3} \\ -\frac{1}{2} & 1 & -\frac{1}{3} \\ -\frac{1}{2} & -\frac{1}{2} & 1 \end{bmatrix}^{-1} \begin{bmatrix} \Lambda_1 \\ \Lambda_2 \\ 0 \end{bmatrix},
$$

i.e., $\underline{\lambda} = ((\mathbf{I} - \mathbf{R})^{\mathrm{T}})^{-1}\underline{\Lambda}$. Given the total flow rates λ, the service rates μ_k can be chosen so that $\mu_k > \lambda_k$ for all queues k to achieve stability (the flow balance equations hold). Finally, note that the mean departure rate to the "outside world," λ_3, will work out from the flow balance equations to be

$$
\lambda_3 r_{30} = \Lambda_1 + \Lambda_2. \tag{5.9}
$$

5.2.2 Open Jackson networks

Suppose that the exogenous arrivals are Poisson and that the service time distributions are exponential. Further suppose that all routing decisions, service times and exogenous (exponential) interarrival times are mutually independent. The resulting network is Markovian and is called an *open Jackson network*. Note that if $X_n(t)$ is the number of packets in station n at time t, then the vector of such processes $\underline{X}(t)$ taking values in $(\mathbb{Z}^+)^N$ is Markovian.

We will now specify a Jackson network's transition rate matrix and stationary distribution on $(\mathbb{Z}^+)^N$. Consider a vector $\underline{x} = (x_1, ..., x_N) \in (\mathbb{Z}^+)^N$ and define the following operator δ mapping $(\mathbb{Z}^+)^N \to (\mathbb{Z}^+)^N$. If $x_m > 0$ and $1 \le n, m \le N$, then $\delta_{m,n}$ represents a packet departing from station m and arriving at station n:

$$
(\delta_{m,n}\,\underline{x})_i = \begin{cases} x_i & \text{if } i \neq m, n, \\ x_m - 1 & \text{if } i = m, \\ x_n + 1 & \text{if } i = n, \end{cases} \tag{5.10}
$$

i.e., $\delta_{m,n}\underline{x} \equiv \underline{x} - \underline{e}_m + \underline{e}_n$. If $x_m > 0$ and $1 \le m \le N$, then $\delta_{m,0}$ represents a packet departing the network to the outside world from station m:

$$
(\delta_{m,0}\,\underline{x})_i = \begin{cases} x_i & \text{if } i \neq m, \\ x_m - 1 & \text{if } i = m. \end{cases}
$$

If $1 \le n \le N$, then $\delta_{0,n}$ represents a packet arriving at the network at station n from the outside world:

$$
(\delta_{0,n}\,\underline{x})_i = \begin{cases} x_i & \text{if } i \neq n, \\ x_n + 1 & \text{if } i = n. \end{cases}
$$

The transition rate matrix of the Jackson network is given by the following equations:

$$
q(\underline{x}, \delta_{m,n}\,\underline{x}) = \begin{cases} \mu_m r_{m,n} & \text{if } 1 \le m \le N, \, 0 \le n \le N, \, x_m > 0, \\ \Lambda_n & \text{if } m = 0, \, 1 \le n \le N. \end{cases}
$$

Theorem 5.2.1. *The stationary distribution of an open Jackson network is*

$$\sigma(\underline{x}) \;=\; \frac{1}{G} \prod_{n=1}^{N} \rho_n^{x_n}, \tag{5.11}$$

where, for all n, the traffic intensity

$$\rho_n \;\equiv\; \frac{\lambda_n}{\mu_n} \;<\; 1$$

for stability and the normalizing term (partition function) is

$$G \;=\; \sum_{\underline{x} \in (\mathbb{Z}^+)^N} \prod_{n=1}^{N} \rho_n^{x_n}.$$

Proof: Recall the balance equations (2.29) for the Jackson network "at" $\underline{x}$, i.e., corresponding to $\underline{x}$'s column in the network's transition rate matrix. To do this, we consider states *from which* the network makes transitions *into* $\underline{x}$. These include:

- $\delta_{n,m}\, \underline{x}$ for stations n such that $x_n > 0$, where

$$q(\delta_{n,m}\, \underline{x}, \underline{x}) \;=\; \mu_m r_{m,n};$$

- $\delta_{0,n}\, \underline{x}$ for all stations n, where

$$q(\delta_{n,0}\, \underline{x}, \underline{x}) \;=\; \Lambda_n;$$

- all other transitions that do not occur in one step, i.e., $q = 0$.

Note that $\delta_{m,n}\delta_{n,m}\, \underline{x} = \underline{x}$. Therefore, the balance equations at $\underline{x}$ are

$$\sum_{\{n \,|\, x_n > 0\}} \left[q(\delta_{n,0}\, \underline{x}, \underline{x})\sigma(\delta_{n,0}\, \underline{x}) + \sum_{m=1}^{N} q(\delta_{n,m}\, \underline{x}, \underline{x})\sigma(\delta_{n,m}\, \underline{x}) \right]$$

$$+ \sum_{m=1}^{N} q(\delta_{0,m}\, \underline{x}, \underline{x})\sigma(\delta_{0,m}\, \underline{x})$$

$$= \left(\sum_{\{m \,|\, x_m > 0\}} \left[q(\underline{x}, \delta_{m,0}\, \underline{x}) \sum_{n=1}^{N} q(\underline{x}, \delta_{m,n}\, \underline{x}) \right] + \sum_{n=1}^{N} q(\underline{x}, \delta_{0,n}\, \underline{x}) \right) \sigma(\underline{x}).$$

Substituting the transition rates we get

$$
\sum_{\{n \mid x_n > 0\}} \left[\Lambda_n \sigma(\delta_{n,0}\, \underline{x}) + \sum_{m=1}^{N} \mu_m r_{m,n} \sigma(\delta_{n,m}\, \underline{x}) \right]
$$

$$
+ \sum_{m=1}^{N} \mu_m r_{m,0} \sigma(\delta_{0,m}\, \underline{x})
$$

$$
= \left(\sum_{\{m \mid x_m > 0\}} \left[\mu_m r_{m,0} + + \sum_{n=1}^{N} \mu_m r_{m,n} \right] + \sum_{n=1}^{N} \Lambda_n \right) \sigma(\underline{x})
$$

$$
= \left(\sum_{\{m \mid x_m > 0\}} \mu_m + \sum_{n=1}^{N} \Lambda_n \right) \sigma(\underline{x}),
$$

where the last equation is (5.7). The theorem is proved if we can show that the distribution σ given in (5.11) satisfies this balance equation at every state $\underline{x}$. Substituting the expression (5.11) for σ and factoring out $\sigma(\underline{x})$ on the left-hand side, we get

$$
\sum_{\{n \mid x_n > 0\}} \left[\Lambda_n \frac{1}{\rho_n} + \sum_{m=1}^{N} \mu_m r_{m,n} \frac{\rho_m}{\rho_n} \right] + \sum_{m=1}^{N} \mu_m r_{m,0} \rho_m = \sum_{\{m \mid x_m > 0\}} \mu_m + \sum_{n=1}^{N} \Lambda_n.
$$

Substituting $\lambda_m = \mu_m \rho_m$, we get

$$
\sum_{\{n \mid x_n > 0\}} \left[\frac{1}{\rho_n} \left(\Lambda_n + \sum_{m=1}^{N} \lambda_m r_{m,n} \right) \right] + \sum_{m=1}^{N} \lambda_m r_{m,0} = \sum_{\{m \mid x_m > 0\}} \mu_m + \sum_{n=1}^{N} \Lambda_n.
$$

Finally, substitution of the flow balance equations (5.7) and (5.8) implies this equation does indeed hold. □

The expression in (5.11) is called a *product form* distribution. Note that the product form implies the queue occupancies are statistically independent in steady state.

■ **EXAMPLE 5.5**

Suppose the network of Example 5.4 is Jacksonian. The steady-state distribution of the number of jobs in the third queue is

$$
\mathsf{P}(Q_3 = k) = \rho_3^k (1 - \rho_3),
$$

where $\rho_3 = \lambda_3/\mu_3 < 1$. Thus, $\mathsf{E}Q_3 = \rho_3$, which is consistent with Little's formula.

Additional details of open Jackson networks and closed (fixed-population) Jackson networks are given in [226].

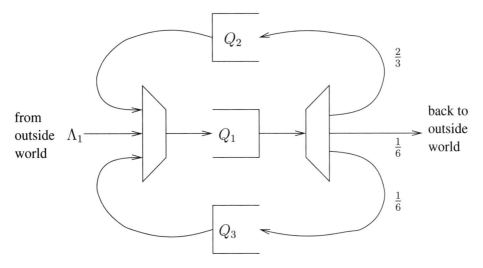

Figure 5.4   A three-node queueing network.

Problems

5.1   Verify the details in the proof of Theorem 5.2.1.

5.2   Give an intuitive explanation for why (5.9) ought to hold.

5.3   Is a Jackson network time reversible in general?

5.4   For the network of three lossless FIFO queues depicted in Figure 5.4, queue 1 has exogenous arrival rate Λ_1 packets per second. Each packet departing from queue 1 has one of three possible fates: It is forwarded to queue 2 with probability $\frac{2}{3}$ and to queue 3 with probability $\frac{1}{6}$ and leaves the network (back to the outside world) with probability $\frac{1}{6}$. All packets departing queues 2 and 3 reenter queue 1. For each queue k ($k = 1, 2, 3$), the mean service rate is μ_k packets per second and the total mean arrival rate is λ_k packets per second.

(a) If all queues are stable, i.e., $\lambda_k < \mu_k$ for all $k = 1, 2, 3$, find λ_k only in terms of Λ_1. So, given Λ_1, find the smallest service rates μ_k^* such that the network is stable whenever $\mu_k > \mu_k^*$ for all queues k.

(b) If $\mu_1 = 7$, $\mu_2 = 3$, and $\mu_3 = 4$, find the largest Λ_1^* such that the queueing network is stable *for all* $\Lambda_1 < \Lambda_1^*$.

Now suppose the network is a Jacksonian and in steady state:

(c) Find the probability that a packet visits only queue 1 (once) *and* experiences no queueing delay.

(d) Find the mean *total* sojourn time of packets in the network, i.e., from the time a packet enters into the first queue from the outside world to the time it finally leaves the network.

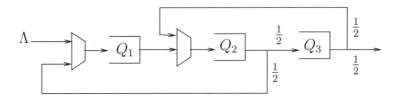

Figure 5.5 An open network of three lossless, FIFO, work-conserving queues.

5.5   For the network of Figure 5.5, half the jobs are routed back into the previous queue, so that half the jobs departing the rightmost queue (indexed 3) leave the system. The exogenous arrival rate (to the leftmost queue indexed 1) is Λ jobs per second.

(a) State and solve the flow balance equations (assuming the queues are all stable). Label Figure 5.5 with the total arrival rate λ_n to each queue n.

(b) Find the smallest number μ_n^* for each queue n such that the network (i.e., every queue) is stable if $\mu_n > \mu_n^*$ for all n.

Now assume the network is Jacksonian and in steady state:

(c) Find the mean sojourn time (queueing delay plus service time) of packets through queue 2 if $\mu_2 = 8\Lambda$.

(d) Additionally if $\mu_1 = 5\Lambda$ and $\mu_3 = 6\Lambda$, find the mean sojourn time of a packet through the entire network, i.e., from the time it arrives to queue 1 from the outside world to the time it completely departs queue 3.

5.6   Consider the context of Section 5.1.1.

(a) Define $Y_l(t)$ as the number of occupied circuits in link l at time t and define the corresponding random vector $\underline{Y}(t)$. Is $\underline{Y}$ a Markov chain? Hint: Consider state transitions when a connection terminates.

(b) Show that *link l's* traffic intensity is

$$\rho_l \equiv \sum_{r \mid l \in r} \frac{\lambda_r}{\mu_r}.$$

5.7   Consider a queueing system with an arrival process that is a stationary marked Poisson process. If the state of the stationary and ergodic (and *causal*) queueing system at time t, X_t, belongs to a set of "blocking states" $\mathcal{B}$, a job arriving at the queueing system at time t is blocked. Let B_t be the number of blocked jobs over $[0, t]$ and let N_t be the number of arriving jobs over $[0, t]$. Show that the stationary probability that an arriving connection is blocked is equal to

$$\mathsf{E}\left(\frac{B_t}{N_t} \mid N_t > 0\right),$$

i.e., when $N_t > 0$, B_t/N_t is an unbiased estimate of the blocking probability. Hint: Condition on N_t and then use the conditional uniformity property to show

$$\mathsf{E}\left(\frac{B_t}{N_t} \mid N_t > 0\right) = \mathsf{P}(X \in \mathcal{B}),$$

the stationary probability that $X \in \mathcal{B}$.

5.8   In the two-dimensional plane, assume nodes are mobile and each takes a roughly direct path through a cell. At a cell boundary, an independent and uniformly distributed random change of direction occurs for each mobile. Assuming the cells are roughly circular, a sample path of a single mobile is depicted in Figure 5.6, where the dot at the center of a cell is its base station. Also, we assume that the average velocities of a mobile through the cells are IID with density $f(v)$ over $[v_{\min}, v_{\max}]$ [98]. The mobiles are initially distributed in the plane according to a spatial Poisson process with density δ nodes per unit area, recall Example 3.1. Finally, assume that the cells themselves are also distributed in the plane so that, at any given time, the total displacements of the mobiles are IID[2] and, consequently, the result of Problem 2.16 applies.

(a) Find the mean rate λ_m of mobiles crossing into a cell of diameter Δ.

(b) How would the expression differ in (a) if velocity and direction through a cell were dependent?

---

[2]The base stations could also be randomly placed according to a spatial Poisson process with density $\delta' \ll \delta$ and the resulting circular cells approximate Voronoi sets about each of them, see Section 7.3.1.

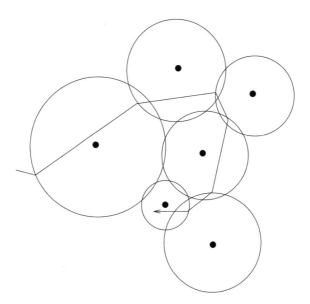

Figure 5.6 A single mobile's motion through circular cells.

CHAPTER 6

DYNAMIC ROUTING AND ROUTING WITH INCENTIVES

In this chapter, we begin with a brief general overview of routing issues. After preliminary material on optimization is given, an introduction to routing with incentives is presented. A section briefly describing an approach to joint scheduling and routing in a multihop wireless context follows. We conclude this chapter with a section on traffic load balancing on multiple paths.

6.1 GENERAL ROUTING ISSUES

In Section 5.1 we assumed a loss network had a constant demand λ_r per route r, i.e., *static routing*. A Jackson network used purely *randomized* routing but with fixed (static) routing probabilities. Conversely, deployed routing algorithms in the Internet or in multihop wireless contexts are *dynamic*, i.e., responsive to changes in network state at all times. Also, routing algorithms in these contexts are highly *distributed* because network operating conditions potentially involve:

- a large scale with respect to traffic volume or geography or both, and/or

- high variability in the traffic volume both at packet and connection/call level on short time-scales (possibly due in part to the routing algorithm itself), and/or

- potentially high variability in the network topology due to, for example, node mobility, channel conditions, or node or link removals because of faults or energy depletion.

157

Optimality results of routing protocols, specifically the Dijkstra and Bellman-Ford algorithms for unicast routing, are described in networking texts such as [139, 220] and in greater theoretical detail in [48, 206]; see Appendix A. These algorithms typically assume that costs (or "metrics") C_r of paths/routes r are additive, i.e.,

$$C_r = \sum_{l \in r} c_l, \tag{6.1}$$

where c_l represents the cost of link l. Such nonnegative link costs include Boolean hops, i.e., $c_l = 1$ for all active links l (leading to path costs C_r that are hop counts as used in the Internet), and those based on estimates of access delays at the transmitting node of the link. Alternatively, path costs could be based on the *bottleneck* link on the path, i.e.,

$$C_r = \max_{l \in r} c_l. \tag{6.2}$$

Such link costs include those based on residual energy e_l, e.g.,

$$c_l = \frac{1}{e_l},$$

or an estimate of the lifetime of the transmitting node of the link [39]. More complex two-dimensional link metrics of the form (c^x, c^y) may be employed to consider more than one quantity simultaneously, delay and energy for example, or hop count and BGP policy domain factors. One can define (lexicographic) order

$$(c_1^x, c_1^y) \leq (c_2^x, c_2^y) \tag{6.3}$$

to mean

$$c_1^x \leq c_2^x \quad \text{or} \quad \{c_1^x = c_2^x \text{ and } c_1^y \leq c_2^y\},$$

and define addition of link metrics (to obtain route costs from link costs) as

$$(c_1^x, c_1^y) + (c_2^x, c_2^y) = (c_1^x + c_2^x, \max\{c_1^y, c_2^y\}); \tag{6.4}$$

see Section 6.4.2 of [195] or Table 1 of [206]. For example, defining $c^x \in \{1, \infty\}$ in order to count hops of a path and basing c^y on the residual energy of the transmitting node, the chosen paths will be those with the highest bottleneck energy among those with the shortest hop count to the destination.

Alternatively, one can determine optimal paths according to one metric (the primary objective) and choose among these paths conditional on another metric (the secondary objective) being less than a threshold. For instance, suppose the primary objective is to minimize (bottleneck) energy costs and suppose a route r has C_r^x hops and C_r^y energy cost according to (6.1) and (6.2), respectively. Now suppose a route $r' = r \cup \{l\}$ is being considered (by appending link l to r). The network will use the (6.4) rule for addition, i.e.,

$$(C_{r'}^x, C_{r'}^y) = (c_l^x + C_r^x, \max\{c_l^y, C_r^y\})$$

if $c_l^x + C_r^x < \theta^x$ for some threshold $\theta^x > 0$. Otherwise it will set

$$(C_{r'}^x, C_{r'}^y) = (\infty, \infty)$$

and, consequently, the network will not use route r' nor any route r^* that uses r' (i.e., $r' \subset r^*$). Similarly, the network can find routes with minimal hop counts (primary objective) while avoiding any link with energy cost $c^y \geq \theta^y > 0$ (i.e., the residual energy of the transmitting node of the link $e \leq 1/\theta^y$).

A survey of routing protocols for (wireless) mobile ad hoc networks (MANETs), in particular Ad Hoc On-Demand Distance Vector (AODV) and Dynamic Source Routing (DSR), is given in [29]. On-demand source routing may be used when, for example, routes need very frequent updating due to node mobility or when forwarding decisions to all destinations is impractical to maintain at each node as may be in the case of a large network with a "flat" address space. Source routing can be implemented with a "threading" approach [71] or more simply as a limited-scope flood when feasible; see Section 7.2.2.

The basic Internet routing protocols, such as the inter-autonomous-system (AS) BGP, intra-AS OSPF protocol, and Internet Group Management Protocol (IGMP multicasting), are described in [139, 172, 220]. A brief overfiew of the OSPF, BGP, and MPLS protocols is given in the following section.

6.1.1   Discussion: IP forwarding

Recall that for Internet (layer 3) routing, a higher layer message is segmented and encapsulated into Internet packets by the transmitting end host. The IP packet headers contain a (destination) 32-bit IPv4 address of the receiving end host. If this address is not cached at the sender or if the message is not in response to another *from* the receiver, it may be determined by the sender via the domain name resolution system (DNS) given the domain name of the receiver. Routers receiving packets make forwarding decisions based on the packets' destination IP addresses. These decisions are determined in a scalably hierarchical fashion typically by the OSPF protocol within an autonomous system (intra-AS, i.e., within a peripheral subnetwork) and by BGP inter-AS. Forwarding works by a longest prefix matching of an arriving packet's destination IP address to the stored entries in a ternary content addressable memory (CAM). The ternary CAM associates address prefixes to output links of the router. These associations are derived from the router's routing information base (RIB).

Under BGP, gateways "advertise" (notify peer routers under BGP) the ASes to which they are directly connected, i.e., for which they are the "origin" routers. More generally, BGP routers advertise to their neighboring peers their shortest (in hops) paths to different groups of ASes. Both gateways and interior routers will update their RIBs in response to such advertisements. Without policy considerations, BGP speaker z will forward packets destined to subnetwork S to z's neighboring (next hop) BGP peer w that is [48]

$$\arg \min_w c_{(z,w)} + C_{(w,S)}, \tag{6.5}$$

where $c_{(z,w)}$ is the hop cost of the link (z, w) between z and its neighboring BGP peer w, and $C_{(w,S)}$ is w's current *path* cost to S as advertised to z. BGP's use of path vectors, wherein the entire AS chain is advertised rather than just the path lengths, allows it to:

- apply policy rules to any AS on the path,

- check for loops, i.e., avoid the situation where the same AS appears two or more times on a single path, and thereby

- avoid potentially slow "count to infinity" convergence problems [139].

Still, the scale of operation and distributed nature of BGP results in issues of convergence and reachability (graph connectedness). Poison reverse, dynamic minimum route advertisement interval (MRAI) adjustments, and other devices to dampen the frequency of route updates trade off responsiveness (to, e.g., changing traffic conditions, link or node withdrawals) and stability/convergence properties. Finally, BGP advertisements (and the resulting RIBs and forwarding decisions) are made economical by aggregating those to ASes with similar routes, in particular those with common address prefixes (stubs).

Within an AS, it is often feasible for routers to periodically flood the network with their link state information. So, each router can build a picture of the entire layer-3 AS graph from which loop-free optimal (minimal-hop-count) intra-AS paths can be found in the manner of Dijkstra-based OSPF protocols. A hierarchical OSPF framework can be employed on the component "areas" of a large AS. Under OSPF, router z will forward packets ultimately destined to router v according to the subpath p to a *neighboring* (predecessor) router r_p of v that is

$$\arg \min_p C_p + c_{(r_p, v)}, \tag{6.6}$$

where C_p is the path cost (hop count) of p. Dijkstra's algorithm works iteratively by calculating optimal paths with increasing distance from the router node at which the algorithm is executing [48]; see Appendix A. A fundamental property of global (network wide) solutions to (6.5) or (6.6) is that all subroutes of any optimal route are themselves optimal. This property, easily proved by contradiction, facilitates "connectionless" (i.e., IP) forwarding along optimal paths; again, see Appendix A.

The 48-bit Ethernet (layer 2) media access control (MAC) addresses are not organized in a hierarchical manner like IP, i.e., Ethernet domains (within an AS) have a flat address space wherein proximal end systems may have numerically unrelated MAC addresses. This is workable since peripheral Ethernet clouds typically connect only on the order of thousands of proximal end systems, as compared to hundreds of thousands of different subnetworks (each designated by an IPv4 address prefix/stub) across the world connected together via IP. Routing in Ethernet works by flooding and self-learning mechanisms ([139], p. 471), where the latter is similar to reverse-path forwarding as described in Section 7.2.2.

We will return to related issues in Chapter 7.

6.1.2 Discussion: MPLS

The operation of MPLS label-switched paths (LSPs) in the Internet, briefly discussed at the end of Section 4.5, is typically achieved via *downstream-unsolicited* label distribution and *ordered control* [153]. Under downstream-unsolicited label distribution:

- labels are assigned (bound) to peripheral IP subnetwork address blocks and are "advertised" *up*stream by egress LERs;

- an upstream LSR simply binds the received labels to new ones in the label set it controls and, in turn, advertises the new ones further upstream toward ingress LERs; and, finally,

- once ingress LERs are in receipt of labels from their downstream, neighboring LSRs, LSPs to IP subnetworks (connected to egress LERs) can be set up by specifying a FEC of packets that are to use them.

Basically, an LSP is requested by specifying a destination IP subnetwork (egress LER), ingress LER, and FEC.

Under ordered control, the process of determining the intermediate LSRs and the set up of the labels that will correspond to a given LSP also begins at the egress LER. Labels are sequentially assigned along the LSP in the opposite direction of the flow of the FEC of data packets it will carry. This is similar to the "receiver-driven" approach of the resource reservation protocol (RSVP) [12, 239].

Alternatively, the Internet's native packet-routing protocols could be used on a "pilot" setup packet to determine the actual path of the LSP in a manner forward from the ingress (source) LER of the LSP. This pilot packet may actually be the first data packet of the FEC so that there could be negligible LSP setup delay. In principle, MPLS can be used by an ISP in concert with BGP to set up a VPN connecting the sites of a customer [187].

6.2 UNCONSTRAINED OPTIMIZATION

In order to be able to discuss revenue maximization in loss networks in the next section, we will now review basic gradient descent/ascent methods for local optimization. Consider a function $f : \mathbb{R}^n \to \mathbb{R}$ to be minimized, i.e., points $\underline{x}^* \in \mathbb{R}^n$ at which f achieves its minimum value(s) are to be found. In the following, we will explain an iterative algorithm that will eventually determine a local minimum point of f.

Lemma 6.2.1. *If the gradient of f at x $\nabla f(\underline{x}) \neq \underline{0}$, then any vector $\underline{h}$ such that $\underline{h}^{\mathrm{T}} \nabla f(\underline{x}) < 0$ is a descent direction of f at $\underline{x}$, i.e., there exists a real $\alpha_{\max} > 0$ such that $f(\underline{x} + \alpha \underline{h}) < f(\underline{x})$ for all $\alpha < \alpha_{\max}$, i.e., $-\nabla f(\underline{x})$ is a descent direction of f at $\underline{x}$.*

Note that $\underline{h}^{\mathrm{T}} \nabla f(\underline{x})$ is the inner (or "dot") product on of the vectors $\underline{h}$ and $\nabla f(\underline{x})$. We say $\underline{x}^*$ is a *local minimizer* of f if there exists a $\delta > 0$ such that

$$f(\underline{x}^*) \ \leq \ f(\underline{x})$$

for all $\underline{x}$ such that $|\underline{x} - \underline{x}^*| < \delta$. If this statement holds for δ arbitrarily large, $\underline{x}^*$ is said to be a *global minimizer*. If this statement holds with strict inequality (for $\underline{x} \neq \underline{x}^*$), then $\underline{x}^*$ is said to be a *strict local minimizer*.

A function f is convex if its $n \times n$ Hessian matrix is positive definite, i.e.,

$$\underline{y}^{\mathrm{T}} \frac{\partial^2 f}{\partial x^2}(\underline{x})\underline{y} \ \equiv \ \sum_{i,j} y_i y_j \frac{\partial^2 f}{\partial x_i \, \partial x_j}(\underline{x}) \ > \ 0$$

for all $\underline{x} \in \mathbb{R}^n$ and $\underline{y} \in \mathbb{R}^n \backslash \underline{0}$; then a local minimizer is a global minimizer. Recall that an equivalent definition for convexity was given at the end of Section 1.6.

Theorem 6.2.1. *If $\underline{x}^*$ is a local minimizer of f, then*

$$\nabla f(\underline{x}^*) \ = \ 0. \tag{6.7}$$

That is, (6.7) is a necessary condition for optimality.

Theorem 6.2.2. $\underline{x}^*$ *is a local minimizer of f if*

$$\nabla f(\underline{x}^*) = 0 \quad and \quad \frac{\partial^2 f}{\partial x^2}(\underline{x}^*) > 0. \tag{6.8}$$

That is, (6.8) is a sufficient condition for optimality.

The following algorithm, called *steepest gradient descent*, will converge from an arbitrary initial point $\underline{x}_0$ to a local minimum of f:

0. Select initial $\underline{x}_0 \in \mathbb{R}^n$ and set index $i = 0$.

1. Compute search direction $\underline{h}_i = -\nabla f(\underline{x}_i)$.

2. Compute the (real-valued) step size

$$\alpha_i \quad \in \quad A(\underline{x}_i) \equiv \arg\min_{\alpha>0} f(\underline{x}_i + \alpha \underline{h}_i).$$

3. Update

$$\underline{x}_{i+1} \quad \equiv \quad \underline{x}_i + \alpha_i h_i.$$

4. Increment index $i \leftarrow i + 1$ and go to step 1.

So, the steepest gradient-descent algorithm generates a sequence $\{\underline{x}_i\}_{i=1}^{\infty}$ in $\mathbb{R}^n$.

An *accumulation point* of a sequence is the limit of a convergent subsequence. See [28, 145, 173] for a proof of the following basic result.

Theorem 6.2.3. *Each accumulation point of the steepest gradient descent algorithm is a local minimizer of f.*

One can also formulate the steepest descent algorithm (with no "gradient" qualifier) by jointly optimizing over the step size and descent direction in step 2. In addition to requiring computation of the gradient of the objective function, steepest gradient descent solves our original unconstrained n-dimensional optimization problem (at least locally) with an iterative algorithm that requires the solution of a one-dimensional optimization problem at each step. The one-dimensional search for the step size required in step 2 of a steepest gradient-descent iteration can be made more practical by discretizing the search space; the resulting algorithm is called the Armijo gradient-descent method [173]. In practice, a gradient-descent iteration can be terminated when the change in f after an iteration, $f(\underline{x}_i) - f(\underline{x}_{i+1})$, becomes sufficiently small. When a function is not unimodal (having more than one local minimum), a better local minimum can perhaps be found by repeating a gradient-descent algorithm at a variety of different (say, randomly) chosen initial states x_0.

6.3 REVENUE MAXIMIZATION FOR LOSS NETWORKS

In this section, we consider the simple problem of tuning a randomized routing policy to maximize a single, global (network wide) revenue objective (6.9) that explicitly depends on steady-state connection blocking rates. A general deficiency of such problem formulations is that they assume a centralized decision maker who knows the network state everywhere and at every given time. Specifically, we consider how randomized routing could be adjusted to maximize the revenue generated by a loss network. Let $\Lambda_{m,n}$ be the intensity of the Poisson connection arrival process between end users n and m and let $\mathcal{R}_{m,n}$ be the set of distinct routes connecting them. Thus,

$$\sum_{r \in \mathcal{R}_{m,n}} \lambda_r = \Lambda_{m,n}.$$

We assume that the mean holding times for all routes in $\mathcal{R}_{m,n}$ are the same, i.e., $\mu_r = \mu_{m,n}$ for all $r \in \mathcal{R}_{m,n}$. In this context, randomized routing determines the component route intensities λ_r of $\Lambda_{m,n}$ for each (unordered) pair of end systems m and n so that the connection arrival process to each route is independent and Poisson. As in the previous chapter, we will find it more notationally convenient to work with traffic load variables $\rho = \lambda/\mu$ than with connection arrival rates λ.

Suppose that the revenue generated by a connection on route r is w_r dollars per second (typically, routes connecting the same end systems will have the same rate of revenue generation). In this section, we assume that the goal of routing is to maximize network revenue as defined below. By Little's formula and PASTA (refer back to Chapter 3), the average number of connections on route r is

$$\lambda_r(1 - B_r(\underline{\rho}, \underline{c})) \frac{1}{\mu_r} = \rho_r(1 - B_r(\underline{\rho}, \underline{c})),$$

where we have explicitly shown the dependence of the blocking probability B_r on the incident route loads $\underline{\rho}$ and the link capacities $\underline{c}$; see Equation (5.4). Thus, the total mean rate of revenue generation in steady state is

$$W(\underline{\rho}, \underline{c}) = \sum_r w_r \rho_r (1 - B_r(\underline{\rho}, \underline{c})). \tag{6.9}$$

With this real-valued objective function, we can study the performance of routing algorithms.

Suppose the connection arrival rate $\Lambda_{m,n}$ has increased by a small amount so that the network must decide how to correspondingly increase the load on a route, or routes, connecting end systems n and m. Further suppose that the route that will be chosen by the network will be the one that results in the greatest increase (or least decrease) in the network revenue rate W. The chosen route will therefore be the route $r \in \mathcal{R}_{m,n}$ for which W has the largest *sensitivity* $(\partial W/\partial \rho_r)$ to ρ_r.

Theorem 6.3.1.

$$\frac{\partial W}{\partial \rho_r}(\underline{\rho}, \underline{c}) = (1 - B_r(\underline{\rho}, \underline{c}))\left(w_r - [W(\underline{\rho}, \underline{c}) - W(\underline{\rho}, \underline{c} - \mathbf{A}\underline{e}_r)]\right).$$

Proof: First note that

$$\frac{\partial W}{\partial \rho_r}(\rho, \underline{c}) = w_r(1 - B_r(\rho, \underline{c})) - \sum_\pi w_\pi \rho_\pi \frac{\partial B_\pi(\rho, \underline{c})}{\partial \rho_r}. \tag{6.10}$$

By direct differentiation,

$$\frac{\partial G(\underline{c})}{\partial \rho_r} = G(\underline{c} - \mathbf{A}\underline{e}_r) \tag{6.11}$$

and, therefore,

$$
\begin{aligned}
\frac{\partial B_\pi(\rho, \underline{c})}{\partial \rho_r} &= -\frac{G(\underline{c} - \mathbf{A}\underline{e}_\pi - \mathbf{A}\underline{e}_r)}{G(\underline{c})} + \frac{G(\underline{c} - \mathbf{A}\underline{e}_\pi)G(\underline{c} - \mathbf{A}\underline{e}_r)}{G^2(\underline{c})} \\
&= -\frac{G(\underline{c} - \mathbf{A}\underline{e}_\pi - \mathbf{A}\underline{e}_r)}{G(\underline{c})} \times \frac{G(\underline{c} - \mathbf{A}\underline{e}_r)}{G(\underline{c} - \mathbf{A}\underline{e}_r)} + \frac{G(\underline{c} - \mathbf{A}\underline{e}_\pi)G(\underline{c} - \mathbf{A}\underline{e}_r)}{G^2(\underline{c})} \\
&= (1 - B_r(\rho, \underline{c}))[(1 - B_\pi(\rho, \underline{c})) - 1 - B_\pi(\rho, \underline{c} - \mathbf{A}\underline{e}_r)].
\end{aligned}
$$

The proof concludes by substituting into (6.10). □

To interpret Theorem 6.3.1, note that the increase in the revenue given by the sensitivity $\partial W/\partial \rho_r$ has two components. The positive quantity $(1 - B_r(\rho, \underline{c}))w_r$ is the increase in revenue from an additional incident unit of load on route r, only the fraction $1 - B_r(\rho, \underline{c})$ of which will be admitted. That is, $(1 - B_r(\rho, \underline{c}))w_r$ is a "benefit." The negative quantity

$$-(1 - B_r(\rho, \underline{c}))[W(\rho, \underline{c}) - W(\rho, \underline{c} - \mathbf{A}\underline{e}_r)]$$

represents the *lost revenue* that this additional unit load on route r precipitates, i.e., the additional load will mean that more circuits on the links of route r will be occupied which will result in increased connection blocking on other routes that share links with r. This negative quantity is called a "shadow cost."

6.4 CONSTRAINED OPTIMIZATION AND DUALITY

We will next consider a kind of *flow-based* network like that of Section 5.2. To do so, some additional material in the theory of optimization is covered in this section. Consider a *primal* optimization problem with a set of m inequality constraints: Find

$$\arg\min_{\underline{x} \in D} f_0(\underline{x}), \tag{6.12}$$

where the constrained domain of optimization is

$$D \equiv \{\underline{x} \in \mathbb{R}^n \mid f_i(\underline{x}) \le 0, \forall i \in \{1, 2, ..., m\}\}.$$

For the example of a loss network, the constraints are

$$f_l(\underline{x}) = (\mathbf{A}\underline{x})_l - c_l = \sum_{r \mid l \in r} x_r - c_l, \tag{6.13}$$

where the index l corresponds to a link and m is the number of links in the network.

To study (6.12), we define the corresponding *Lagrangian* function on $\mathbb{R}^{n+m}$:

$$L(\underline{x}, \underline{v}) \equiv f_0(\underline{x}) + \sum_{i=1}^{m} v_i f_i(\underline{x}), \qquad (6.14)$$

where, by implication, the vector of *Lagrange multipliers* is $\underline{v} \in \mathbb{R}^m$. Let

$$\underline{v} \geq 0$$

connote that all of the m Lagrange multipliers are nonnegative, i.e., $\underline{v} \in [0, \infty)^m$.

Theorem 6.4.1.

$$\min_{\underline{x} \in \mathbb{R}^n} \max_{\underline{v} \geq 0} L(\underline{x}, \underline{v}) = \min_{\underline{x} \in D} f_0(\underline{x}) \equiv p^*.$$

Proof:

$$\max_{\underline{v} \geq 0} L(\underline{x}, \underline{v}) = \begin{cases} \infty & \text{if } x \notin D, \\ f_0(\underline{x}) & \text{if } x \in D, \end{cases} \qquad (6.15)$$

as desired. □

So, by Theorem 6.4.1, we can maximize the Lagrangian in an *unconstrained* fashion to find the solution to the primal problem (6.12).

Define the maximizing values of the Lagrange multipliers,

$$\underline{v}^*(\underline{x}) \equiv \arg\max_{\underline{v} \geq 0} L(\underline{x}, \underline{v})$$

and note that the *complementary slackness* conditions

$$v_i^*(\underline{x}) f_i(\underline{x}) = 0 \qquad (6.16)$$

hold for all $\underline{x} \in D$ and $i \in \{1, 2, ..., m\}$. That is, if there is slackness in the ith constraint, i.e., $f_i(\underline{x}) < 0$, then there is no slackness in the constraint of the corresponding Lagrange multiplier, i.e., $v_i^*(\underline{x}) = 0$. Conversely, if $f_i(\underline{x}) = 0$, then the *optimal* value of the Lagrange multiplier $v_i^*(\underline{x})$ is not relevant to the Lagrangian. Complementary slackness conditions lead to the Karush-Kuhn-Tucker necessary conditions for optimality of the primal solution [28, 145, 173].

Now define the *dual* function of the primal problem:

$$g(\underline{v}) = \min_{\underline{x} \in \mathbb{R}^n} L(\underline{x}, \underline{v}). \qquad (6.17)$$

Note that $g(\underline{v})$ may be infinite for some values of $\underline{v}$ and that g is always concave.

Theorem 6.4.2. *For all $\underline{x} \in D$ and $\underline{v} \geq 0$,*

$$g(\underline{v}) \leq f_0(\underline{x}).$$

Proof: For $\underline{v} \geq 0$,

$$g(\underline{v}) \leq L(\underline{x}, \underline{v}) \leq \max_{\underline{v} \geq 0} L(\underline{x}, \underline{v}) = f_0(\underline{x}),$$

where the last equality is (6.15) assuming $\underline{x} \in D$. □

So, by Theorem 6.4.2, if we solve the *dual problem*, i.e., find

$$d^* \equiv \max_{\underline{v} \geq 0} g(\underline{v}),$$

then we will have obtained a (hopefully good) lower bound to the primal problem, i.e.,

$$d^* \leq p^*.$$

Under certain conditions in this finite dimensional setting, in particular when the primal problem is convex and a *strictly feasible* solution exists, the *duality gap*

$$p^* - d^* = 0; \tag{6.18}$$

see [28]. To use duality to find p^* and $\arg\max_{\underline{x} \in D} f_0(\underline{x})$ in this case, suppose that a *slow* ascent method is used to maximize g,

$$\underline{v}_n = \underline{v}_{n-1} + \alpha_1 \nabla g(\underline{v}_{n-1}), \tag{6.19}$$

and between steps of the ascent method a *fast* descent method is used to evaluate $g(\underline{v}_n)$ by minimizing $L(\underline{x}, \underline{v}_n)$,

$$\underline{x}_k = \underline{x}_{k-1} - \alpha_2 \nabla_{\underline{x}} L(\underline{x}_{k-1}, \underline{v}_n). \tag{6.20}$$

The process described by (6.19) and (6.20) is called an iterative subgradient method. Note that the step size α_1 may need to be chosen so that $\underline{v}_n \geq 0$ for all n.

Comprehensive treatments of optimization using gradient methods are given in [28, 145, 173].

6.5 A DISTRIBUTED PRICING AND RESOURCE MANAGEMENT FRAMEWORK

We now consider a kind of *flow-based* network like that of Section 5.2. Recall the introduction to constrained optimization and duality in Section 6.4 and consider a group of R users sharing a network consisting of m links (hopefully without cycles) connecting a pair of nodes. We identify a single fixed route r with each user, where, again, a route is simply a group of connected links. Thus, the user associated with each route could, in reality, be an aggregation of many individual flows of smaller users. Each link l has a capacity of c_l bits per second and each user r transmits at x_r bits per second. Link l charges $\kappa_l x$ dollars per second to a user transmitting x bits per second over it.

Suppose that user r derives a certain benefit from transmission of x_r bits per second on route r. The value of this benefit can be quantified as $U_r(x_r)$ dollars per second. The user *utility* function U_r is often assumed to have the following properties: $U_r(0) = 0$, U_r is nondecreasing, and, for *elastic* traffic, U_r is concave; recall Section 4.6. The concavity property is sometimes called a principle of diminishing returns or diminishing marginal utility. The nondecreasing and concave assumption may not be valid for individual users with applications requiring precise amounts of bandwidth [140]; in some cases, one can aggregate such inelastic demand applications into a *call center* which then may be modeled with an elastic utility [110].

Note that user r has *net* benefit (net utility)

$$U_r(x_r) - x_r \sum_{l \in r} \kappa_l.$$

Suppose that, as with the loss networks, the network wishes to select its prices $\underline{\kappa}$ so as to optimize the total benefit derived by the users, i.e., the network wishes to *maximize* "social welfare," for example,

$$-f_0(\underline{x}) \;\equiv\; \sum_{r=1}^{R} U_r(x_r), \tag{6.21}$$

subject to the link capacity constraints

$$f_l(\underline{x}) \;=\; (\mathbf{A}\underline{x})_l - c_l \;\leq\; 0 \text{ for } 1 \leq l \leq m. \tag{6.22}$$

We can therefore cast this problem in the primal form using the Lagrangian defined in (6.14), i.e., maximizing

$$\sum_{r=1}^{R} U_r(x_r) \tag{6.23}$$

is equivalent to minimizing $f_0(\underline{x})$.

Since all of the individual utilities U_r are assumed concave functions on $\mathbb{R}$, f_0 is convex on $\mathbb{R}^n$. Since the inequality constraints f_i are all linear, the conditions of (6.18) are satisfied. So, we will now formulate a distributed solution to the dual problem in order solve the primal problem. First note that, because of convexity, a necessary *and sufficient* condition to minimize the Lagrangian $L(\underline{x}, \underline{v})$ over $\underline{x}$ (to evaluate the dual function g) is

$$\nabla_{\underline{x}} L(\underline{x}^*(\underline{v}), \underline{v}) = 0.$$

For the problem under consideration,

$$\frac{\partial L(\underline{x}, \underline{v})}{\partial x_r} \;=\; -U_r'(x_r) + \sum_{l \in r} v_l$$
$$= \; -U_r'(x_r) + (\mathbf{A}^{\mathrm{T}}\underline{v})_r.$$

Therefore, for all r,

$$
\begin{aligned}
x_r^*(\underline{v}) &= (U_r')^{-1}\left(\sum_{l \in r} v_l\right) \\
&= (U_r')^{-1}((\mathbf{A}^{\mathrm{T}}\underline{v})_r),
\end{aligned}
\tag{6.24}
$$

where the right-hand side of (6.24) is made unambiguous by the above assumptions on U_r.

Assume that, at any given time, user r will act (select x_r) so as to maximize their net benefit, i.e., select

$$
\arg\max_{x \geq 0} U_r(x) - x\sum_{l \in r} \kappa_l = (U_r')^{-1}\left(\sum_{l \in r}\kappa_l\right).
\tag{6.25}
$$

By (6.24), the quantity in (6.25) is simply $x_r^*(\underline{\kappa})$, i.e., the prices κ correspond to the Lagrange multipliers v. A user acting in this manner is sometimes said to be *greedy*. Therefore, by the statement of Equation (6.24) and recalling the dual function g of (6.17),

$$
g(\underline{\kappa}) = L(\underline{x}^*(\underline{\kappa}), \underline{\kappa}),
\tag{6.26}
$$

i.e., *for fixed link costs $\underline{\kappa}$, the decentralized actions of greedy users minimize the Lagrangian and, thereby, evaluate the dual function.*

Following the framework of the dual algorithm (6.19) and (6.20), suppose now that the network slowly modifies its link prices to maximize $g(\underline{\kappa})$, where by "slowly" we mean that the greedy users are able to react to a new set of link prices well before they change again. To apply (6.19) as the method of modifying the link prices, we need to evaluate the gradient of g to obtain the ascent direction. Differentiating (6.26) we get

$$
\begin{aligned}
\frac{\partial g(\underline{\kappa})}{\partial \kappa_l} &= [(\mathbf{A}\underline{x}^*(\underline{\kappa}))_l - c_l] - \sum_r U_r'(x_r^*(\underline{\kappa}))\frac{\partial x_r^*(\underline{\kappa})}{\partial \kappa_l} + \sum_{l'}\kappa_{l'}\sum_{r|l' \in r}\frac{\partial x_r^*(\underline{\kappa})}{\partial \kappa_l} \\
&= (\mathbf{A}\underline{x}^*(\underline{\kappa}))_l - c_l,
\end{aligned}
$$

where the second equality is a result of (6.24). Thus, for *each link l*, (6.19) becomes

$$
(\kappa_l)_n = (\kappa_l)_{n-1} + \alpha_1\left((\mathbf{A}\underline{x}^*(\underline{\kappa}_{n-1}))_l - c_l\right)
\tag{6.27}
$$

or, in vector form,

$$
\underline{\kappa}_n = \underline{\kappa}_{n-1} + \alpha_1(\mathbf{A}\underline{x}^*(\underline{\kappa}_{n-1}) - \underline{c}).
\tag{6.28}
$$

Note that the link price updates on (6.27) depend only on "local" information such as link capacity and price and link demand, $(\mathbf{A}\underline{x}^*(\underline{\kappa}_{n-1}))_l$, where the latter can be empirically evaluated.

Suppose that we initially begin with very high prices $\underline{\kappa}_0$ so that demands $\underline{x}^*(\kappa)$ are very small. The action of (6.28) will be to lower prices and, correspondingly, increase demand. The prices will try to *converge* to a point $\underline{\kappa}^*$, where supply $\underline{c}$ equals demand $\mathbf{A}\underline{x}^*(\underline{\kappa}^*)$.

Note that in the present problem formulation the action of greedy users and that of the network attempting to maximize its revenue based on perceived supply and demand levels result in the maximization of social welfare f_0. In [157], a passive framework was considered wherein round-trip delays, estimated by the users of TCP sessions, were used instead of prices. Maximizing "social welfare" (6.23) may likely *not* be an objective of a practical system. Instead, a network may simply attempt to maximize its revenue by, say, controlling its price charged to end users for access, possibly subject to government regulations and to competitive networking market forces. Obviously, by selecting higher prices, it will lose some customers but make more money on those "premium" customers that remain (i.e., those that can afford the higher prices). A network's additional desire to maximize utilization of its resources (or government regulation) may lead to service differentiation involving an affordable flat-rate best-effort service in addition to more dynamically usage-priced premium services.

6.6 DISCUSSION: JOINT SCHEDULING AND ROUTING IN MULTIHOP WIRELESS NETWORKS

Consider a network of N nodes with a set of L (one-hop) links and a set of F active end-to-end unidirectional, unicast flows. The rth flow requires an allocation of bandwidth that is proportional to the integer k_r and uses unidirectional (one-hop) links $l \in r$. Finally, suppose that the local medium access control is round-robin TDMA.

Our objective in this section is to briefly describe the problem of formulating a schedule of round-robin link transmissions subject to the constraint that, at any given time slot, a node can either receive or transmit but not both, i.e., a node must avoid self-interference. By synchronizing local scheduling, this can be broken down to a bipartite graph-matching problem as discussed in Section 4.1.3. That is, in any given "global" time slot t, the N nodes are matched to themselves as specified by an $N \times N$ matrix $\mathbf{M}(t)$ of Boolean entries $m_{i,j}(t)$, where

$$m_{i,j}(t) \;=\; \begin{cases} 1 & \text{if node } i \text{ transmits to } j \text{ in time slot } t, \\ 0 & \text{otherwise.} \end{cases}$$

The duration of the time slots can be sized to account for transmission of acknowledgments by a receiving node upon correct reception of a data frame. A global schedule $\mathcal{M}$ of length T time slots is a set of T such schedules, i.e.,

$$\mathcal{M} \;=\; \{\mathbf{M}(1), \mathbf{M}(2), ..., \mathbf{M}(T)\}.$$

The desired global schedule must meet the needs of the flows, of course. To this end, we can decompose each flow $r \in F$ into a set of $k_r \cdot |r|$ *one-hop* unidirectional flows, i.e., k_r subflows for each link $l \in r$. So, we require that

$$\sum_{t=1}^{T} m_{i,j}(t) \;=\; \sum_{r \in F} k_r \mathbf{1}\{(i,j) \in r\}$$

for all links $l = (i,j)$, where i is the transmitting node and j is the receiving node of link l in this notation. Naturally, the goal is to obtain the shortest possible schedule T satisfying this constraint. Note that the bandwidth allocation of a flow r will be roughly $k_r B/T$, where B is the channel bandwidth. That is, each hop of r will have access to the channel the fraction k_r/T of the time.

In a multihop wireless setting there are additional constraints that need to be considered in the formulation of a schedule $\mathcal{M}$. For example, certain pairs of links associated with proximal nodes may interfere with each other and therefore cannot be scheduled in the same time slot. More specifically, if links (i, j) and (a, b) interfere, then

$$m_{i,j}(t)m_{a,b}(t) \neq 1$$

for all $1 \leq t \leq T$. Note that this notion for a pairwise "interference" relation between links is more general than that considered in Section 4.1.3, i.e., two links *need not* necessarily have only transmitting nodes (e.g., i, a) or receiving nodes (e.g., j, b) in common to interfere. Centralized and distributed cross-layer designs in different networking contexts, including those addressing versions of this scheduling problem, are described in, e.g., [65, 66, 91, 132, 142] and in recent overviews [81, 144]. A typical but suboptimal approach would be to completely refresh the link layer schedule only periodically, i.e., as fast as existing computational resources will allow for such a complex problem. A period between refreshes could have two phases: In the first phase, a quick and feasible "incremental" modification of the current schedule would occur to accommodate recently arrived and account for recently departed connections. In the second phase, no new connections are admitted and a refreshed schedule is computed based on the existing connections at the end of the first phase of the period. Clearly, connections arriving at the network during the second phase of a period may suffer significantly more setup delay.

6.7   MULTIPATH LOAD BALANCING

Reliability in the presence of faults and attacks is often achieved by proactively allocating redundant (backup) resources (e.g., bandwidth, computation, memory/state, energy) and possibly even setting up independent backup processes in their entirety [10]. For example, proactive setup, use, and maintenance of multiple paths between a source and destination for a single unicast session is required when issues of network reliability are important. When a path fails or is significantly disrupted, immediate switch-over to an alternative path is possible. This motivates the need for partial or total link or node disjointness of the paths. In an ad hoc wireless context, multipath setup is discussed in [16, 96, 108, 148, 167, 229].

Given multiple paths connecting a transmitting/source node to a receiving/destination node, the source can

- transmit exclusively on one path,

- load balance by dynamically selecting one path for each packet or consecutive group of packets to be transmitted (one can also envision this as a scheduling problem with multiple servers), or

- transmit each packet on more than one path.

Transmitting the same packet on multiple paths results in more reliable delivery of the packet at the cost of greater bandwidth resource expenditure of course.

The focus of this section will be on load balancing based on the "biomimetic" notion of *pheromone* state, assuming that the performance (cost) of the links is not affected by the load balancing decisions under consideration. Moreover, the actual performance of the links need to be *learned*. Packets are interpreted as ants that associate pheromone with paths [8, 17, 34, 87]. More specifically, for a given pair of nodes, we explain a convergence

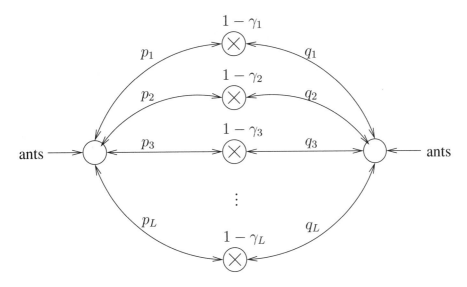

Figure 6.1 Simplified network topology.

result [107, 233] resolving a path that is optimal in terms of throughput using an approach based on "regular" ants (messages) [213].

Consider two nodes connected with L disjoint, bidirectional paths as in Figure 6.1. At one node, the total transmission rate is $1 - \alpha$ ants per unit time,[1] with $0 < \alpha < 1$, and the routing probabilities on the L paths are $\underline{p} = (p_1, \ p_2, \ ..., \ p_L)$, where $\sum_{i=1}^{L} p_i = 1$, i.e., $\underline{p} \in \Sigma_L$, the L-dimensional simplex. At the other node, the total transmission rate is α ants per unit time but the routing probabilities are $\underline{q}$. Let $1 - \gamma_i$ be the probability that an ant on path i is dropped (irrespective of its direction of travel on the path) and assume that such transmission and dropping decisions are mutually independent. We further assume that there is no time decay mechanism for pheromone levels and that the path-dropping probabilities $1 - \gamma_i$ are negligibly affected by changes in $\underline{p}$ or $\underline{q}$, i.e., in the forwarding decision node by the source-destination pair shown in Figure 6.1.

So, the joint process $\underline{x} \equiv (\underline{p}, \underline{q})$ can be modeled as a discrete-time Markov process on $\Sigma_L \times \Sigma_L$ [233]. The state transition

$$(\underline{p}, \underline{q}) \ \rightarrow \ (\underline{\phi}^i(\underline{p}), \underline{q}) \tag{6.29}$$

occurs with probability $\alpha q_i \gamma_i$, where

$$\phi_j^i(\underline{p}) \ \equiv \ \begin{cases} \dfrac{p_i + C}{C + 1} & \text{if } j = i, \\ \dfrac{p_j}{C + 1} & \text{else,} \end{cases}$$

and a constant pheromone $C > 0$. Similarly,

$$(\underline{p}, \underline{q}) \ \rightarrow \ (\underline{p}, \underline{\phi}^i(\underline{q})) \tag{6.30}$$

occurs with probability $(1 - \alpha) p_i \gamma_i$. Note that this process is time homogeneous. Let T be the time of the first transition (or "jump") of the Markov process, i.e., T is the smallest

---

[1]Note that ants can be piggybacked on data packets.

positive time such that $\underline{x}(T) \neq \underline{x}(0)$. Suppose that $\underline{x}(0) = (\underline{p}, \underline{q})$ for some known initial set of routing probabilities and let $(\tilde{\underline{p}}, \tilde{\underline{q}}) = \mathsf{E}(\underline{x}(T) \mid \underline{x}(0) = (\underline{p}, \underline{q}))$. Define

$$< \underline{p}, \underline{\gamma} > \; \equiv \; \mathsf{E}_{\underline{p}}\underline{\gamma} \; \equiv \; \sum_{i=1}^{L} p_i \gamma_i \quad \text{and} \quad < \underline{p}, \underline{\gamma}^2 > \; \equiv \; \mathsf{E}_{\underline{p}}(\underline{\gamma}^2) \; \equiv \; \sum_{i=1}^{L} p_i \gamma_i^2.$$

Theorem 6.7.1. *For any $0 < \alpha < 1$ and $p, q, \gamma \in \Sigma_L$,*

$$(1 - \alpha)\mathsf{E}_{\tilde{\underline{p}}}\underline{\gamma} + \alpha\mathsf{E}_{\tilde{\underline{q}}}\underline{\gamma} \; \geq \; (1 - \alpha)\mathsf{E}_{\underline{p}}\underline{\gamma} + \alpha\mathsf{E}_{\underline{q}}\underline{\gamma}.$$

Proof: We are given that $\underline{x}(0) = (\underline{p}, \underline{q})$. First define

$$p_i^* = \frac{(1 - \alpha)p_i \gamma_i}{(1 - \alpha)\mathsf{E}_{\underline{p}}\underline{\gamma} + \alpha\mathsf{E}_{\underline{q}}\underline{\gamma}} \quad \text{and} \quad q_i^* = \frac{\alpha q_i \gamma_i}{(1 - \alpha)\mathsf{E}_{\underline{p}}\underline{\gamma} + \alpha\mathsf{E}_{\underline{q}}\underline{\gamma}}.$$

Correspondingly define the L-vectors $\underline{p}^*$ and $\underline{q}^*$. The transition (6.29) of the *jump* process of the discrete-time Markov process occurs with probability q_i^* and, similarly, (6.30) occurs with probability p_i^*. By definition,

$$
\begin{aligned}
\tilde{\underline{p}} &= \sum_{i=1}^{L} \underline{\phi}^i(\underline{p}) \, q_i^* + \sum_{i=1}^{L} \underline{p} \, p_i^* \\
&= \frac{(1 - \alpha)\mathsf{E}_{\underline{p}}\underline{\gamma} + \dfrac{1}{C+1}\alpha\mathsf{E}_{\underline{q}}\underline{\gamma}}{(1 - \alpha)\mathsf{E}_{\underline{p}}\underline{\gamma} + \alpha\mathsf{E}_{\underline{q}}\underline{\gamma}}\underline{p} + \frac{C}{C+1}\underline{q}^*.
\end{aligned}
$$

Therefore,

$$
\begin{aligned}
\mathsf{E}_{\tilde{\underline{p}}}\underline{\gamma} &= \left(1 - \frac{C}{C+1} \cdot \frac{\alpha\mathsf{E}_{\underline{q}}\underline{\gamma}}{(1 - \alpha)\mathsf{E}_{\underline{p}}\underline{\gamma} + \alpha\mathsf{E}_{\underline{q}}\underline{\gamma}}\right) \mathsf{E}_{\underline{p}}\underline{\gamma} + \frac{C}{C+1}\mathsf{E}_{\underline{q}^*}\underline{\gamma} \\
&= \mathsf{E}_{\underline{p}}\underline{\gamma} + \frac{C}{C+1} \cdot \frac{\alpha}{(1 - \alpha)\mathsf{E}_{\underline{p}}\underline{\gamma} + \alpha\mathsf{E}_{\underline{q}}\underline{\gamma}} \cdot (\mathsf{E}_{\underline{q}}\underline{\gamma}^2 - \mathsf{E}_{\underline{q}}\underline{\gamma}\mathsf{E}_{\underline{p}}\underline{\gamma}). \quad (6.31)
\end{aligned}
$$

Similarly,

$$
\mathsf{E}_{\tilde{\underline{p}}}\underline{\gamma} = \mathsf{E}_{\underline{p}}\underline{\gamma} + \frac{C}{C+1} \cdot \frac{1 - \alpha}{(1 - \alpha)\mathsf{E}_{\underline{p}}\underline{\gamma} + \alpha\mathsf{E}_{\underline{q}}\underline{\gamma}} \cdot (\mathsf{E}_{\underline{p}}\underline{\gamma}^2 - \mathsf{E}_{\underline{q}}\underline{\gamma}\mathsf{E}_{\underline{p}}\underline{\gamma}). \quad (6.32)
$$

Adding $1 - \alpha$ times (6.31) to α times (6.32) and using the fact that

$$
\begin{aligned}
\mathsf{E}_{\underline{p}}\underline{\gamma}^2 + \mathsf{E}_{\underline{q}}\underline{\gamma}^2 - 2\mathsf{E}_{\underline{q}}\underline{\gamma}\mathsf{E}_{\underline{p}}\underline{\gamma} &\geq (\mathsf{E}_{\underline{p}}\underline{\gamma})^2 + (\mathsf{E}_{\underline{q}}\underline{\gamma})^2 - 2\mathsf{E}_{\underline{q}}\underline{\gamma}\mathsf{E}_{\underline{p}}\underline{\gamma} \\
&= (\mathsf{E}_{\underline{p}}\underline{\gamma} - \mathsf{E}_{\underline{q}}\underline{\gamma})^2 \\
&\geq 0 \quad\quad\quad\quad\quad\quad\quad\quad (6.33)
\end{aligned}
$$

proves the theorem. $\square$

This theorem implies that the inner product of the vectors $\underline{\gamma}$ and $\underline{x}(t)$,

$$\underline{\gamma}^{\mathrm{T}}\underline{x}(t) \equiv (1-\alpha)\mathsf{E}_{\underline{p}(t)}\underline{\gamma} + \alpha\mathsf{E}_{\underline{q}(t)}\underline{\gamma},$$

is a submartingale. Note that the first inequality of (6.33) is strict whenever γ is not constant $\underline{p}$ almost surely and $\underline{q}$ almost surely. So, assuming that initially $\underline{\gamma}^{\mathrm{T}}\underline{x}(0)$ is not zero on the subset of $\Sigma_L \times \Sigma_L$ wherein $\underline{\gamma}^{\mathrm{T}}\underline{x}$ is maximal, we can use the martingale convergence theorem 2.9.1 to show that $\underline{\gamma}^{\mathrm{T}}\underline{x}(t)$ converges almost surely to a random variable that is constrained to this subset, i.e., to the *optimal* paths. See [233] for similar proofs of convergence of "uniform" and "synchronous" ant routing algorithms.

In this section, we considered forwarding on multiple paths, where path costs had to be learned and did not depend on the forwarding decisions. This approach, based on positive reinforcement in the reverse directions, found the optimal paths for forwarding. To relate this problem formulation to that of Section 6.3, suppose that a total transmission rate X is to be divided among L unidirectional paths whose loss rates are assumed to be both known and load dependent. The transmission rate assigned to path i is $x_i \geq 0$, where

$$\sum_{i=1}^{L} x_i = X. \tag{6.34}$$

Suppose that lost packets are selectively retransmitted so that in order to obtain an error-free throughput (or "goodput") of x_i on path i, the transmission rate into path i needs to be

$$\frac{x_i}{1 - \gamma_i(x_i)}, \tag{6.35}$$

where $\gamma_i(x_i)$ is the loss probability of path i such that γ_i is nondecreasing, $\gamma_i(0) = 0$, and $\gamma_i(x) \to 1$ as $x \to \infty$. We can define a "soft" capacity of path i as, for example,

$$c_i \equiv \gamma_i^{-1}(0.05),$$

i.e., the transmission rate at which the loss rate is 5%. Such capacities obviously depend on the existing load and available bandwidth especially at bottleneck nodes of the path. The objective now is to minimize the total transmission rate

$$G(\underline{x}) = \sum_{i=1}^{L} \frac{x_i}{1 - \gamma_i(x_i)}$$

subject to (6.34).

To further simplify matters, assume there is a single loss function model γ such that $\gamma_i(x) \equiv \gamma(x/\alpha_i)$ for all paths i, where we note that

$$\alpha_i = \frac{c_i}{c},$$

where c is the capacity when $\alpha = 1$. Now consider the Lagrangian

$$G(\underline{x}) + v\left(X - \sum_{i=1}^{L} x_i\right), \tag{6.36}$$

where we note that the equality constraint (6.34) can be replaced in the problem formulation by the inequality constraint

$$\sum_{i=1}^{L} x_i \geq X$$

because G is increasing in all of its arguments. Defining

$$\Gamma(x) \equiv \frac{d}{dx}\left(\frac{x}{1 - \gamma(x)}\right) \geq 0,$$

it can be directly shown that the rates optimizing (6.36) are

$$x_i^* = \alpha_i \Gamma^{-1}(v) \tag{6.37}$$

for all paths i, where the Lagrange multiplier v is chosen so that (6.34) holds. Thus,

$$x_i^* = \frac{\alpha_i}{\alpha_1 + \alpha_2 + \cdots + \alpha_L} X = \frac{c_i}{c_1 + c_2 + \cdots + c_L} X$$

for all paths i, i.e., all paths are utilized (in proportion to capacity), not just those of maximal capacity.

Problems

6.1 Prove that the dual function g defined in (6.17) is always concave.

6.2 Prove f_0 as defined in (6.21) is convex on $\mathbb{R}^n$.

6.3 Prove (6.37).

6.4 Consider a total demand of Λ between two network end systems having R disjoint routes connecting them. On route r, the service capacity is c_r and the fraction of the demand applied to it is π_r, where $\sum_r \pi_r = 1$. Find the routing decisions that minimize the average delay

$$D(\underline{\pi}) = \sum_r \frac{\pi_r}{c_r - \pi_r \Lambda},$$

where this expression is clearly derived from that of an M/M/1 queue.
Note: This problem was extended to include the consideration of end-user dynamics in [134].

6.5 Consider the special case of the network of Section 6.5 that consists of just a single link l with capacity c so that the common charge per unit bandwidth on the link is $\kappa_l = M_r \equiv M$ for all users r.

(a) Show that the solution $\underline{x}$ maximizing (6.21) subject to (6.22) satisfies

$$U_r'(x_r) \begin{cases} = M & \text{if } x_r > 0, \\ \leq M & \text{if } x_r = 0. \end{cases}$$

(b) Now consider an iteration, where at the nth step each user rth requests an allocation

$$w_r^n = \arg\max_w U_r\left(\frac{w}{M^{n-1}}\right) - w$$

(i.e., user r "bids" w_r^n given price M^{n-1}) and then the network sets its price at

$$M^n = \frac{\sum_r w_r^n}{c} \tag{6.38}$$

and allocates $\underline{x}^n = \underline{w}^n/M^n$ to the users. Assuming there exists a unique solution $M = M^*$ to

$$\sum_r (U_r')^{-1}(M) = c$$

and that the corresponding $x_r^* > 0$ for all r, show that M^* is an equilibrium solution to the iteration above wherein (6.21) is maximized subject to (6.22).

6.6   For the context of the previous problem, suppose each user is aware of the pricing strategy (6.38). So, each user r can infer the sum of the other users' bids from their own:

$$\begin{aligned} W_{-r} &\equiv \sum_{i\neq r} w_i \\ &= cM - w_r \\ &= \left(\frac{c}{x_r} - 1\right) w_r. \end{aligned}$$

The following iterative bidding strategy can then be defined: The nth bid of the rth user is

$$w_r^n = \arg\max_w U_r\left(\frac{w}{w + W_{-r}^{n-1}}c\right) - w.$$

(a) Show that the Nash equilibrium point $\underline{w}^*$ of this game satisfies

$$U_r'(x_r^*)\left(1 - \frac{x_r^*}{c}\right) \begin{cases} = M^* & \text{if } x_r^* > 0, \\ \leq M^* & \text{if } x_r^* = 0, \end{cases}$$

where $M^* = \sum_r w_r^*/c$ and $\underline{x}^* = \underline{w}^*/M^*$.

(b) Letting $\hat{M}$ denote the equilibrium price for the scenario of Problem 6.5(b), show that $M^* \leq \hat{M}$.

It was shown in [112] that such user knowledge of the pricing strategy will result in a reduction in social welfare $\sum_r U_r(x_r)$ of no more than 25%.

CHAPTER 7

PEER-TO-PEER FILE SHARING WITH INCENTIVES

Loosely interpreted, almost all systems involving a plurality of processes participating in a somewhat "symmetric" protocol can be interpreted in peer-to-peer (P2P) terms. An example of an *a*symmetric protocol is that governing client-server transactions wherein only the clients initiate transactions at any given time and the "always-on" servers respond to them. P2P systems have been used to implement name resolution services (e.g., for the Skype voice-over-IP system [18]), application layer multicast for content distribution [11, 82, 135, 143], and distributed computing [75]. P2P systems are also employed for management of Web caching [116]. An instance of a P2P content distribution network (CDN) could be a federated server farm that resolves queries for data objects (or "content") from the public Internet to a server that possesses the requested content; see, e.g., [212]. Also, "structured" P2P systems have been proposed to facilitate applications, such as mobile computing and multicasting, via the notion of address indirection [210, 218].

We will specifically focus on large-scale distributed P2P file-sharing networks involving peers that are not equally cooperative or trustworthy, though the discussion will be relevant to other applications of P2P frameworks. More general overviews of P2P networking systems are given in [6, 169, 191]. In this chapter, query resolution (also known as application layer routing, anycasting, or just search) will be discussed. Performance issues for unstructured and structured designs will be explored. The chapter is concluded by sections discussing incentives for cooperation in the downloading of data objects, focusing on cumulative reputation systems.

7.1 SUMMARY OF QUERY RESOLUTION

In this section, we briefly summarize the performance issues that are common among file-swapping systems. A peer requesting a data object will launch a query among its fellow peers to identify peers that possess the object. As such, query resolution is seen to be performed at a protocol layer above that of TCP/IP, i.e., an "application layer" search. Once a query is resolved, a separate transaction typically occurs wherein the querying peer directly requests the object of interest from the identified "provider" peer and, if the provider agrees, downloads the object from (or swaps pieces of the object with) the provider peer. Both search and downloading phases will rely on the layer 3 routing underlay of the Internet.

For file-sharing systems, performance metrics from a query's point of view include:

- query resolution latency in terms of time or forwarding hops;

- query loss probability, where loss could be due to TTL expiration or mistakenly forwarding to an inactive peer;

- the quantity or quality of the provider peers in the response, where quality could refer to willingness to upload, uplink bandwidth allocated for the upload, and other factors (like proximity [212]) that affect the upload performance; and

- the quality of the obtained data object itself.

Performance metrics also include measures of the resources consumed by the individual peers to resolve queries, i.e.,

- forwarding load and

- acquisition and maintenance of related information.

Corresponding system-wide measures (totals or averages) can also be considered. A measure of "fairness" could be the variation in query resolution overhead experienced by the peers, possibly normalized by the quantity of their own requests.

In addition, file-sharing systems need to be robust in the face of problems such as:

- peer churn (nodes frequently leaving and joining),

- the spread of false and potentially harmful data objects (spam and other content pollution, or malware),

- the spread of false routing or name resolution information,

- peers employing false or multiple identities, and

- peers otherwise trying to undermine the systems in place to promote cooperation.

Sometimes these problems are due to faulty peers. Sometimes they are deliberately caused by selfish or malicious peers. Defense against such activities may require significant overhead of the peers. For example, peers may be compelled to announce their departure beforehand and, if this rule is not well observed, a proactive "heartbeat" or periodic pinging system could be used to detect departed peers more quickly than a system based on observations of routing failures due to their departures. Some of these problems are further discussed later in the chapter, Section 7.5.3 in particular.

7.2 UNSTRUCTURED QUERY RESOLUTION

We first discuss approaches to "unstructured" query resolution that differ in the degree to which they operate in a decentralized fashion.

7.2.1 A centralized approach to search

Napster performed query resolution with the aid of centralized content registries residing on Napster-owned servers that kept track of which peers currently held what data objects. The search mechanism of the Napster client contacted a centralized registry and the registry responded with a list of peers that likely possessed the desired data object.

Under BitTorrent [23], the group of peers that are actively uploading and downloading a given data object are known as a "swarm" (for that data object). Peers search the Web and download a ".torrent" file corresponding to the data object of interest. The peer can then connect to a "tracker" that informs it of other peers currently participating in the swarm for the data object. Decentralized (trackerless) versions of BitTorrent employ a structured P2P system; see Section 7.3.4.

7.2.2 A decentralized approach to search: Limited-scope flooding and reverse-path forwarding

Gnutella used a decentralized approach involving *limited-scope flooding*. Essentially, each query was initially sent by the source (original querying) peer to a small number of peers (in this case just seven), i.e., a breadth limit to the flooding tree. If a queried peer did not have the data object and was not previously queried by a particular limited-scope flooding process, it in turn forwarded the query to seven more peers for that process. A single query thread was prevented from being forwarded more than 10 times by a TTL counter carried along each query message that was decremented each time the query was relayed, i.e., depth limits to the flooding tree. A single flood identifier, that may be randomly chosen by the source, is carried on every query packet of a given flood and enables peers to easily detect reception of the same query forwarded by different peers.

If a queried peer possessed the desired data object, it would communicate back to the original querying peer via *reverse-path forwarding* [54]. Under reverse-path forwarding, a query is forwarded but not before the relaying peer appends its identifier to the query. Once resolved, a query response travels back along the path of peers that previously relayed it so that they can all learn about the data object's provider peers.

Gnutella's performance was improved through the actions of "superpeers" (or "supernodes"), i.e., cooperative, long-lived peers typically with significant resources (memory, computation and network access bandwidth) so that they were able to effectively handle very high amounts of query resolution traffic. One may interpret a P2P system that heavily relies on superpeers as only partially decentralized. Again, once the querying peer has identified peer(s) that possess its desired data object, it then contacts them directly to request download of the data object.

Freenet [47, 237] is a P2P system that employs limited-scope flooding and reverse-path forwarding to find *and* distribute data objects. That is, the data object itself can be sent along the reverse path of the query for it, and is potentially cached by intermediate Freenet nodes, thereby obfuscating the peer that originally uploaded it, and thus protecting the privacy of (anonymizing) transactions especially with respect to entities outside the Freenet community. Also, the query originator may obfuscate his or her identity by varying the initial value of the query message's TTL. Peers are connected so as to create a "small world" effect in order to reduce search time; see the end of Section 7.3.3.

When items are cached, the age, size, and possibly frequency at which the item changes (i.e., is updated) factor into caching strategies. The age of a item in the cache can refer to the last time it was accessed. Clearly, to improve system performance, peers will prefer to cache the items that are popular (frequently requested and, hence, "younger"), small in size (so that they do not consume significant memory and bandwidth resources), and largely static (do not require frequent updating to maintain consistency in the distributed cache). In Freenet, the data object itself may be the subject of caching and, in this case, the size of the item cached will be more of an issue than for the cases where only the identity of peer(s) that are providers for certain data objects are cached. Mechanisms for updating or discarding stale items in a cache may rely on set lifetimes or explicit notifications of item expiration in whole or part. When the cache is full, a "least recently used" rule may be employed to decide which cache entry to overwrite, i.e., overwrite the oldest entry. Again, this rule may be modified to consider the sizes and mean and variance of interupdate times of the affected entries [190].

7.2.3   A partially centralized approach to search

The popular file-sharing system KaZaA employs a partially centralized query resolution strategy. That is, certain peers become superpeers each handling a group of (nonsuper) peers that are assigned to it. The superpeers are aware of the IP addresses and content of all of its assigned peers. Also, superpeers are aware of the identity of other superpeers in order to quickly resolve queries for data objects that its peer group does not possess.

The voice-over-IP system Skype involves a similar group of superpeers for name resolution, i.e., mapping the Skype login name of the desired recipient of a call to the corresponding end system's IP address. In addition, a special Skype server interacts with client peers for login, public-key encryption, and possible billing purposes [18]. Once the destination end system of a call is identified, packets containing encrypted (for privacy) and encoded voice are transmitted between the peers over the commodity Internet.

In the GIA system [40], a topology adaptation framework is used to "bias" the random walk to superpeers and thereby significantly reduce the overhead as compared to the limited-scope flooding approach of Gnutella. A peer estimates the query-processing rates of other peers and tries to associate itself with peers that are no slower than itself, i.e., it avoids sending to and relaying queries from peers that are relatively slower. This system creates a hierarchical query-forwarding topology in which peers of similar query processing rates are grouped. Also, GIA employs a tit-for-tat token system to reward cooperative peers; that is, tokens are accrued by a peer when it forwards relays and tokens can thereafter be redeemed by that peer when she or he wishes to launch queries of their own.

7.2.4   An example of search by random walk

Consider a query resolution system that involves reverse-path forwarding. In particular, consider a series of queries, assumed not overlapping in time, from a peer population w that are launched for a single piece of information (say the identity of any member of a swarm of peers that are actively acquiring and disseminating a certain data object) that is known by a population f. For simplicity of the following model, suppose for each peer that each entry in its forwarding table (of other known peers) experiences a lifetime with mean

$$\frac{1}{\mu} \tag{7.1}$$

irrespective of the frequency at which the entry was accessed or the time of the last access. Peers join the system via a randomly chosen access point in the $f + w$ population. In addition, define:

- λ is the total external arrival rate of new peers to the system (specifically to the $f + w$ population),

- $q < \lambda$ is the per-node rate at which queries are spawned from the population w for the swarm under consideration, and

- δ is the per-node rate at which peers leave the system, i.e., $1/\delta$ is the mean lifetime of a peer.

Finally, suppose that search is conducted in a distributed fashion via a single memoryless random walk through the forwarding tables of the peers and that, at each step of this search, any remaining peer is equally likely to be chosen. Such a single-thread search may require less overhead than a limited-scope flooding approach but will result in longer query resolution times.

Given f and w, the mean number of hops to resolve the query is

$$h(w, f) \quad \equiv \quad 1\frac{f}{w - 1 + f} + 2\frac{w - 1}{w - 1 + f} \cdot \frac{f}{w - 2 + f} + \cdots + w\frac{1}{\binom{w-1+f}{w-1}}.$$

Note that $h(w, f)$ is equal to the mean number of w-population peers visited including the querying peer. By reverse-path forwarding, on average $h(w, f)$ peers will leave the w population and join the f population. We further simplify the model by assuming peers that have launched a query, joined the f population as a result, and then reverted back to the w population may thereafter launch the same query again. The following deterministic, continuous ("fluid") model summarizes the dynamics of the system:

$$\frac{dw}{dt} = \lambda\frac{w}{w + f} - qh(w, f) - \delta w + \mu f, \tag{7.2}$$

$$\frac{df}{dt} = \lambda\frac{f}{w + f} + qh(w, f) - \delta f - \mu f. \tag{7.3}$$

Note that with regard to the exogenous arrival rate (λ) terms, $f/(w + f)$ is the probability that the entry point is in the f population. This system is depicted in Figure 7.1. Specifying a stochastic Markovian version of this model is left as an exercise. In [191], a scenario is described where the fraction of peers that can resolve the query is proportional to the square root of the querying rate, i.e., $f/(f + w) \propto \sqrt{q}$; see Problem 7.1. In practice, a

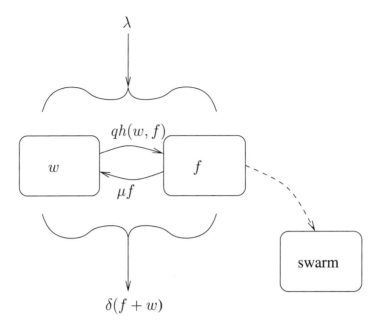

Figure 7.1   Randomized search with reverse-path forwarding.

swarm may experience an exponentially increasing rather than constant (λ) arrival rate of new peers in the initial stages of its lifetime, followed by a decline in arrivals as interest dwindles in the data object that is the subject of the swarm.

7.3   STRUCTURED QUERY RESOLUTION

Structured systems assign data objects *and* peers to points in a discrete metric space. The *common* (standard) name used for any given data object, say i, is mapped by a hash function/table h to an element of a "key space", $h(i)$. Note that a name resolution process may be required to discover the common name of a data object. Each peer is assigned a segment of the key space, nearby its own assigned key or keys, and is directly responsible for resolving queries of all data objects that map to an element of their segment.

Structured P2P systems employ "consistent" [116] distributed hashing tables (DHTs) to distribute the load required for query resolution among the participating peers in a balanced way and to facilitate peers leaving and joining. Under consistent hashing, peers leaving and joining do not significantly affect the keys assigned to data objects and to the remaining peers so that the overhead associated with peer node churn is localized. In some consistent DHT systems, each key is 160 bits (40 hexadecimal digits) long so that key space $\{0, 1\}^{160}$ has 2^{160} elements. When each peer is assigned a single key, it is possible that the segments assigned to peers will significantly vary in size; to reduce any resulting unfairness, multiple keys can be assigned to each peer [117] so that each peer's assigned portion of key space is a union of disjoint segments about its assigned keys (i.e., the peer's "virtual nodes" in key space); see Problem 7.3.

When the data object of a query is not in the segment(s) of a queried peer, it should know of a peer that does know (or is more likely to know) and forward the query accordingly. Some of this information is acquired directly upon initialization of the peer. That is, with the aid of existing peers or by special-purpose servers, a newly arrived peer is set up with an appropriate forwarding (or "finger") table of keys *and* IP addresses of other peers in the system. Once established, a peer can periodically query other peers to update such information and to ensure that peers in its forwarding table have not left the system. Also, the identities/keys of other active peers can be acquired indirectly by observing specific queries and their responses, both of which may be labeled by the addresses of the originating and/or forwarding peers under reverse-path forwarding. Observed problems with queries (say timeouts in waiting for responses to arrive via reverse-path forwarding) may be indicative of stale forwarding table entries. A peer can emit "probe" queries with destination keys close to its own simply in order to identify neighboring peers in key space from the response. A peer with multiple keys assigned may elect to use only one of them for *forwarding* queries [117].

There are many possible strategies for the management of both tables of data objects and tables of fellow peers for forwarding purposes. Clearly, entries that are known to be stale (e.g., peers that are known to have departed the system) should be removed from forwarding tables. Typical trade-offs are in play in the sizing of such caches: Larger forwarding tables will result in fewer querying hops/relaying but will require more memory, maintenance overhead, longer look-up times per node, and possibly more overhead in setting up new peers.

In summary, from a data object's point of view there are peers:

- that possess the object,

- that do not possess the object but know about peers that do, and

- that neither possess the object nor know about peers that do and hence must forward a query for that object to another peer.

From a peer's point of view there are:

- data objects it possesses,

- a table (or "registry") of data objects nearby in the key space together with the identities of known peers that possess them, and

- a forwarding table of other known peers.

In the following, we explore structured P2P query resolution for a specific example that is related to those described in [143, 160]. The section concludes with a discussion of the distance metrics used by Chord [89, 211] and Kademlia [152]. For additional reading, see the discussion given in [216] comparing Chord, Kademlia and continuous-discrete [160]. Other well-known structured P2P systems are described in the general references [169, 6, 191], in particular Pastry [196] and Tapestry [240].

7.3.1 A structured P2P framework using Voronoi cells

For the purposes of discussion, suppose a data object has:

- at least one *provider* peer that possess the object (and can provide it to others).

Also, for query resolution, suppose a data object has:

- at least one *primary* peer whose identity is, by some chosen metric, typically closest to the object in key space (more than one primary is possible in the case where distances are tied) and

- several possible *secondary* peers whose identities are closest to the primary peer(s) in key space.

Both the primary and secondary peers (collectively called "index" peers) of an object are aware of one or more of its provider peers. Each peer therefore has a table of nearby data objects (i.e., for which they are either the primary or a secondary) and one or more provider peers for each object.

The secondary peers offer an amount of redundancy that is required to facilitate management of peer departures, especially when departures are abrupt due to, for example, a fault. That is, when a peer node departs, its closest neighbors in key space can immediately take over its query resolution responsibilities, assuming the departure is detected in a timely fashion. In addition to reliability, secondary peers of a data object may elect to respond to queries for it, thereby improving search performance (during times of high demand for the data object in particular). This rule can be extended to allow popular but distant data objects to be stored in secondary registries.

To join a peer group, an end system could contact an existing peer, superpeer, or server to obtain the client application and the key it will subsequently use. Peer keys can be assigned:

- close in key space to that of the peer assisting in setup,

- with the IP address, public encryption key, or physical location of the joining peer in mind,

- by explicit consideration of load balancing across the key space, or

- by sampling the key space at random (which may also have load-balancing benefits).

In this process, the new peer's IP address and key are initially known to at least one other peer and can be disseminated by that peer to others, particularly those that are close to the new peer in key space. Given the identities of its neighboring peers in key space, a newly set-up peer can query them for their tables of data objects and peers, in particular to determine the objects to which it is closest in key space and primarily responsible for query resolution [143]. Implicitly in the following, when we state that a primary or secondary peer is aware of an object, we mean that it is aware of providers of that object.

7.3.2 Specific approaches using Voronoi cells

Suppose that hashing maps both peer and object names to identifiers in a key space

$$\mathcal{K} \subset \mathcal{S}^d,$$

where $\mathcal{S}^d$ is the surface of a $(d \geq 2)$-dimensional hypersphere, i.e., $\mathcal{K}$ is a finite, $(d-1)$-dimensional set. Let

- $X \subset \mathcal{K}$ be the set of peer identifiers and

- $\Omega \subset \mathcal{K}$ be the set of data object identifiers.

Note that the number of bits required to codify peer and object keys will need to be large enough to accommodate the peers and data objects. This is, of course, not a problem when the size of the key space is 2^{160}, as in the previously mentioned example (wherein the key space can be interpreted as belonging to a circle by mod 2^{160} arithmetic). Indeed, it is likely that a 160-bit key space will be very sparsely populated with data objects and peers.

The objects A_x of primary responsibility for peer x are those closest to it in key space, i.e.,

$$A_x \equiv \{w \in \Omega \mid x = \arg\min_{y \in X} |y - w|\}.$$

Thus, the convex *Voronoi cells* A_x partition Ω, i.e., they are mutually disjoint and

$$\bigcup_{x \in X} A_x = \Omega.$$

Let

$$N_x \subset X$$

be the nearest neighbors of peer $x \in \mathcal{K}$, i.e., $y \in N_x$ if and only if A_y and A_x touch (share portions of their boundaries). Note that in two dimensions $|N_x|$ is simply the number of edges (or vertices) of the polygon (Voronoi cell) A_x. Define the content "view" of a peer x as the combination of its primary and secondary sets of data objects:

$$V_x \equiv A_x \cup \bigcup_{y \in N_x} A_y.$$

That is, each peer x maintains knowledge of peers that possess all objects in V_x. In the two-dimensional key space example of Figure 7.2, the first-order neighboring peers of the center (black) peer are shaded and all of their cells are completely depicted. Clearly, for a one-dimensional key space, $|N_x| = 2$. For a two-dimensional key space, $\mathsf{E}|N_x| = 6$; see [163]. That is, with regard to the definition of secondary peers and *local* forwarding decisions, additional dimensionality in the key space obviously increases the number of one-hop neighbors. Additional redundancy may be achieved by expanding the secondary assignments to include neighbors of neighbors (i.e., second-order neighbors), or third-order neighbors, etc. For the case of second-order neighbors,

$$V_x = \bigcup_{y \in N_x} \bigcup_{z \in N_y} A_z. \tag{7.4}$$

Again, a peer may include in its table the keys of distant but popular data objects so as to improve the performance of the system (note the concept of "unidirectionality" described in Section 7.3.4 below). Such information could be obtained by reverse-path forwarding of queries, recall Section 7.2. That is, a portion of the secondary data object registry could be employed in "most recently seen" mode to deal with flash crowds for data objects, irrespective of their distance to the peer.

When a peer joins the network, a protocol among it and its neighbors in key space will result in the creation of its primary and secondary lists of objects and corresponding

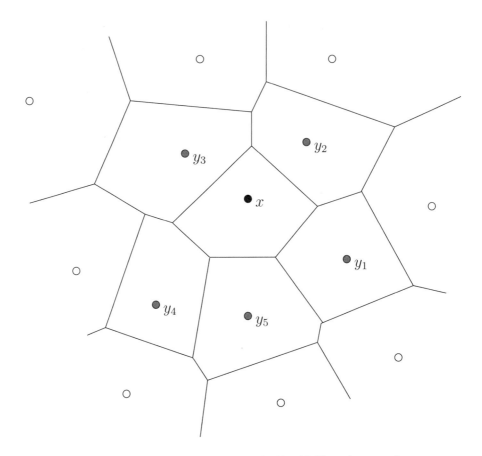

Figure 7.2   Two-dimensional Voronoi cells with $N_x = \{y_1, ..., y_5\}$.

modification of those of its neighbors [143, 160]. Construction of Voronoi diagrams, and the "dual" Delaunay graphs having links between all pairs of neighboring peers, is described in, e.g., [86, 143]. Upon departure, all of the peers whose "views" contained objects that *primarily* belonged to x must adjust their object lists. In particular, the immediate (first-order) neighbors of x must negotiate to adjust their *primary* list of objects. This is graphically depicted for the two-dimensional case in Figure 7.3.

To describe a *local* forwarding rule for this system, suppose that a peer with key x desires an object with key w. So, x needs to find a primary or secondary peer of w. Query resolution can operate so as to select the known *neighboring* peer y of x whose identifying key is closest to that of the data object w. Assuming "closest" is determined by simple arithmetic (Euclidean) distance and ignoring the boundary effects of modulo arithmetic, one can determine forwarding decisions by performing a longest prefix match of the key of the requested data object against the forwarding table of peer keys.

If each forwarding step is to a peer that has at least one more (most) significant bit in common with that of w, then the maximum number of hops for any query will be bounded by the minimum of the number of peers and the size of the address space in bits. In the system proposed in [143], mean query latencies (network diameters) that were of the order of $\sqrt{|X|/4}$ hops were observed.

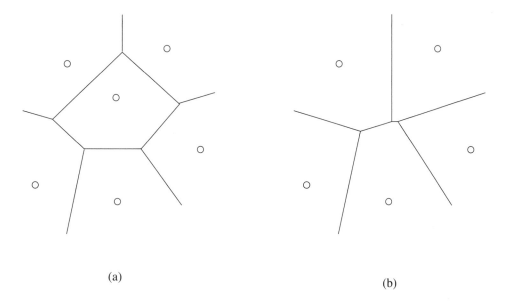

(a)

(b)

Figure 7.3   Two-dimensional Voronoi cells of (first-order) neighbors with and without the peer at the center.

In the CAN system [178], a joining peer is assigned an address in key space z selected at random. The new peer then discovers the identity of the existing peer x that is the primary for its assigned address, i.e., $z, x \in A_x$, say by querying a data object with key equal to its own address. The set A_x is then partitioned into two sets A'_z and A'_x so that

- all primary sets are hypercubes aligned parallel to the axes of key space and

- x and z are reassigned to addresses x' and z' inside their respective primary sets, i.e., $z' \in A'_z = A_{z'}$ and $x' \in A'_x = A_{x'}$.

The process is reversed (primaries are merged) when a peer leaves. Clearly, if the new addresses x', z' are chosen at the center of their primary sets, then the primaries are Voronoi sets generated by the addresses of the peers in key space.

7.3.3 Variations in the design of search, including Chord

We have thus far described an approach that is similar to a distance vector method in that queries are forwarded to neighboring nodes in key space based on information that is local to the forwarding peer in key space, noting that, in application layer routing, neighboring peers in key space are not necessarily physically proximal (as they would be in a "spatial" graph), i.e., we are assuming just a "relational" graph connecting peers in key space. Also note that the primary table of data objects A_x could instead correspond to a fixed region about x, thereby requiring more careful assignment of key space identifier(s) of peers so that the key space is completely covered by the A_x and so that there is adequate redundancy. If the number of objects $|\Omega|$ and peers $|X|$ are large, the former may be achieved with high probability by a uniform "randomness" of the hash function assigning keys to data objects; again see Problem 7.3. One can envision a highly decentralized and dynamic "opportunistic" system in which peers may cache the identities of any distant (in the key space) peers, information that may be obtained through reverse-path forwarding of queries. Typically in a highly decentralized system, it is also clearly of interest to include mechanisms to avoid loops in forwarding paths. As in IP routing, a TTL mechanism could be used to abort queries that have been excessively (unsuccessfully) forwarded.

In this section, "long-distance" entries in forwarding tables will be considered. Assume a one-dimensional 160-bit key space and suppose that every peer $x \in X$:

- is a primary peer for $D = |A_x|$ data objects and

- is aware of K other peers for forwarding purposes, i.e., forwarding tables of size K.

That is, the peer x is primary for all data objects with keys that have

$$160 - \log_2 D$$

most significant bits in common with x (again, ignoring boundary effects when $x \approx 2^{160}$). Further suppose that the kth entry of its forwarding table is a peer z in the interval

$$[(x + 2^{k-1}D) \bmod 2^{160}, \quad (x + 2^k D - 1) \bmod 2^{160}], \tag{7.5}$$

where

$$2^K D = 160,$$

i.e., we logarithmically partition the key space about x and assume the peer is aware of another in each of the K elements of the partition, as in the manner of Chord [211] (wherein z is chosen as the smallest known peer identifier in its interval). Again, queries for data objects y are relayed to peers whose keys are closest to $y \pmod{2^{160}}$ among those stored in the forwarding table. For this system, the following result follows by simply showing that each forwarding step results in halving the distance between the peer's address and the data object every time the query is forwarded [211].

Theorem 7.3.1. *Every query under Chord will be resolved within K hops (relays), where K is the size of the forwarding tables of the peers.*

■ **EXAMPLE 7.1**

Suppose a query for a data object with key y is launched by peer x_0. The case where $D = 2^{156}$ and $K = 4$ is depicted in Figure 7.4, i.e., the primary domain of a peer, indicated as a bold line segment in the figure, is greatly exaggerated and the size of the forwarding table is chosen small for the purposes of illustration. The partition of the key space of the forwarding table of peers x_0 and x_1 are depicted in Figures 7.4(a) and (b), respectively. Key space is typically depicted as a circle (the bottom of Figure 7.4) to reflect modulo arithmetic operations on it. Note that each of the forwarding decisions, e.g., $x_0 \rightarrow x_1$ and $x_1 \rightarrow x_2$, result in at least halving the distance between the current peer handling the query and the data object, i.e., the progress of the distance is such that

$$|y - x_{i+1}| \leq \tfrac{1}{2}|y - x_i|,$$

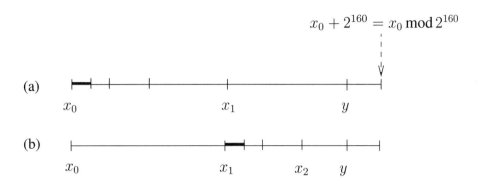

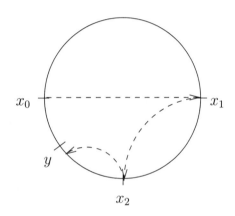

Figure 7.4   A 160-bit key space partition of (a) peer x_0 and (b) peer x_1.

where x_i is the ith peer to relay the query. Also note how search is conducted only in the clockwise direction in Figure 7.4; see Problem 7.5.

A point here is that (one-hop) forwarding decisions are not necessarily to neighboring peers. That is, in this approach, each peer needs to be aware of a larger community of peers so that not only nearby peers in key space are eligible for forwarding decisions. Hybrid approaches involving both local and nonlocal forwarding have been proposed, e.g., Pastry [196], hierarchical search structures [191], and small-world graphs [222, 103]. In one of the networks of [131], key space is a two-dimensional lattice with the l_1 metric

$$d(\underline{x}, \underline{y}) \quad \equiv \quad |x_1 - y_1| + |x_2 - y_2|,$$

peers are aware of their immediate neighbors, and peers have just one long-distance connection to a peer chosen at random. In this setting, a query process itself is a Markov chain and the proof of querying performance in [131] involves a logarithmic partition of key space (about the destination y) that is similar to the "deterministic" finger table structure later used by Chord for the peers.

Non-local forwarding potentially reduces search delays but may have disadvantages when handling peer arrivals and departures (churn). Recall that under the "Voronoi" approach described earlier, peers in the forwarding table can be polled to recover from the departure of a neighboring peer. Again, a peer can *react* to a detected departed entry in its forwarding table by querying for a data object (possibly a fictitious one) whose key is close to that of a desired peer in key space and rely on reverse-path forwarding information in the response, or by simply querying known long-lived superpeers [152, 218]. Alternatively, peers may *proactively* identify multiple peers in each element of their partition of key space under Chord as mentioned at the start of this section. Clearly, for many different contexts both structured and not, given a critical mass of densely connected superpeers, routing is facilitated by simply forwarding the query to the nearest superpeer and letting them do most of the work.

7.3.4 The Kademlia example

In this section, we briefly discuss the Kademlia structured P2P file-sharing system [152], on which a recent "trackerless" version of the popular file-swapping system BitTorrent is based. Under Kademlia, data objects and peers are assigned to elements of an n-bit key space. Kademlia uses a bitwise exclusive OR (XOR) distance d between points in key space:

$$d(x, y) \;\equiv\; x \oplus y \tag{7.6}$$

for all $x, y \in \{0, 1\}^n$. For example, if $n = 5$, $x = 01101$ (13 in decimal), and $y = 10100$ (20 in decimal), then

$$d(01101, 10100) \;=\; 11001 \text{ (25 in decimal)}.$$

It is left as an exercise to show that d satisfies the formal properties of a metric on the key space, i.e., that

$$\begin{aligned}
d(x, y) &> 0 \quad \text{for all } x \neq y \in \{0, 1\}^n, \\
d(x, y) &= 0 \;\Leftrightarrow\; x = y, \\
d(x, y) &= d(y, x) \quad \text{for all } x, y \in \{0, 1\}^n, \\
d(x, y) + d(y, z) &\geq d(x, z) \quad \text{for all } x, y, z \in \{0, 1\}^n,
\end{aligned}$$

where the second-to-last property is symmetry and the last property is the triangle inequality.

Suppose the peer with key x_k receives a query for a data object with key y. Moreover, suppose that peer x_k is not aware of a provider for y and so must relay the query. Peer x_k will search its forwarding table for the identity of another peer x_{k+1} that is closest to y according to the XOR metric so that $d(x_k, y) \geq d(x_{k+1}, y)$. Note that this metric benefits from a "unidirectional" property, as does that of Chord, i.e., given a key y and distance $\Delta \geq 0$, there is a unique solution x to

$$d(x, y) \;=\; \Delta. \tag{7.7}$$

Under Kademlia, a peer node becomes aware of such information by queries for content each of which is assumed to be labeled with the sending peer's key and responses that also have the recipient's key, as in reverse-path forwarding. Also, a peer node can perform remote procedure calls (RPCs) to ask its fellow peers for such information and can ping peers to check whether they are still "on" the network [152]. Peer nodes with long-term presence, i.e., those with well-developed lists, are important to such systems. The distribution of the lifetimes L of peers of file-sharing networks was empirically observed to satisfy the following property [198]:

$$f(t) \quad \equiv \quad \mathsf{P}(L > t + 60 \mid L > t)$$

is nondecreasing and $f(100 \text{ minutes}) \approx 0.8$. For this reason, Kademlia does not delete peer nodes from a ("K-bucket") forwarding list even if they have not been been recently observed participating in a query or response, i.e., "stale" peers are potentially removed only when the list overflows. Similar reliance on powerful and key space knowledgeable superpeers has been proposed for other systems, e.g., a kind of hierarchical version of Chord called Iridium [170]. It may be feasible that small communities of superpeers may continually exchange significant amounts of up-to-date key space information, i.e., tables of data objects and keys of active "regular" peers.

Note that the unidirectionality of the metric d implies that all queries for a given data object will converge along the same paths to it. So, peers along those paths that cache look-ups (again facilitated by reverse-path forwarding) may alleviate hot spots. Also note that resistance to the distribution of phony data objects can be achieved in a decentralized fashion by downloading the same content from more than one peer, an objective that unidirectionality may make difficult to achieve. One simple work-around is to respond to a query and, in addition, continue to forward the query but with an indication in it that a response has been previously issued, together with the identity of the providing peer given in that response, to ensure that a different providing peer can be given in subsequent responses. In this context, reverse path forwarding may not necessarily be in effect for all queries. Finally, note that multidimensional key spaces tend to have path diversity, instead of unidirectionality, which may be valuable for load-balancing purposes, especially in the presence of a flash crowds of high demand for certain data objects.

7.3.5   Discussion: Spatial neighbor-to-neighbor graphs

Note that thus far we have not necessarily associated the key space identifier of a peer with that of its IP address or physical location, i.e., "proximity" routing. Recall that in the Internet, BGP economically forwards packets based on address prefixes (stubs) that correspond to a group of subnetworks that lie in the same direction (output link) from a given router's point of view. In terms of latency and bandwidth consumption performance, such an association would be beneficial for, for example:

- multicasting in which physically proximal peers are also proximal in the multicast tree [11, 43, 82, 135, 143],

- individual downloads from decentralized content distribution networks (i.e., resolving queries for data objects to servers that are physically close to the querying peers) [212], and

- route-to-location services of a sensor network (e.g., to resolve a query for a temperature reading at a certain location) [59].

On the other hand, by leveraging superpeers one may be able to feasibly perform large-scale routing in "flat" address spaces; see, e.g., [32, 218]. Also, there may be reliability disadvantages of high correlation of peer keys with physical location; see the next section. A hybrid relational/spatial addressing system is also possible using a two-dimensional key with only one component having spatial properties; forwarding could be performed by a lexicographic rule as discussed in Chapter 6 at Equation (6.3).

7.4   DISCUSSION: SECURITY ISSUES

In this section, we will give an overview a variety of security issues that P2P overlay systems face.

7.4.1   The querying process

Attacks on the query resolution system itself are considered in, e.g., [72, 203, 204]. These attacks can be conducted by single peers or by a group of colluding peers. Specific tactics include:

- misforwarding queries (or responses) and/or modifying them, e.g., forwarding away from the data object key, modifying the TTL, or modifying the forwarding record on each query (affecting the reverse-path forwarding mechanism);

- generating a great quantity of phony queries to deplete the system's available resources for query processing;

- replying with stale or erroneous information when polled for forwarding table entries; and

- simply discarding queries (or responses) rather than relaying them.

Peers can *assess* their fellow peers not only by examination of the fate of their own queries but also by examination of all query and response traffic they receive. These assessments can be maintained in the form of "reputations" that can be pooled (for improved accuracy) by trusted peers and employed to detect malicious or faulty peers; see the next section. Peers with low reputations can be removed from forwarding tables and a "blacklist" of low-reputation (suspected) peers can be included, in a secure fashion, on each forwarded query thereby warning trusted peers that subsequently handle the query. In [235], a reputation overlay system is proposed to secure BGP. In [218], a method of "indirection" and authentication for secure routing is proposed wherein the identity of a peer is decoupled from its encryption key (signing identity), thereby facilitating periodic replacement of the encryption key.

In [13, 125], security systems are proposed that can protect availability of content (data objects) in the face of denial-of-service attacks targeting individual peers, groups of peers, or areas of key space. Suitably redundant tables of data objects that can be cached among peers that are not proximal to try to thwart a single denial-of-service attack localized in space (as discussed earlier in the context of load balancing for flash crowds).

Tor [60] is an onion routing system for anonymous Web surfing that employs both short-term and long-term encryption keys. Recall that Freenet, briefly described in Section 7.2.2

above, anonymizes file sharing within its community. Also, the privacy-preserving Tarzan system [77] uses, for example, additional "cover" traffic to mask certain activity. Such systems trade off anonymity with efficient use of resources.

7.4.2 The downloading process

With regard to the security of the downloading process itself, content pollution (ranging from spam to malware) is a potentially significant problem [221]. In the case of spam, it is possible that the data object may be easily perceived by the end user as not authentic. In the case of malware, a downloaded data object may be a trojan for an embedded virus; once the user accesses the data object, the malware may discreetly or overtly harm his or her computer and be spread further by the normal file-sharing operations of the P2P system or by other means. Instead of downloading the same data object from multiple peers, instances of a popular data object acting as a trojan for a virus can be potentially detected by applying a known hash function to the downloaded data object and comparing the result against that of the true, unmodified version of the data object; the legitimate hash values could be obtained from a secure website or trusted (super)peer.

An interesting discussion of the potential for automated malware (worm) spread through P2P file-sharing systems is given in [223]. Such worms exploit vulnerabilities in the client applications of P2P systems. Collectively, the clients of a given P2P system may form a "monoculture" on the Internet with common vulnerabilities. The forwarding tables are built-in "hit lists" for the worm potentially enabling extremely rapid spread. Note that effective defenses to such worms need to detect and securely propagate (e.g., configure firewalls) faster than the worm itself.

Some issues related to the security of cumulative reputation systems (in the context of promoting cooperation in uploading data objects) are discussed in Section 7.5.3.

7.5 INCENTIVES FOR COOPERATION WHEN UPLOADING

Systems to provide incentives for cooperation during the actual act of sharing (uploading) of data objects in P2P networks can be classified into three groups [7]:

- monetary systems based on a global currency,

- systems based on cumulative reputations (or cumulative tokens or credits) and associated referrals within trust groups, and

- rule-based systems with memoryless "tit-for-tat" transactions.

Using a global currency (e.g., a micropayments system [156, 185]), cooperative behavior of peers is rewarded with a form of payment that can be redeemed anywhere else in the P2P network, i.e., currency can even be used to make payment to peers with whom no previous contact has occurred. If significant amounts of currency are in play, an authentication mechanism may be required. Authentication can be implemented by a banking (certification and accounting) node or system.

Alternatively, the outcomes of transactions between a pair of peers, say A and B, can result in an adjustment of a tally of credits, tokens or reputations that A and B maintain *with respect to each other*. That is, if A successfully downloads a data object from B in a timely fashion, then A will reward B with credits or tokens or will increase B's reputation. Thus, if in the not-too-distant future B requests a data object of A, then A will comply if B's reputation is sufficiently high or if B can redeem enough tokens or credits previously accrued. Moreover, A may belong to a trust group of peers that (securely) pool their reputation information so that B can redeem credits accrued servicing A with another peer in A's trust group; see Section 7.5.3. A superpeer in the trust group could maintain a single account of credits or tokens for each peer B outside the group so that any peer A within the trust group can (securely) deposit tokens into B's account. Moreover, the manner in which credits accumulate over time could be such that the results of recent transactions are weighted more than those from the more distant past. Thus, this incentive system looks less tit-for-tat and more like a local currency system within the trust group. Such issues are discussed in greater detail in [93, 92, 217].

Incentive systems typically possess an "initialization" problem that impedes the first transaction involving a specific peer or trust group. Typically, each peer is given some initial measure of trust (a benefit of the doubt), for example, a peer is given a small initial token allotment [64] or is "optimistically unchoked" [23]. Such systems can be abused by so-called Sybil attacks [36] where a single peer assumes multiple identities in the P2P system in order to accumulate these small initial measures of trust for the purposes of free-riding, i.e., extracting significant benefit from the P2P system without contributing and cooperating in return. When peers unwittingly extend trust to Sybil attackers, or to peers colluding with physically different peers for the purposes of free-riding, the overall performance of the network can significantly degrade. A typical solution to Sybil attacks involves a centralized *registration* server that authenticates a unique identifier for each peer when it joins. Some of these issues are described further in Sections 7.5.3 (at the end) and 7.5.4.

In the remainder of this section, we briefly describe rule-based incentives for BitTorrent-like swarms and then give a detailed description of a specific cumulative reputation system. The section concludes with a discussion of game-theoretic frameworks that employ such incentives.

7.5.1 Rule-based incentives of BitTorrent-like swarms

Recall the brief discussion of search under BitTorrent at the end of Section 7.2.1. BitTorrent employs rule-based incentives wherein data objects are segmented into chunks (pieces) for the purposes of individual transactions that typically involve chunk *swapping* rather than single-chunk (i.e., client-server) transfers. For the purposes of distributing a given data object, a separate swarm of interested peers is formed. Peers that require significant numbers of chunks to complete the data object are called "leechers." Under a *locally rarest first* strategy, "seed" peers, possessing most or all of the chunks comprising the swarm's data object, tend to first distribute the chunks that are rarest held (most demanded) by leechers.

Since the peer arrival rate to a swarm may initially experience exponential growth [88, 19], dealing with free riders is important (recall the initialization problem mentioned above in particular). In addition to efficient chunk swapping, BitTorrent employs a peer "choking" mechanism to deter free riders (briefly described in Section 7.5.4 at the end of this chapter).

Avalanche [11] proposes a *network-coding* approach to facilitate multicast dissemination of content that is segmented. Under Avalanche, each peer can distribute a single message that is an algebraic combination of all of the different chunks he or she has received so far, together with a specification of exactly how the chunks were combined. As with a FEC framework, the data object can be reconstituted upon receipt of a sufficiently large number of *any* such messages (whether unmodified chunks or messages formed by combining many chunks and other messages together) [76]. In a large-scale distributed system, the method of combining may be chosen at random to ensure, with minimal overhead, that a maximal number of received messages are linearly independent.

7.5.2 A cumulative reputation system to observe the level of peer cooperation

Consider a group of N peer end systems that subject one another to queries for data objects. A query (say from peer i to j) together with a response (j's response to i's query) forms a *transaction*. For $i \neq j$, let R_{ij} be the *normalized reputation* of end system j from the point of view of end system i, i.e., it will always be the case that

$$\sum_{j,\ j\neq i} R_{ij} \ = \ 1 \quad \text{for all end systems } i. \tag{7.8}$$

As transactions occur, these reputation states will change. In particular, if i queries j and the subsequent response is that j gives i the requested data object (i.e., responds *positively*), then R_{ij} will increase. In the following, we will study a specific kind of reputation system that estimates the propensity of end systems to cooperate (respond positively to queries).

We begin with a set of definitions. Without consideration of reputation, let $\pi_j > 0$ be the fixed probability that end system j will respond positively to a query, i.e., j's propensity to cooperate. In the following, a *sequence of assumed-independent transactions* is considered with $R_{ij}(n)$ representing the reputation of j from i's point of view after the nth transaction. We assume that transactions are independent so that the $N(N-1)$ vector **R** of reputation states R_{ij} will be a Markov chain on $(\Sigma_{N-1})^N$, where Σ_{N-1} is the N-dimensional simplex; see (7.8). The process **R** makes a transition upon the conclusion of each successful transaction. Let

$$\bar{R}_i(n) \ \equiv \ \frac{1}{N-1} \sum_{k,\ k\neq i} R_{ki}(n) \tag{7.9}$$

be the mean reputation of i after the nth transaction and let the *response function*

$$G(\pi_j, \bar{R}_i)$$

be the probability that j responds positively to i's query, where G is generally nondecreasing in both arguments. Also, $G(\pi, \bar{R}) = 0$ only if $\bar{R} = 0$. That is, end system j obtains and averages the reputations R_{ki} from all other peer end systems k and modifies its intrinsic probability of responding positively, π_j, accordingly.

Now a specific mechanism for updating reputations as a result of transactions will be defined. If the nth transaction involves i querying j, then, with probability $G(\pi_j, \bar{R}_i(n-1))$,

$$
R_{ik}(n) \quad = \quad
\begin{cases}
\dfrac{R_{ij}(n-1) + C}{1 + C} & \text{if } k = j \neq i, \\[2ex]
\dfrac{R_{ik}(n-1)}{1 + C} & \text{if } k \neq j, i,
\end{cases}
\tag{7.10}
$$

for some fixed $C > 0$, i.e., R_{ij} becomes relatively larger only when the transaction ij succeeds. With probability $1 - G(\pi_j, \bar{R}_i(n-1))$:

$$
R_{ij}(n) \quad = \quad R_{ij}(n-1) \text{ for all } i \neq j,
$$

i.e., if the transaction fails (the data object is not transferred as requested), then there is no change in the reputation. Note that reputations of end systems may (relatively) decrease upon positive transactions that do not involve them.

Let ρ_{ij} be the probability that a transaction involves i querying j so that

$$
\sum_i \sum_{j,\, j \neq i} \rho_{ij} \quad = \quad 1.
$$

For $n \geq 1$, we can now directly derive

$$
\begin{aligned}
&\mathsf{E}(R_{ij}(n) \mid \mathbf{R}(n-1)) \\[1ex]
&= \left(1 - \sum_{k,\, k \neq i} \rho_{ik}\right) R_{ij}(n-1) \\[1ex]
&\quad + \rho_{ij}[R_{ij}(n-1)(1 - G_j(\pi_j, \bar{R}_i(n-1))) + \frac{R_{ij}(n-1) + C}{1 + C} G_j(\pi_j, \bar{R}_i(n-1))] \\[1ex]
&\quad + \sum_{k,\, k \neq i,j} \rho_{ik}[R_{ij}(n-1)(1 - G_k(\pi_k, \bar{R}_i(n-1))) + \frac{R_{ij}(n-1)}{1 + C} G_k(\pi_k, \bar{R}_i(n-1))] \\[1ex]
&= \left(1 - \frac{C}{1 + C} \sum_{k,\, k \neq i} \rho_{ik} G_k(\pi_k, \bar{R}_i(n-1))\right) R_{ij}(n-1) \\[1ex]
&\quad + \frac{C}{1 + C} \rho_{ij} G_j(\pi_j, \bar{R}_i(n-1)).
\end{aligned}
\tag{7.11}
$$

In the first equality above, the nth transaction does not involve i querying in the first term, involves i querying $j \neq i$ in the second term, and involves i querying $k \neq j$ in the third term.

We will say that the response function G is ε-*bounded* if it satisfies the following property: There is a strictly positive $\varepsilon \ll 1$ such that, for all $0 \leq \pi, \bar{R} \leq 1$,

$$
\varepsilon \pi \quad \leq \quad G(\pi, \bar{R}) \quad \leq \quad \pi.
\tag{7.12}
$$

Also, G is said to be *separable* if

$$
G(\pi, \bar{R}) \quad = \quad \pi g(\bar{R})
$$

for nondecreasing g, where, by (7.12), $g(0) \geq \varepsilon$ and $g(1) \leq 1$. For example, $g(\bar{R}) \equiv \varepsilon + \bar{R}(1 - \varepsilon)$.

Theorem 7.5.1. *If the response function G is separable and ε-bounded, then*

$$\lim_{n \to \infty} \mathsf{E}(R_{ij}(n) \mid \mathbf{R}(0)) \;=\; \frac{\rho_{ij}\pi_j}{\sum_{k,k \neq i}\ \rho_{ik}\pi_k} \ \text{for all } i \neq j.$$

Proof: For separable G, define

$$X_{ij}(n) \;\equiv\; \frac{\rho_{ij}\pi_j}{\sum_{k,k \neq i}\ \rho_{ik}\pi_k} - R_{ij}(n) \ \ \text{for all } i \neq j \text{ and } n \geq 0.$$

By (7.11),

$$\mathsf{E}(X_{ij}(n) \mid \mathbf{R}(n-1)) \;=\; \left(1 - \frac{C}{1+C} \sum_{k,\ k \neq i} \rho_{ik}G(\pi_k, \bar{R}_i(n-1))\right) X_{ij}(n-1),$$

where (7.12) allows division by $g(\bar{R}_i(n-1)) > 0$. Since

$$\frac{C}{1+C} \sum_{k,\ k \neq i} \rho_{ik}G(\pi_k, \bar{R}_i(n-1)) \;\geq\; \frac{C\varepsilon}{1+C} \sum_{k,\ k \neq i} \rho_{ik}\pi_k \equiv \alpha$$

and $1 > \alpha > 0$,

$$\mathsf{E}(|X_{ij}(n)| \mid \mathbf{R}(n-1)) \;\leq\; (1-\alpha)|X_{ij}(n-1)|.$$

Now, define the random vector $\mathcal{F}_n = (\mathbf{R}(0), \mathbf{R}(1), ..., \mathbf{R}(n))$ for notational convenience. Note that

$$\begin{aligned}
\mathsf{E}(|X_{ij}(n)| \mid \mathcal{F}_{n-2}) &= \mathsf{E}(\mathsf{E}(|X_{ij}(n)| \mid \mathcal{F}_{n-1}) \mid \mathcal{F}_{n-2}) \\
&\leq (1-\alpha)^2|X_{ij}(n-2)|.
\end{aligned}$$

Repeating this standard conditioning operation iteratively gives

$$\mathsf{E}(|X_{ij}(n)| \mid \mathcal{F}_0) \;\leq\; (1-\alpha)^n|X_{ij}(0)|$$

from which the theorem statement follows since $X_{ij}(0)$ is bounded and $1 > \alpha > 0$. $\qquad\square$

Interpreting Theorem 7.5.1, the reputation $\mathsf{E}R_{ij}$ is a *consistent* estimator of "intrinsic" mean rate $\rho_{ij}\pi_j$ of successful transactions ij. One can modify this reputation framework to observe more complex kinds of transaction outcomes. For example, the querying peer can estimate their download *rate* r (say in megabytes per second) and use r in (7.10) instead of the fixed constant C for "successful" transactions. Assuming that the transmission rate of a transaction is generally determined by the upload bandwidth (r) that the *providing* peer allocates to the file-sharing network[1], this reputation system will estimate the relative values of quantity $\pi_j r_j$ for each peer j.

---

[1]This assumption is supported by asymmetric residential broadband Internet access in which the downlink bandwidth is typically much larger than that of the uplink.

7.5.3 Modeling trust groups

In this section, we discuss scalability and security problems facing deployed reputation systems. We also describe how to model a distributed, cumulative reputation system that could be implemented and secured by a referral system based on trust groups and light-weight message authentication and peer registration mechanisms; see, e.g., [31, 114, 115].

Potential attacks on cumulative distributed reputation systems include, but are not limited to, badmouthing and ballot-box stuffing, which are variations of Byzantine attacks [78], i.e., false reputation referrals and associated collusions. For the example of KaZaA, the reputation of each peer is stored in its own client. This fully decentralized approach can be subverted as seen with the KaZaA Lite client [121] which always reports a high reputation for itself. eBay reputations are centrally stored but are not therefore immune to attack via the methods described above [181, 182].

Similar to [31, 115, 149, 234], we can account for misrepresentation and subsampling of reputations by using the following instead of $\bar{R}_i$ in the reputation model:

$$\bar{R}_{ji}(n) = \frac{\sum_{k,k\neq i} \lambda_{jki} h(R_{jk}(n)) R_{ki}(n)}{\sum_{k,k\neq i} h(R_{jk}(n))}, \tag{7.13}$$

where the terms λ_{jki} can be used to represent how node k may misrepresent when polled by j for i's reputation, i.e., $\lambda_{jki} \in [0, 1/R_{ki}(n)]$ and misrepresentation occurs when $\lambda_{jki} \neq 1$. The h-function parameters can be used to weight reputation information by the reputation of the pollee [149] (such reputation "weightings" can also be used in more general voting systems for distributed decision making). Examples are $h(R_{jk}) \equiv \mathbf{1}\{R_{jk} > \theta_j\}$ and $h(R_{jk}) \equiv R_{jk}\mathbf{1}\{R_{jk} > \theta_j\}$, where $\theta_j \geq 0$ is a reputation *threshold* that may be used by node j to define "trust". Trust and reputation are discussed in [57, 141].

Since the terms $\lambda_{jki} h(R_{jk}(n)) \geq 0$ depend on reputations only through $\mathbf{R}(n)$, we can generalize the model (7.11) to account for misrepresentation and subsampling of reputations by replacing in (7.11) the $\bar{R}_i$ as defined in (7.9) with $\bar{R}_{ji}$ as defined in (7.13), i.e.,

$$\mathsf{E}(R_{ij}(n) \mid \mathbf{R}(n-1)) = \left(1 - \frac{C}{1+C}\sum_{k,\ k\neq i} \rho_{ik}G_k(\pi_k, \bar{R}_{ki}(n-1))\right) R_{ij}(n-1)$$

$$+ \frac{C}{1+C}\rho_{ij}G_j(\pi_j, \bar{R}_{ji}(n-1)). \tag{7.14}$$

As a special case, we can model federations of peers that are formed in part to pool reputation information in a more reliable manner, i.e., trust groups. That is, consider M groups $\{\mathcal{N}_m\}_{m=1}^{M}$ of peers, where

$$\bigcup_{m=1}^{M} \mathcal{N}_m$$

is the set of all N peers and $|\mathcal{N}_m| \geq 2$ for all m. This is modeled by taking

$$h(R_{jk}) \equiv \begin{cases} 1 & \text{if } j, k \in \mathcal{N}_m \text{ for some } m, \\ 0 & \text{else.} \end{cases}$$

Note that $\{\mathcal{N}_m\}_{m=1}^{M}$ need not be a partition, i.e., a single peer j could belong to more than one group (and note that we clearly need to assume that the denominator of (7.13) is always strictly positive for all i, j, n). Such local trust repositories can be securely implemented using one of a variety of existing light-weight authentication techniques within each group in a distributed or centralized fashion [25, 46, 179]. Obviously, the implicit assumption of any trust group m (assumed small enough to allow complete sharing of reputation information among its peers) is that, for all appraised nodes $i, \lambda_{jki} \approx 1$ for all nodes $j, k \in \mathcal{N}_m$. In a very large-scale P2P network, a deeper hierarchy of trust groups would form a complex "social" network. Instead of simply allocating an unknown peer a small reputation value (recall our response function $G(\pi, R) > \varepsilon\pi > 0$ for all reputations R in (7.12)), a reputation for a querying peer could be determined by a routing operation through the social network [131, 222], i.e., one search process determines the providing peer for the querying peer and then another search process determines a reputation of the querying peer for the providing peer.

Finally, recall Sybil attacks, which were briefly described for the context of the peer initialization problem at the start of Section 7.5. Again, a Sybil attacker employs many different identities and can try to create a phony "mutual admiration" society or attempt to harm the reputation of other peers through falsely negative referrals. Note that the reputation accrued by a Sybil attacker through cooperative action (uploading data objects) may be diluted among his or her multiple identities. A system of federated trust can limit the scope of harm of a Sybil attacker to within the trust group(s) to which he or she belongs, and specific strategies have been proposed to thwart Sybils within a group [58].

7.5.4   Discussion: Game-theoretic models of P2P systems

Game-theoretic models of communication networks typically involve end users that behave in a rationally selfish manner. For P2P query resolution, recall the token-based system of GIA mentioned at the end of Section 7.2.3. Games modeling the sharing of data objects typically involve a mechanism that is designed to provide incentives for peers to cooperate, as discussed at the beginning of Section 7.5.

Several authors have explored game models in which peers file share and adjust their reputation estimates of each other [68, 146, 147, 158, 159]. For a given transaction between two peers, the cooperation level of one peer will depend on the reputation of the other as described above. In the game, peers may modify their own "default" cooperation level (deciding, for example, whether to comply with a request, π, and/or how much uplink bandwidth to assign to the transaction) in order to change their own reputation and thereby achieve a desired utility from the system (e.g., their target query success rate or mean data-object download time). Practical challenges to such game formulations include calibration of reputation levels (i.e., determining specifically what reputation levels correspond to a "cooperative" user [158]), and reconciling the time scales that are required to accurately estimate reputations, the time scales that are required to make decisions (transactions), and those of peer churn. Similar time-scale issues were behind the "quasi-stationary" ALOHA example of Section 4.6 wherein users act based on assumed accurate estimates of steady-state received quality of service θ for a given set of decision variables $\underline{\lambda}$ and a fixed user population.

Under rule-based BitTorrent, a peer may employ a "choking" algorithm to periodically refuse to upload to certain uncooperative peers, e.g., peers that are perceived to have allocated little uplink bandwidth in recent transactions. BitTorrent peers may "optimistically" unchoke certain peers, a policy that is especially beneficial to potentially cooperative peers that have recently joined a swarm (and have little to share) or to potentially rehabilitated free-riders that have increased their uplink (transmission) rates.

Problems

7.1   Consider a simplified version of the query forwarding scenario of Section 7.2.4 wherein there is a fixed population of peers, i.e., $\lambda = \delta = 0$ so that $N \equiv f + w$ is constant. Let $p = \mathsf{E} f / N$ be the fraction of peers that have cached the specific information that is the objective of the queries under consideration. Given f, simply suppose that before a query is resolved (i.e., received by a peer of the population f), it will be forwarded to N/f peers in the $w = N - f$ population of peers that do not possess the information of interest. Using Little's formula, show that

$$p \;\geq\; \sqrt{\frac{q}{N\mu}}\,.$$

7.2   Specify a Markovian model corresponding to the deterministic equations (7.2) and (7.3) for search by random walk with reverse-path forwarding. Carefully handle how the Markov chain behaves near $f = 0$ so that this state is not "absorbing."

7.3   Consider n peers whose keys are chosen independently and uniformly at random on a unit circle and assign to each peer the arc segment for which its key is the left boundary point. Let A_n be a random variable representing lengths of arc segments.

(a) Prove $\mathsf{E} A_n = 2\pi / n \approx \sigma(A_n)$, where σ is standard deviation and the approximation is close for large n.
Hint: first argue that

$$\mathsf{P}(A_n > x) \;=\; \left(\frac{2\pi - x}{2\pi}\right)^{n-1}.$$

So, the standard deviation of the segment size is comparable to its mean.

(b) Now suppose that each peer has k keys assigned, where all nk keys are chosen and arc segments are assigned as for part (a). Let $B_{n,k}$ be a random variable representing the total lengths of the k arc segments of a peer. Clearly, $\mathsf{E} B_{n,k} = k \mathsf{E} A_{nk} = 2\pi / n = \mathsf{E} A_n$, i.e., the mean total arc length assigned to a peer does not depend on k. *Assuming that the lengths of the arc segments assigned to a peer are uncorrelated,* prove

$$\sigma(B_{n,k}) \;\approx\; \frac{\sigma(A_n)}{\sqrt{k}}.$$

Hint: Recall the law of large numbers from Section 1.11. Note: Chord suggests $k = O(\log n)$ [117], and one can use the conditional uniformity property (recall Problem 2.14) to show that $B_{n,k}$ is actually beta distributed with $\sigma^2(B_{n,k}) \sim (n^2 k)^{-1}$ as $n \to \infty$.

7.4   Suppose $|X|$ peers belong to a P2P system with addresses chosen in one-dimensional key space of size $|\mathcal{K}|$ independently uniformly at random. Also suppose that each peer is primary for a set of keys of fixed size $2r$ about the peer and that there are no secondary assignments. Find the probability that a region of key space of size $k < |\mathcal{K}|$ is not known to any of the peers, where $k \gg r$.

7.5   Consider $N \gg 1$ peers (points) residing on a circle with unit radius. They are evenly spaced, i.e., the (shortest) arc length between nearest neighbors is $\varepsilon \equiv 2\pi/N$. Each peer can forward messages to either of his nearest neighbors. Also, each peer x can forward messages to $\nu \geq 1$ long-distance peers $L_i(x)$, $1 \leq i \leq \nu$, each of whose position on the circle is chosen independently and uniformly at random. Let $D(m) \equiv d(x(m), y) \leq \pi$ be the *shortest* arc length (in any direction) between peer $x(m)$ and data object y on the circle. Assuming that peers are aware of the position in the circle of a peer to which they want to send a query, a query from peer $x(m)$ for y is forwarded to the peer $x(m+1)$ in its forwarding table that is closest to y, where peer $x(0)$ originally launched the query for y.

(a) Assuming for simplicity that $D(m) \gg \varepsilon$ and that the distribution of the position of the long-distance peers on the circle is continuous ($\varepsilon \ll 1$), show that

$$E(D(m+1) \mid x(m)) \quad = \quad \frac{\pi}{\nu+1}\left(1 - \left(1 - \frac{D(m)}{\pi}\right)^{\nu+1}\right) \qquad (7.15)$$

$$= \quad D(m) - \nu\frac{D^2(m)}{2\pi} + \mathrm{o}\left(\left(\frac{D(m)}{\pi}\right)^2\right).$$

(b) Repeat (a) for the case where $D(m)$ approaches ε.

(c) Compare the search performance to Chord with similarly sized finger table at each node (especially as $D(m)$ approaches ε).

Hint: Find $\Phi(z) \equiv P(\min_{1 \leq i \leq \nu} d(L_i(x), y) > z)$ and argue that the quantity of interest in (7.15) is $-\int_0^{D(m)} z \, d\Phi(z) - D(m)\int_{D(m)}^\pi d\Phi(z)$. The second equality is Taylor's theorem.

7.6   With regard to the system and statement of Theorem 7.3.1, suppose that the key space is instead partitioned into equal-sized (rather than logarithmicly increasing) elements for the purposes of forwarding. How would the statement of Theorem 7.3.1 change?

7.7   Consider the bitwise XOR distance of Equation (7.6).

(a) Prove that it is a formal metric on $\{0,1\}^N$. Hint: To show the triangle inequality, argue that $d(x, z) = d(x, y) \oplus d(y, z)$ and $a + b \geq a \oplus b$ for all $a, b \geq 0$ [152].

(b) Prove (7.7).

(c) Explore the possibility of using the Hamming distance instead of an arithmetic (Euclidean) or XOR metric, i.e., $d(x, y)$ is the *number* of different bit positions in which the binary representations of x and y differ. In particular, how do the "neighborhoods" in key space differ?

7.8   Consider an overlay network of n peers for which there is a large number R of distinct routes, i.e., $R = O(n^2) \gg L$, where L is the number of (one-hop) bidirectional "links" directly connecting a pair of nodes. Suppose that the links are unreliable, where each link l has a message-dropping probability b_l. Assuming the message dropping events are independent, the route-dropping probabilities B_r satisfy

$$1 - B_r \quad = \quad \prod_{l \in r}(1 - b_l) \quad = \quad \prod_{l \in \mathcal{L}} a_{r,l}(1 - b_l),$$

which implies

$$\Delta_r \equiv \log(1 - B_r) \quad = \quad \sum_{l \in r} a_{r,l} \log(1 - b_l) \equiv \sum_{l \in r} a_{r,l} \delta_l,$$

where we are recalling the notation of Section 5.1. So, we can write this succinctly in vector form as

$$\underline{\Delta} = \mathbf{A}^{\mathrm{T}} \underline{\delta},$$

where $\mathbf{A}^{\mathrm{T}}$ is an $R \times L$ matrix. Suppose that the link-dropping rates, represented by $\underline{\delta}$, are fixed but unknown. The problem formulated in [42] is to determine $\underline{\delta}$ from a small number $k < L$ of "probe" routes for which the route-dropping probabilities are measured. Explain how this can be done. Hint: In one method, a $k \times L$ submatrix $\tilde{\mathbf{A}}^{\mathrm{T}}$ of $\mathbf{A}^{\mathrm{T}}$ that is of full row rank k is first found.

7.9   Verify the claim at the end of Section 7.5.2 regarding the reputation system estimating $\pi_j r_j$ for peers j, where r_j is the uplink bandwidth (transmission rate) allocated by peer j for file sharing.

7.10   Suppose the reputations are not normalized by $1 + C$ in (7.10), so that they simply accumulate the reward C for each successful transaction, and that the outcome of the transactions do not depend on the reputations of the querying peers, i.e., $G(\pi, R) \equiv \pi$. Use the law of large numbers (Section 1.11) to show that

$$\lim_{n \to \infty} \frac{R_{ij}(n)}{n} \quad = \quad \frac{\rho_{ij} \pi_j}{\sum_{k, k \neq i} \rho_{ik} \pi_k} \quad \text{for all } i \neq j.$$

APPENDIX A

ADDITIONAL BACKGROUND ON

ROUTING

A.1 NETWORK GRAPH TERMINOLOGY

Consider the network graph depicted in Figures A.1 and A.2. Note that it has unidirectional links (edges) that come in pairs, i.e., there is a link *from* node (vertex) v *to* node u if and only if there is a link from u to v as well. A node is responsible for and immediately cognizant of the *costs* of usage associated with all of its outbound links. Let $\mathcal{L}(v)$ be the set of outbound links of a node. Thus, $\mathcal{L}^{-1}(l)$ is the single node for which l is an outbound link, i.e., the node transmits out on l. For example, in Figure A.1,

$$\mathcal{L}(f) = \{6, 8\} \quad \text{and} \quad \mathcal{L}^{-1}(2) = b.$$

Let $\mathcal{N}(v)$ be the set of nodes that are immediate neighbors (connected by a single outbound link) of node v, e.g., in Figures A.1 and A.2, the neighborhood of node a is

$$\mathcal{N}(a) = \{b, f, d\}.$$

We can use this definition to define a neighborhood of a set S of nodes:

$$\mathcal{N}(S) = \bigcup_{v \in S} \mathcal{N}(v).$$

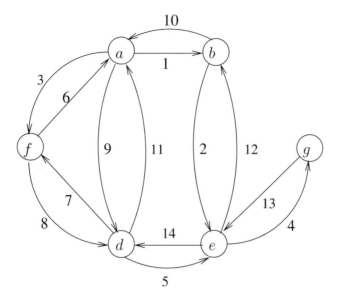

Figure A.1   A network graph with unidirectional links labeled by their *index l*.

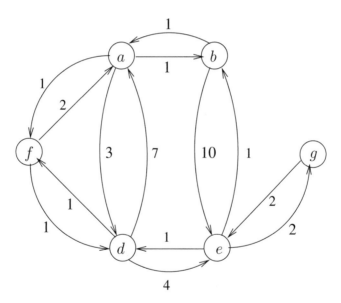

Figure A.2   A network graph with unidirectional links labeled by their *cost c_l*.

Note that by definition

$$v \notin \mathcal{N}(v),$$

but it may be the case that

$$S \cap \mathcal{N}(S) \neq \emptyset.$$

A unidirectional route (path) from node u to node v consists of a series of unidirectional links in the usual way. For the example in Figure A.1, the route labeled $r = \{1, 2, 4\}$ connects node a to g. Alternatively, we can specify a route using nodes, e.g., $r = \{a, b, e, g\}$, where we note that the ordering of nodes matters in this notation e.g., route

$$\{3, 8\} = \{a, f, d\} \quad \neq \quad \{f, a, d\} = \{6, 9\}.$$

Given a measure of cost borne by a node/link to support a traffic flow on a route, one can define optimal (minimal cost) routes. To this end, let $C(r)$ be the cost of a route r determined by the costs (or "weights" or "metrics") c_l of its component links $l \in r$. Note that (unidirectional) links connecting the same pair of nodes do not necessarily have the same associated costs.

We will consider two general ways to determine $C(r)$ from the c_l, $l \in r$. The first way is when the costs are *additive*, i.e.,

$$C(r) \quad = \quad \sum_{l \in r} c_l. \tag{A.1}$$

The second way is when the route cost is the maximum of the associated link costs, i.e.,

$$C(r) \quad = \quad \max_{l \in r} c_l. \tag{A.2}$$

In the following, the link costs are always assumed to be nonnegative, i.e.,

$$c_l \quad \geq \quad 0 \quad \text{for all links } l.$$

■ **EXAMPLE A.1**

Recalling Jackson networks, if we associate a mean delay cost with each link, then the mean delay of a route is clearly the sum of those of its component links. Recalling loss networks, if we associate a loss (blocking) rate c_l with each link and assume that loss events are independent and that that $\sum_{l \in r} c_l \ll 1$, then the route cost is approximately additive, i.e.,

$$C(r) \quad = \quad 1 - \prod_{l \in r} (1 - c_l)$$

$$\approx \quad \sum_{l \in r} c_l.$$

■ **EXAMPLE A.2**

In addition to or instead of delay considerations, a normalized *energy* cost associated with link l can be the basis of routing. For example, define

$$c_l \quad = \quad \frac{\tau_l}{b_{\mathcal{L}^{-1}(l)}},$$

where b_v is the energy (residual battery level) in node v which is available for transmission and τ_l is the energy required to transmit a frame on link l [39]. In this case, we could identify route cost with that of the *bottleneck* link:

$$C(r) \;=\; \max_{l \in r} c_l.$$

Note how an attribute of the *node* $\mathcal{L}^{-1}(l)$ affects the cost associated with link l. An *optimal* route in this context would have *maximal* bottleneck energy (or, equivalently, minimal cost C). That is, among a set of routes $\mathcal{R}$ connecting a pair of nodes, the routing algorithm would want to find

$$\min_{r \in \mathcal{R}} C(r) \;=\; \min_{r \in \mathcal{R}} \max_{l \in r} c_l \tag{A.3}$$

$$= \; \max_{r \in \mathcal{R}} \min_{l \in r} \frac{b_{\mathcal{L}^{-1}(l)}}{\tau_l}.$$

Other nonnegative link costs decreasing in $b_{\mathcal{L}^{-1}(l)}$ and increasing in τ_l could be used, including simply $c_l = 1/b_{\mathcal{L}^{-1}(l)}$ or $c_l = \tau_l$, the latter resulting in an additive route cost. Hybrid delay and energy considerations are discussed in, e.g., [70, 108]. Finally, the assigned energy costs can be made more sensitive to current traffic load by substituting τ_l for the current energy dissipation rate, i.e., the product of τ_l and the frame transmission rate on the link. In [199], how such link costs lead to maximization of network lifetime is studied.

Let

$$a \to_r c$$

be the *subroute* of r connecting node a to node c, where a and c are nodes that are along path r implicitly by this notation, i.e., $a, c \in r$. Let $\alpha(r)$ be the origin (source) node of route r and $\omega(r)$ be the destination (sink) node of route r. Thus, by the above notation,

$$r \;\equiv\; \alpha(r) \to_r \omega(r).$$

For example, in Figure A.2, the route $r = \{b, a, f, d\}$, $\alpha(r) = b$, $\omega(r) = d$, and the subroute $a \to_r f$ is just the link indexed $l = 3$.

Lemma A.1.1. *All subroutes of a minimum-cost route connecting two nodes in a network are themselves minimum-cost routes.*

Proof: Consider two nodes, a and f, along the (unidirectional) route r that is a minimum-cost route connecting node $\alpha(r)$ to node $\omega(r)$. Suppose that $a \to_r f$ is *not* a minimum cost route connecting a to f, i.e., there is another route s connecting a to f such that $C(s) < C(a \to_r f)$. Therefore, the route r' created by connecting together routes $\alpha(r) \to_r a$, s and $f \to_r \omega(r)$ has lower cost than r, which contradicts r's optimality. Consequently, the above assumption that $a \to_r f$ is not a minimum-cost path is false.   □

For example, in Figure A.2, route $r = \{b, a, f, d, e\}$ (with $C(r) = 7$) is, by inspection, a minimum-cost route from b to e. Note that this route costs less than the direct (single-link) route from b to e ($c_2 = 10$). Also note that the alternative (direct/single-link) subroute $\{a, d\}$ from a to d has higher cost ($c_9 = 3$) than the optimal subroute $\{a, f, d\}$ used by r (with $C(\{a, f, d\}) = 2$).

A *loop* is a route r that begins and ends at the same point, i.e., $\alpha(r) = \omega(r)$. A route is said to "possess a loop" if one of its subroutes is a loop.

Lemma A.1.2. *Among minimum-cost routes connecting two nodes in a network, there exists one that possesses no loops.*

Proof: By simply deleting a loop from a route r, we form a route r' that connects $\alpha(r)$ to $\omega(r)$ but with $C(r') \leq C(r)$, where equality holds only if the loop has zero cost. That is, removal of links from a route will reduce the cost for both (A.2) and (A.1). $\square$

For example, from Figure A.2, route $\{b, a, f, d, a, f, d, e\}$ connecting b to e has a loop $\{a, f, d, a\}$. Removing the loop yields the loop-free route $\{b, a, f, d, e\}$ also connecting b to e. For the remainder of this appendix, additive path costs (A.1) are assumed. Showing how the following results hold for path costs defined by (A.2) is left as an exercise.

A.2 LINK STATE ALGORITHMS

In link state routing approaches, nodes flood the network with the current costs of their outbound links; see Section 7.2.2. The flooding could take place periodically and/or whenever an outbound link's cost changes state. Suppose that each node v is currently in receipt of such link state information from every other node in the network graph. The nodes can therefore create a diagram of the entire network and label it with the (current) link costs, as in Figure A.2. Assume an at least temporarily static link state scenario in which each node has constructed the same diagram of the network. The objective of Dijkstra's algorithm described in this section is that each node finds the optimal (minimum-cost) route to every other node in the network. Thus, for each packet, a node can make an optimal forwarding decision (first hop along the optimal path) to one of its neighbors. It then relies on Lemma A.1.1 to ensure that each neighbor will continue to forward the packet along the optimal route.

The *predecessor* of node g on route r is denoted by $\pi_r(g)$. Because we assume that there is at most one (unidirectional) link from one given node to another, a special case of Lemma A.1.1 is:

Corollary A.2.1. *If r is a minimum-cost (unidirectional) route connecting node u to v, then $u \to_r \pi_r(v)$ is a minimum-cost route.*

With this corollary to Lemma A.1.1, we can state Dijkstra's algorithm as it operates in *every* node given current link-state information for the entire network. At node x, let $S \subset V$ be the set of nodes to which a minimum-cost path has been determined, where V is the complete set of nodes in the network graph. The idea of Dijkstra's algorithm is inspired by the previous corollary to build minimum-cost paths from the set S to neighboring nodes in $V \backslash S$, i.e., nodes that have a predecessor node in S to which minimum-cost routes from x have been found. For each node $y \in S$, Dijkstra's algorithm maintains the predecessor node $\pi(y)$ along the minimum-cost route from x. Dijkstra's algorithm is iterative and, so, we define ν as the node most recently added to the set S. Finally, let $\kappa(z)$ be the cost of the best *known* path from x to $z \notin S$ so far and let $c_{\nu \to z}$ be the cost of the (single) link from ν to z (i.e., implicitly, ν and z are neighbors).

Dijkstra's algorithm operating at node x is:

0. Initialize: $S = \{x\}$, $\nu = x$, $\kappa(x) = 0$, $\kappa(z) = \infty$ for all $z \neq x$, and $\pi(z) = x$ for all $z \in V$.

1. For all $z \in \mathcal{N}(\nu) \backslash S$, if

$$\kappa(z) \;>\; \kappa(\nu) + c_{\nu \to z}, \tag{A.4}$$

then set:

    1.1. $\pi(z) = \nu$ and

    1.2. $\kappa(z) = \kappa(\nu) + c_{\nu \to z}$.

2. For the node $y \in \mathcal{N}(S) \backslash S$ for which $\kappa(y)$ is minimal:

    2.1. $\nu = y$ and

    2.2. $S = S \cup \{y\}$.

3. If $S = V$, then stop, else go to Step 1.

The initialization step simply states that the minimum-cost cost path from x to x has no links and zero cost. Step 1 determines whether better routes to destination nodes in $\mathcal{N}(\nu) \backslash S$ are obtainable via the most recently added node to S, ν, acting as a predecessor to a destination node. Note that a minimum-cost path to a new node y in step 2 may have been discovered by the current or by a previous iteration's Step 1, i.e., we select among $y \in \mathcal{N}(S) \backslash S$ not necessarily $y \in \mathcal{N}(\nu) \backslash S$. It is left as a simple exercise to show (by contradiction using Lemma A.1.1) that the path to node y selected in step 2 is optimal. Also, it is left as an exercise to modify Dijkstra's algorithm for path costs are defined as the maximum of their component link costs. Dijkstra's algorithm is described in greater detail in [3, 48].

■ **EXAMPLE A.3**

The following table shows the operation of Dijkstra's algorithm at node a of Figure A.2. The states given are those found at the end of step 1 of each iteration. Iteration 0 is the initialization. With regard to iteration 1, note that the immediate neighbors of a are $\mathcal{N}(a) = \{b, d, f\}$. Finally note that at iteration 6, $S = V$, the entire set of nodes.

Iteration	S	$\pi, \kappa(a)$	$\pi, \kappa(b)$	$\pi, \kappa(d)$	$\pi, \kappa(e)$	$\pi, \kappa(f)$	$\pi, \kappa(g)$
0	a	$a, 0$	∞	∞	∞	∞	∞
1	a	$a, 0$	$a, 1$	$a, 3$	∞	$a, 1$	∞
2	a, b	$a, 0$	$a, 1$	$a, 3$	$b, 11$	$a, 1$	∞
3	a, b, f	$a, 0$	$a, 1$	$f, 2$	$b, 11$	$a, 1$	∞
4	a, b, f, d	$a, 0$	$a, 1$	$f, 2$	$d, 6$	$a, 1$	∞
5	a, b, f, d, e	$a, 0$	$a, 1$	$f, 2$	$d, 6$	$a, 1$	$e, 8$
6	a, b, f, d, e, g	$a, 0$	$a, 1$	$f, 2$	$d, 6$	$a, 1$	$e, 8$

By considering the predecessor nodes of optimal paths found by Dijkstra's algorithm, one can construct a tree rooted at node a that spans the entire graph and summarizes the forwarding decisions from a. In this example, the optimal spanning tree rooted at a has two branches: $a \to f \to d \to e \to g$ and $a \to b$. Thus, all packets relayed or spawned by a that are destined to nodes f, d, e or g are forwarded by a to f. One can easily check that Dijkstra's algorithm at f will result in a spanning tree that contains the branch $f \to d \to e \to g$ consistent with the optimal spanning tree rooted at a.

As mentioned previously, a node could flood the network immediately after one of its (outbound) links changes state, where individual floods may be made economical with the use of flood identifiers, TTL mechanisms (see Section 7.2.2) and a kind of reverse-path forwarding [139]. But to further economize on routing overhead and to make routes less sensitive to, say, faulty links whose costs may change frequently, a node could be permitted to only periodically flood the network with its link state information. The resulting staleness in link state information (even for small periods of time) may, however, lead to the temporary use of suboptimal routes or attempted use of no-longer existing routes.

A.3 DISTANCE VECTOR ALGORITHMS

Distributed Bellman-Ford algorithms involve exchanges of *routing tables* only among neighbors instead of link state information flooding the network. The routing table of a node x would have an entry for each destination node $z \neq x$ consisting of its best route r to z and the cost $C(r)$ of that route. Suppose x is in receipt of the current routing tables of all of its neighbors. For a given destination node z, node x considers the routes to z *via* each of its neighbors $y \in \mathcal{N}(x)$, i.e., the first hop $y \in \mathcal{N}(x)$ after the origin x is considered rather than the predecessor $\pi(z)$ to the destination z.

Assuming additive link costs, let $C(y \to z)$ be the *current* minimum cost among routes from y to z as advertised by y to x. Under the Bellman-Ford algorithm, node x computes

$$\min_{y \in \mathcal{N}(x)} c_{x \to y} + C(y \to z)$$

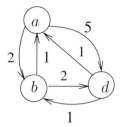

Figure A.3   A network graph with unidirectional links labeled by their cost c_l.

for each destination node z. The route that achieves the minimum becomes the entry for destination z in x's own routing table. The route minimum costs thus computed are advertised to x's neighbors in turn.

■ **EXAMPLE A.4**

The action of the distributed Bellman-Ford algorithm for the three-node network of Figure A.3 is given in Figure A.4. The entries in the *distance vectors* that are exchanged are indicated by circles. For example, after the initial step 1, node a transmits this distance (route cost) vector to each of its neighbors:

Destination	Route Cost
b	2
d	5

After step 2, there are no further changes to the routing tables of the nodes for the static network of Figure A.3.

The following result can also be argued by contradiction and its proof is left as an exercise.

Theorem A.3.1. *For a given, fixed set of link costs, the distributed Bellman-Ford algorithm will not terminate before optimal routes have been determined by all of the network's nodes.*

A distributed Bellman-Ford algorithm can be designed in which only the next-hop-from-the-origin node is kept in the routing tables rather than the complete route. In this case, the entries in the exchanged routing tables are simply pairs of destination node and route cost, i.e., distance vectors. Link costs may be very sensitive to traffic load, i.e., sensitive to the routing decisions themselves. Links may even be severed (their costs become infinite) by excessive traffic load, hardware or software faults, and, especially in a wireless

DISTANCE VECTOR ALGORITHMS **211**

At Node	Step 1			Step 2		
	Next Hop	Dest.	Route Cost	Next Hop	Dest.	Route Cost
a	b	b	2	b	b	2
	d	b	∞	d	b	6
	b	d	∞	b	d	4
	d	d	5	d	d	5
b	a	a	1	a	a	1
	d	a	∞	d	a	3
	a	d	∞	a	d	6
	d	d	2	d	d	2
d	a	a	1	a	a	1
	b	a	∞	b	a	2
	a	b	∞	a	b	3
	b	b	1	b	b	1

Figure A.4 Action of link-state algorithm.

setting, environmental conditions or node mobility. In response to changing link costs, the use of distributed distance vector routing may result in slow convergence to optimal routes (especially when link costs increase) because routes with loops are not immediately excluded from consideration. Simple techniques exist to address these problems [139, 172]. For example, if x itself is y's next hop to destination z, then y advertises infinite cost to z when it sends its distance vector table to x. Thus, x will not use y as its next hop to z, avoiding a possible two-hop loop back to x. This technique is called *poison reverse*. Other techniques such as DSDV [171] and hold-down (delaying updates; see p. 358 of [172]) also address the problem of route loops. BGP avoids loops by carrying (entire AS) path vectors rather than just distance vectors [101, 180].

APPENDIX B

SOLUTIONS OR REFERENCES FOR

SELECTED PROBLEMS

Chapter 1

1.12 Note that if either one of the nonnegative quantities $E(X\mathbf{1}\{X > 0\})$ or $E(-X\mathbf{1}\{X < 0\})$ is finite, we can define

$$EX \;=\; E(X\mathbf{1}\{X > 0\}) - E(-X\mathbf{1}\{X < 0\}).$$

1.13 The values of a and b that minimize the MSE are

$$b \;=\; E(X - aY) \;=\; EX - aEY,$$
$$a \;=\; \frac{\operatorname{cov}(X,Y)}{\operatorname{var}(Y)}.$$

1.15 The MGF of a binomial random variable is

$$m_{n,q}(\theta) \;=\; \sum_{k=0}^{n}\binom{n}{k}(q\mathrm{e}^{\theta})^{k}(1-q)^{n-k}$$
$$=\; (q\mathrm{e}^{\theta} + 1 - q)^{n}$$
$$=\; \left[(1 + q(\mathrm{e}^{\theta} - 1))^{1/(q(\mathrm{e}^{\theta}-1))}\right]^{nq(\mathrm{e}^{\theta}-1)}.$$

Therefore, as $q \to 0$ and $n \to \infty$ in such a way that $nq \to \lambda$,

$$m_{n,q}(\theta) \quad \to \quad \exp(\lambda(e^{\theta} - 1)),$$

which is the Poisson MGF as desired.

1.16   (a) Y_{λ} is Poisson distributed with $\lambda = EY$.

$$
\begin{aligned}
EY_{\lambda}^2 &= e^{-\lambda} \sum_{n=1}^{\infty} \frac{n^2 \lambda^n}{n!} \\
&= \lambda e^{-\lambda} \sum_{n=1}^{\infty} \frac{n \lambda^{n-1}}{(n-1)!} \\
&= \lambda e^{-\lambda} \frac{d}{d\lambda} \left(\sum_{n=1}^{\infty} \frac{\lambda^n}{(n-1)!} \right) \\
&= \lambda e^{-\lambda} \frac{d}{d\lambda} (\lambda e^{\lambda}) \\
&= \lambda^2 + \lambda.
\end{aligned}
$$

Thus, $\text{var}(Y_{\lambda}) = EY_{\lambda}^2 - (EY_{\lambda})^2 = \lambda$.

(b) Let m_{λ} be the MGF of $Z_{\lambda} = (Y_{\lambda} - \lambda)/\sqrt{\lambda}$. Since the MGF of Y_{λ} is $\exp(\lambda(e^{\theta} - 1))$,

$$m_{\lambda}(\theta) = \exp(-\sqrt{\lambda}\theta + \lambda e^{\theta/\sqrt{\lambda}} - \lambda).$$

Expanding about $\theta = 0$, we get

$$e^{\theta/\sqrt{\lambda}} = 1 + \frac{\theta}{\sqrt{\lambda}} \times \frac{\theta^2}{2\lambda} + o\left(\frac{1}{\lambda}\right)$$

where we recall that $o(x)$ ("little oh x") is a function satisfying $o(x)/x \to 0$ as $x \to 0$. After substituting this expansion, we get

$$
\begin{aligned}
m_{\lambda}(\theta) &= \exp\left(\frac{\theta^2}{2} + \lambda + o\left(\frac{1}{\lambda}\right)\right) \\
&\to \exp\left(\frac{\theta^2}{2}\right) \quad \text{as } \lambda \to \infty,
\end{aligned}
$$

which is the standard Gaussian MGF.

1.19 Recall that a CDF is a nondecreasing mapping $F : \mathbb{R} \to [0, 1]$. Thus,

$$P(F^{-1}(U) \le x) = P(U \le F(x)) = F(x)$$

where the second equality is simply due to the fact that U is uniform on $[0, 1]$.

1.20 The probability that all have a unique birthdays is

$$\frac{\binom{365}{n}}{365^n/n!} = 1\left(1 - \frac{1}{365}\right)\left(1 - \frac{2}{365}\right) \cdots \left(1 - \frac{n-1}{365}\right), \qquad \text{(B.1)}$$

where the quantity in the denominator of (B.1) is that obtained by choosing *with* replacement. So the answer is obtained by setting 1 minus the quantity in (B.1) to 0.5 and solving for n.

1.21 The likelihood that one spoofed response fails to match any of the transaction IDs of all of the forwarded queries is $x \equiv (1 - 2^{-16})^q$. So, the likelihood that all spoofed responses fail is x^s. So, solving

$$(1 - 2^{-16})^{qs} = (1 - 2^{-16})^{n^2} = 0.5$$

gives $n = \sqrt{\log(0.5)/\log(1 - 2^{-16})}$ rounded up to the nearest integer. See [208].

Chapter 2

2.3 Consider a differentiable function Φ on $\mathbb{R}^+$ satisfying

$$\Phi(0) = 1, \tag{B.2}$$
$$\lim_{x \to \infty} \Phi(x) = 0, \tag{B.3}$$
$$\Phi(x + y) = \Phi(x)\Phi(y) \quad \text{for all } x, y \in \mathbb{R}^+. \tag{B.4}$$

So, we can interpret $\Phi = 1 - F$, where F is the CDF of a continuous, nonnegative random variable with the memoryless property. We are required to show that, for $x \in \mathbb{R}^+$,

$$\Phi(x) = \exp(x\Phi'(0)),$$

where $\Phi'(0) < 0$. We can do this by differentiating (B.4) with respect to y, evaluating the result at $y = 0$, and then integrating with respect to x. That is, beginning with (B.4) above,

$$\Phi'(x + y) = \Phi(x)\Phi'(y)$$
$$\Rightarrow \Phi'(x) = \Phi(x)\Phi'(0).$$

Therefore, by integrating, we get

$$\Phi(x) = A \exp(x\Phi'(0))$$

for some constant A. Finally, (B.2) above implies that $A = 1$ and (B.3) implies that $\Phi'(0) < 0$ as desired.

2.5

$$
\begin{aligned}
P(X_1 + X_2 \leq \varepsilon) &= \int_0^\varepsilon \int_{x_1}^\varepsilon \lambda_1 e^{-\lambda_1 x_1} \lambda_2 e^{-\lambda_2 x_2} \, dx_2 \, dx_1 \\
&= \int_0^\varepsilon \lambda_1 e^{-\lambda_1 x_1} \left(e^{-\lambda_2 x_1} - e^{-\lambda_2 \varepsilon} \right) dx_1 \\
&= \frac{\lambda_1}{\lambda_1 + \lambda_2} \left(1 - e^{-(\lambda_1 + \lambda_2)\varepsilon} \right) - e^{-\lambda_2 \varepsilon} \left(1 - e^{-\lambda_1 \varepsilon} \right) \\
&= \frac{\lambda_1}{\lambda_1 + \lambda_2} ((\lambda_1 + \lambda_2)\varepsilon + o(\varepsilon))(1 - \lambda_2 \varepsilon + o(\varepsilon)) \\
&\quad \times (\lambda_1 \varepsilon + o(\varepsilon)) \\
&= \lambda_1 \varepsilon - \lambda_1 \varepsilon + o(\varepsilon) \\
&= o(\varepsilon).
\end{aligned}
$$

2.6 Find the only $n \times n$ matrix R such that $\underline{\pi}_0^{\mathrm{T}} R = \underline{\sigma}^{\mathrm{T}}$ for all initial distributions $\underline{\pi}_0$.

2.14 Hint:

$$P(X_i \in (x_i, x_i + \mathrm{d}x_i), \ i = 1, ..., n, \ N(I) = n)$$

$$= \lambda e^{-\lambda x_1}\,\mathrm{d}x_1 \cdot \left(\prod_{i=2}^{n} \lambda e^{-\lambda(x_i - x_{i-1})}\,\mathrm{d}x_i \right) \cdot e^{-\lambda(T - x_n)}$$

and $N(I)$ is Poisson distributed with parameter λT.

2.16 Using the hint and substituting $p \equiv |I|/|\hat{I}|$ give

$$
\begin{aligned}
E \exp(sN^Y(I)) &= \sum_{r=0}^{\infty} (pe^s + 1 - p)^r \frac{(\lambda|\hat{I}|)^r e^{-\lambda|\hat{I}|}}{r!} \\
&= e^{-\lambda|\hat{I}|} \sum_{r=0}^{\infty} \frac{(\lambda(|I|e^s + |R_Y|))^r}{r!} \\
&= \exp(\lambda|I|(e^s - 1))
\end{aligned}
$$

as desired.

2.22 See [130].

2.23 $\mathbf{P}_{0,1} = \frac{2}{5}$, $\mathbf{P}_{0,2} = \frac{3}{5}$, $\mathbf{P}_{1,2} = 1$, $\mathbf{P}_{2,0} = 1$, otherwise $\mathbf{P}_{n,m} = 0$.

Chapter 3

3.6

$$
\begin{aligned}
P(W(t) \le x) &= P\left(\sum_{j=1}^{Q(t)} \tilde{S}_j \le x \right) \\
&= \sum_{n=0}^{\infty} P\left(\sum_{j=1}^{n} \tilde{S}_j \le x \right) P(Q(t) = n) \\
&= e^{-\rho} + \sum_{n=1}^{\infty} \frac{\rho^n e^{-\rho}}{n!} \int_0^x \frac{\mu^n y^{n-1} e^{-\mu y}}{n!}\,\mathrm{d}y.
\end{aligned}
$$

3.8 (c) Let W be distributed as the steady-state workload and X be an exponentially distributed random variable independent of W. By PASTA, upon arrival of a typical *batch*, the workload distribution is that of W. But, the *second* job of the typical batch sees a distribution of $W + X$. Thus, the distribution of the workload upon arrival of a typical *job* is that of $W + X/2$.

3.9 (b) $3\lambda < \mu$.

(c) $P(Q > 0) = 1 - \rho = 1 - 3\lambda/\mu$.

(d) $q_{1,0} = \mu > 0$ but $q_{0,1} = 0$. So, the detailed balance equation $\sigma_0 q_{0,1} = \sigma_1 q_{1,0}$ is not true and, therefore, the Markov chain is not time reversible.

(f) $0 = \sum_n \sigma_n q_{n,3}$, i.e.,

$$
\begin{aligned}
0 &= q_{0,3}\sigma_0 - (q_{3,4} + q_{3,2})\sigma_3 + q_{4,3}\sigma_4 \\
&= \lambda\sigma_0 - (\lambda + 2\mu)\sigma_3 + 2\mu\sigma_4.
\end{aligned}
$$

(g) Considering the likelihood that an arriving job is blocked and using PASTA to condition on the queue backlog upon arrival of a batch,

$$\tfrac{1}{3}\sigma_2 + \tfrac{2}{3}\sigma_3 + \sigma_4.$$

3.10 Consider a real time $t \geq \theta$ and let $i = A[\theta, t]$. For an arbitrary single-server queue,

$$W(t) = (W(a) - (t-a))^+,$$

where $a \leq t$ is the most recent (largest) job arrival time prior to time t; see Figure 3.5. In this case

$$a = \theta + \frac{i-1}{\lambda}.$$

By taking expectations of both sides of the previous equation for W, we get

$$EW(t) = E(W(a) - (t-a))^+.$$

To conclude, recall that $t - a$ is uniformly distributed on $[0, 1/\lambda]$ (since t is a "typical" time).

3.14 (a) By PASTA, the blocking probability is

$$b \equiv \frac{\rho^K}{1 + \rho + \rho^2 + \cdots \rho^K};$$

see Section 2.5.1.

(b) The net arrival rate is $(1-b)\lambda$ jobs per second. So, by Little's theorem, the sojourn time of jobs not blocked is

$$(1-b)\lambda \times \frac{\sum_{k=1}^{K} k\rho^k}{\sum_{k=0}^{K} \rho^k}.$$

3.15 See Examples 5-12 and 5-13 of [226].

Chapter 4

4.1 See [127].

4.3 (a) For the packet of length l arriving at time T, compute its delay

$$\delta \equiv \max\{d, T\} + \frac{l}{\rho} - T.$$

If $\delta > \sigma/\rho$ then discard the packet, else set

$$d = \delta + a.$$

Thus, only a single state variable, d, is required.

4.8 See [73, 227].

4.10 See [109].

4.11 See [109, 110].

4.12 Assuming the nodes are ordered, the number of conflict-free assignments is $K(K-1)(K-2)\cdots(K-N+1)$. Thus, the probability of collision in a time slot is

$$1 - \frac{K!/N!}{N^K}.$$

4.13 (a) The vector $\underline{s}$ has entries $s_j = \gamma_j R_j \sigma^2 / (W h_{b_j j})$ and the matrix A has entries $A_{j,j} = 0$ and $A_{j,k} = \gamma_j R_j h_{b_j k} / (W h_{b_j j})$ for $j \neq k$.

(b) If $\det(A) \neq 1$, then the unique fixed point for the unconstrained dynamics exists:

$$\underline{p}^* \;=\; (I-A)^{-1}\underline{s}.$$

(c) If the eigenvalues of A all have modulus < 1 (equivalently, A is doubly substochastic), the unconstrained iteration $\underline{p}^i$ will converge to $\underline{p}^*$.

See [228].

Chapter 5

5.3 A detailed balance equation when $x_n > 0$ is

$$\sigma(\underline{x})\mu_n r_{n,m} = \sigma(\delta_{n,m}\underline{x})\mu_m r_{m,n}.$$

After substitution of the product form expression for σ and cancellation, we get

$$\lambda_n r_{n,m} \;=\; \lambda_m r_{m,n}.$$

This is clearly *not* true in general, so the Jackson network is not time reversible in general.

5.7 Following the hint,

$$\mathsf{E}\left(\frac{B_t}{N_t}\Big| N_t > 0\right) \;=\; \mathsf{E}\left(\mathsf{E}\left(\frac{B_t}{N_t}\Big| N_t\right)\Big| N_t > 0\right)$$

$$= \; \mathsf{E}\left(\frac{1}{N_t}\mathsf{E}(B_t \mid N_t)\Big| N_t > 0\right).$$

So, by the conditional uniformity property of a Poisson process,

$$\mathsf{E}(B_t \mid N_t) \;=\; N_t \mathsf{E}\frac{1}{t}\int_0^t \mathbf{1}\{X(s) \in \mathcal{B}\}\mathrm{d}s$$

$$= \; N_t \mathsf{P}(X \in \mathcal{B}).$$

where the last equality is due to the stationarity of X. Substituting this into the previous equation gives

$$E\left(\frac{B_t}{N_t} \,\Big|\, N_t > 0\right) = P(X \in \mathcal{B}).$$

The desired result then follows from PASTA. See the appendix of [150].

5.8 (a) At any given time, the average number of mobiles in the cell is

$$L \;:=\; \delta\pi(\Delta/2)^2.$$

The average sojourn time of a mobile in a cell is

$$
\begin{aligned}
W &\equiv \int_{v_{\min}}^{v_{\max}} \int_0^\pi \frac{\Delta \sin\theta}{v} \frac{d\theta}{\pi} f(v) dv \\
&= \frac{2\Delta}{\pi} \int_{v_{\min}}^{v_{\max}} \frac{1}{v} f(v) dv,
\end{aligned}
$$

where $2\Delta/\pi$ is the average length of a chord in a circle of diameter Δ. Thus, by Little's formula,

$$\lambda_m \;=\; \frac{L}{W} \;=\; \frac{\delta\pi^2}{8\beta}\Delta,$$

where $\beta := \int_{v_{\min}}^{v_{\max}} \frac{1}{v} f(v) dv$ is assumed finite. Clearly, the calculation also works if velocity and direction of a mobile in a cell are dependent.

(b) In this case, simply replace the term $f(v)/\pi$ in the first expression for W above by the joint distribution $f(\theta, v)$.

Chapter 6

6.5 See [124].

6.6 (b) $U_r'(x_r^*) = M^* + U_r'(x_r^*)x_r^*/c \geq M^*$ and, since U_r' is decreasing (U_r is concave), this implies $(U_r')^{-1}(M^*) \geq x_r^*$. Summing over r gives $V(M^*) \geq c = V(\hat{M})$, where the function $V \equiv \sum_r (U_r')^{-1}$. Finally, note that V is a decreasing function.

Chapter 7

7.1 Since each query results in an average of $E(N/f)$ new cache entries in the peer group N,

$$Ef = Np = \frac{1}{\mu}(qE\frac{N}{f}) \geq \frac{q}{\mu} \cdot \frac{N}{Ef} = \frac{q}{\mu p},$$

where the second equality is Little's theorem and the inequality is Jensen's.

7.3   (a) It is straightforward to check that

$$\mathsf{E}A_n \;=\; \int_0^{2\pi} \mathsf{P}(A_n > x)\,\mathrm{d}x \;=\; \frac{2\pi}{n}.$$

To compute the standard deviation $\sigma(A_n)$, compute the PDF $-\frac{\mathrm{d}}{\mathrm{d}x}\mathsf{P}(A_n > x)$, directly evaluate $\mathsf{E}A_n^2$ (integrate by parts twice), and substitute into $\sigma^2(A_n) = \mathsf{E}A_n^2 - (\mathsf{E}A_n)^2$.

(b) Since the variance of the sum of uncorrelated random variables is the sum of their variances,

$$\sigma^2(B_{n,k}) = k\sigma^2(A_{nk}).$$

7.5 Note that

$$\Phi(z) \;=\; \left(\frac{2\pi - 2z}{2\pi}\right)^{\nu}$$

and follow the hint.

7.8 Consider a $k \times L$ submatrix $\tilde{\mathbf{A}}^{\mathrm{T}}$ of $\mathbf{A}^{\mathrm{T}}$ with rank $k = \mathrm{rank}(\tilde{\mathbf{A}}) < L$ and the corresponding subvector $\underline{\tilde{\Delta}}$ whose entries are all estimated, i.e.,

$$\underline{\tilde{\Delta}} \;=\; \tilde{\mathbf{A}}^{\mathrm{T}}\underline{\delta}.$$

An estimate of the link dropping rates can then be computed via a generalized inverse of $\tilde{\mathbf{A}}^{\mathrm{T}}$ giving the minimum-norm solution to the underdetermined set of equations above [30]:

$$\underline{\tilde{\delta}} \;=\; \tilde{\mathbf{A}}(\tilde{\mathbf{A}}^{\mathrm{T}}\tilde{\mathbf{A}})^{-1}\underline{\tilde{\Delta}}.$$

REFERENCES

1. E. Aarts and J. Korst. *Simulated Annealing and Boltzmann Machines*. Wiley, New York, 1989.

2. Agilent, Inc. Internet packet length distribution. Available: http://advanced.comms.agilent.com/insight/2001-08/Questions/traffic_gen.htm, 2001.

3. R.K. Ahuja, T.L. Magnanti, and J.B. Orlin. *Network Flows*. Prentice-Hall, Englewood Cliffs, NJ, 1993.

4. V. Anantharam and T. Konstantopoulos. A methodology for the design of optimal traffic shapers in communication networks. *IEEE Trans. Automatic Control*, Vol. 44, No. 3:583–586, Mar. 1999.

5. V. Anantharam and T. Konstantopoulos. Optimality and interchangeability of leaky buckets. In *Proc. 32nd Allerton Conference*, Monticello, IL, Oct. 1994, pp. 235–244.

6. S. Androutsellis-Theotokis and D. Spinellis. A survey of peer-to-peer content distribution technologies. *ACM Comput. Surv.*, Vol. 36, No. 4:335–371, 2004.

7. P. Antoniadis, C. Courcoubetis, and R. Mason. Comparing economic incentives in peer-to-peer networks. *Computer Networks*, Vol. 46, No. 1:133–146, 2004.

8. P. Arabshahi, A. Gray, I. Kassabalidis, A. Das, S.Narayanan, M. El-Sharkawi, and R. Marks II. Adaptive routing in wireless communication networks using swarm intelligence. In *Proc. 9th AIAA Int. Communications Satellite Systems Conf.*, Toulouse, France, Apr. 2001, pp. 17–20.

9. S. Asmussen. *Applied Probability and Queues*. Wiley, Chichester West Sussex, 1987.

10. H. Attiya and J. Welch. *Distributed Computing: Fundamentals, Simulations, and Advanced Topics*, 2nd ed. Wiley, Hoboken, NJ, 2004.

11. Avalanche: File swarming with network coding, http://research.microsoft.com/~pablo/avalanche.aspx.

12. D. Awduche, L. Berger, D. Gan, T. Li, V. Srinivasan, and G. Swallow. RSVP-TE: Extensions to RSVP for LSP tunnels. *IETF RFC 3209*, Available: http://www.ietf.org, Dec. 2001.

13. D. Awerbuch and C. Scheideler. Towards a scalable and robust DHT. In *Proc. 18th ACM SPAA*, 2006.

14. F. Baccelli and P. Brémaud. *Elements of Queueing Theory*, 2nd ed. Springer-Verlag, New York, 2003.

15. F. Baccelli, S. Machiraju, D. Veitch, and J. Bolot. The role of PASTA in network measurements. In *Proc. ACM SIGCOMM*, Pisa, Sept. 2006.

16. C. Balasubramanian and J.J. Garcia-Luna-Aceves. Shortest multipath routing using labeled distances. In *Proc. IEEE MASS*, Oct. 2004.

17. J. Baras and H. Mehta. A probabilistic emergent routing algorithm for mobile ad hoc networks. In *Proc. Workshop on Modeling and Optimization in Mobile, Ad Hoc and Wireless Networks*, Sophia-Antipolis, France, Mar. 2003.

18. S.A. Baset and H. Schulzrinne. An analysis of the Skype peer-to-peer Internet telephony protocol. Available: http://www.citebase.org/cgi-bin/citations?id=oai:arXiv.org:cs/0412017, 2004.

19. A.R. Bharambe, C. Herley, and V.N. Padmanabhan. Analyzing and improving a BitTorrent network's performance mechanisms. In *Proc. IEEE INFOCOM*, Barcelona, 2006.

20. B.N. Bhattacharya and E.C. Waymire. *Stochastic Processes and Applications*. Wiley, New York, 1990.

21. R.N. Bhattacharya. On the functional central limit theorem and the law of the iterated logarithm for Markov processes. *Z. Wahrsheinlichkeitstheorie verw. Gebiete*, Vol. 60:185–201, 1982.

22. G. Bianchi. Performance analysis of the IEEE 802.11 distributed coordination function. *IEEE J. Selected Areas Commun. (JSAC)*, Mar. 2000.

23. BitTorrent, http://www.bittorrent.com.

24. S. Blake, D. Black, M. Carlson, E. Davies, and Z. Wang. An architecture for Differentiated Services. *IETF RFC 2475*, Available: http://www.ietf.org, Dec. 1998.

25. M. Blaze, J. Feigenbaum, and A.D. Keromytis. The role of trust management in distributed systems security. In G. Vitek and C.D. Jensen (Eds.), *Secure Internet Programming*, Springer LNCS Vol. 1603. Springer, Berlin, 1999, pp. 185–210.

26. C. Bordenave, S. Foss, and V. Shneer. A random multiple access protocol with spatial interactions. In *Proc. Workshop on Spatially Stochastic Wireless Networks (SpaSWiN)*, Cyprus, Apr. 2007.

27. K.C. Border. *Fixed Point Theorems with Applications to Economics and Game Theory*. Cambridge University Press, London, 1985.

28. S. Boyd and L. VandenBerghe. *Convex Optimization*. Cambridge University Press, London, 2004.

29. J. Broch, D.A. Maltz, D.B. Johnson, Y.-C. Hu, and J. Jetcheva. A performance comparison of multi-hop ad hoc network routing protocols. In *Proc. ACM MobiCom*, 1998.

30. W.L. Brogan. *Modern Control Theory*. Prentice-Hall, Englewood Cliffs, NJ, 1991.

31. S. Buchegger and J.-Y. Le Boudec. Robust reputation system for P2P and mobile ad-hoc networks. In *Proc. 2nd Workshop on Economics of Peer-to-Peer Systems*, Berkeley, CA, June 2004.

32. M. Caesar, T. Condie, J. Kannan, K. Lakshminarayanan, S. Shenker, and I. Stoica. Routing on flat labels. In *Proc. ACM SIGCOMM*, Pisa, 2006.

33. F. Cali, M. Conti, and E. Gregori. IEEE 802.11 protocol: Design and performance evaluation of an adaptive backoff mechanism. *IEEE J. Selected Areas Commun. (JSAC)*, Sept. 2000.

34. G. Di Caro and M. Dorigo. Mobile agents for adaptive routing. In *Proc. of the 31st Annual Hawaii International Conference on System Sciences(HICSS)*, Kohala Coast, HI, 1998.

35. C.G. Cassandras. *Discrete Event Systems: Modeling and Performance Analysis.* Irwin, Homewood, IL, 1993.

36. M. Castro, P. Druschel, A. Ganesh, A. Rowstron, and D.S. Wallach. Security for structured peer-to-peer overlay networks. In *Proc. 5th USENIX Symposium on Operating Systems Design and Implementation (OSDI)*, Boston, MA, Dec. 2002.

37. C.-S. Chang, D.-S. Lee, and C.-M. Lien. Load balanced Birkoff-von Neumann switches, part I: One-stage buffering. *Computer Commun.*, Vol. 25, No. 6, 2002.

38. C.-S. Chang, D.-S. Lee, and C.-M. Lien. Load balanced Birkoff-von Neumann switches with resequencing, part II: Multistage buffering. *Computer Commun.*, Vol. 25, No. 6, 2002.

39. J.-H. Chang and L. Tassiulas. Energy conserving routing in wireless ad-hoc networks. In *Proc. IEEE INFOCOM*, Tel Aviv, Israel, Mar. 2000.

40. Y. Chawathe, S. Ratnasamy, L. Breslau, N. Lanham, and S. Shenker. Making Gnutella-like P2P systems scalable. In *Proc. Conf. on Application Technologies, Architectures and Protocols for Computer Communications*, 2003.

41. X. Chen and J. Heidemann. Detecting early worm propagation through packet matching. Technical Report ISI-TR-2004-585. University of Southern California, ISI, Feb. 2004.

42. Y. Chen, D. Bindel, and R.H. Katz. Tomography-based overlay network monitoring. In *Proc. Internet Measurement Conference (IMC)*, Miami Beach, FL, Oct. 2003.

43. Y. Chu, A. Ganjam, T.S.E. Ng, S.G. Rao, K. Sripanidkulchai, J. Zhan, and H. Zhang. Early experience with an Internet broadcast system based on overlay multicast. In *Proc. USENIX*, June 2004.

44. K. L. Chung. *A Course in Probability.* Academic, San Diego, CA, 1974.

45. S.-P. Chung and K. Ross. Reduced load approximations for multirate loss networks. *IEEE Trans. Commun.*, Vol. 41:1222-1231, 1993.

46. D. Clarke, J.-E. Elien, C. Ellison, M. Fredette, A. Morcos, and R.L. Rivest. Certificate chain discovery in SPKI/SDSI. *Journal of Computer Security*, Vol. 9, No. 4:285-322, Jan. 2001.

47. I. Clarke, S.G. Miller, O. Sandberg, B. Wiley, and T.W. Hong. Protecting freedom of information online with Freenet. *IEEE Internet Computing*, Jan. 2002.

48. T. Cormen, C. Leiserson, and R. Rivest. Introduction to Algorithms. MIT Press, Cambridge, MA, 1990.

49. T.M. Cover and J.A. Thomas. *Elements of Information Theory*, Wiley Series in Telecommunications. Wiley, New York, 1991.

50. R.L. Cruz. Service burstiness and dynamic burstiness measures: A framework. *J. High-Speed Networks*, Vol. 1, No. 2:105–127, 1992.

51. R.L. Cruz. SCED+: Efficient management of quality of service guarantees. In *Proc. IEEE INFOCOM*, San Francisco, Mar. 1998.

52. R.L. Cruz and A.P. Blanc. A service abstraction with applications to network calculus. In *Proc. Allerton Conf.*, Allerton, IL, Oct. 2003.

53. J.N. Daigle and J.D. Langford. Models for analysis of packet voice communication systems. *IEEE J. Selected Areas Commun. (JSAC)*, Vol. 6:847–855, 1986.

54. Y.K. Dalal and R.M. Metcalfe. Reverse path forwarding of broadcast packets. *Commun. of the ACM*, Vol. 21, No. 12:1040–1048, Dec. 1978.

55. D.J. Daley and D. Vere-Jones. *An Introduction to the Theory of Point Processes.* Springer-Verlag, New York, 1988.

56. W.J. Dally and B. Towles. *Principles and Practices of Interconnection Networks.* Morgan Kaufmann, San Francisco, 2004.

57. D. DeFigueiredo, E.T. Barr, and S.F. Wu. Trust is in the eye of the beholder. Technical Report CSE-2007-9. Computer Science Dept, UC Davis, March 2007.

58. D. DeFigueiredo and E.T. Barr. TrustDavis: A non-exploitable online reputation system. In *Proc. 7th IEEE International Conference on E-Commerce Technology (CEC)*, July 2005.

59. M. Demirbas and H. Ferhatosmanoglu. Peer-to-peer spatial queries in sensor networks. In *Proc. Peer-to-Peer Computing*, 2003.

60. R. Dingledine, N. Mathewson, and P. Syverson. Tor: The second-generation onion router. In *Proc. 13th USENIX Security Symposium*, Aug. 2004.

61. R.O. Duda, P.E. Hart, and D.G. Stork. *Pattern Classification*, 2nd ed. Wiley, New York, 2001.

62. R. Durrett. *Probability: Theory and Examples.* Wadsworth and Brooks, Pacific Grove, CA, 1991.

63. R. Durrett. *The Essentials of Probability.* Duxbury, Belmont, CA, 1994.

64. eDonkey, http://www.edonkey.com.

65. T. ElBatt and A. Ephremides. Joint scheduling and power control for wireless ad hoc networks. In *Proc. IEEE INFOCOM*, 2002.

66. A. Eryilmaz and R. Srikant. Joint congestion control, routing and MAC for stability and fairness in wireless networks. In *Proc. Int. Zurich Seminar on Commun.*, Feb. 2006.

67. L. Feinstein, D. Schackenberg, R. Balupari, and D. Kindred. Statistical approaches to DDoS attack detection and prevention. In *Proc. DARPA Information Survivability Conference and Exposition*, Apr. 2003.

68. M. Feldman, K. Lai, I. Stoica, and J. Chuang. Robust incentive techniques for peer-to-peer networks. In *Proc. 5th ACM Conference on Electronic Commerce*, New York, NY, 2004, pp. 102–111.

69. W. Feller. *An Introduction to Probability Theory and Its Applications.* Wiley, New York, 1968.

70. G. Feng and C. Douligeris. Fast algorithms for delay-constrained unicast QoS routing. In *Proc. INFORMS*, Miami, FL, Nov. 2001.

71. D. Ferrari and D.C. Verma. A scheme for real-time channel establishment in wide-area networks. *IEEE J. Selected Areas Commun. (JSAC)*, Vol. 8, No. 3:368–379, 1990.

72. A. Fiat, J. Saia, and M. Young. Making Chord robust to Byzantine attacks. In *Proc. 13th Annual European Symposium on Algorithms (ESA)*, Springer LNCS Vol. 3669. Springer, Berlin, 2005, pp. 803–814.

73. N.R. Figueira and J. Pasquale. An upper bound on delay for the VirtualClock service discipline. *IEEE/ACM Trans. Networking*, Vol. 3, No. 4:399–408, Aug. 1995.

74. G.F. Fishman. *Monte Carlo Concepts, Algorithms, and Applications.* Springer-Verlag, New York, 1995.

75. I. Foster and A. Iamnitchi. On death, taxes, and the convergence of peer-to-peer and grid computing. In *Proc. IPTPS*, Berkeley, CA, Feb. 2003.

76. C. Fragouli, J.-Y. Le Boudec, and J. Widmer. Network coding: An instant primer. *ACM SIGCOMM: Computer Commun. Rev.*, Vol. 36, No. 1:63–68, Jan. 2006.

77. M.J. Freedman, E. Sit, J. Cates, and R. Morris. Tarzan: A peer-to-peer anonymizing network layer. In *Proc. First International Workshop on Peer-to-Peer Systems*, Cambridge, MA, 2002.

78. J.A. Garay and Y. Moses. Fully polynomial Byzantine agreement for $n > 3t$ processors in $t+1$ rounds. *SIAM Journal on Computing*, Vol. 27, No. 1:247-290, 1998.

79. M.R. Garey and D.S. Johnson. *Computers and Intractability.* W.H. Freeman and Co., 1979.

80. L. Georgiadis, R. Guerin, V. Peris, and K.N. Sivarajan. Efficient network QoS provisioning based on per node traffic shaping. *IEEE/ACM Trans. Networking*, Vol. 4, No. 4:482–501, Aug. 1996.

81. L. Georgiadis, M.J. Neely, and L. Tassiulas. Resource allocation and cross-layer control in wireless networks. *Found. Trends Networking*, Vol. 1, No. 1:1–144, 2006.

82. C. Gkantsidis and P.R. Rodriguez. Network coding for large scale content distribution. In *Proc. IEEE INFOCOM*, Miami, FL, 2006.

83. J. Goldman. Stochastic point processes: Limit theorems. *Ann. Math. Stat.*, Vol. 38:721–729, 1967.

84. S.J. Golestani. A framing strategy for congestion management. *IEEE J. Selected Areas Commun. (JSAC)*, Vol. 9, No. 7:1064–1077, Sept. 1991.

85. R.M. Gray. *Entropy and Information Theory*. Springer Verlag, 1991.

86. L. Guibas, D. Knuth, and M. Sharir. Randomized incremental construction of Delaunay and Voronoi diagram. *Algorithmica*, Vol. 7:381–413, 1992.

87. M. Gunes, U. Sorges, and I. Bouazizi. ARA–The ant-colony based routing algorithm for MANETs. In *Proc. of International Conference on Parallel Processing Workshops (ICPPW)*, Vancouver, B.C., Canada, Aug. 2002.

88. L. Guo, S. Chen, Z. Xiao, E. Tan, X. Ding, and X. Zhang. Measurements, modeling and analysis of BitTorrent-like systems. In *Proc. Internet Measurement Conference (IMC)*, Oct. 2005.

89. R. Gupta and A.K. Somani. An incentive driven lookup protocol for chord-based peer-to-peer (p2p) networks. In *Proc. International Conference on High Performance Computing*, Bangalore, India, Dec. 2004.

90. B. Hajek. Cooling schedules for optimal annealing. *Math. Oper. Res.*, Vol. 13, No. 2:311–329, 1988.

91. B. Hajek and G. Sasaki. Link scheduling in polynomial time. *IEEE Trans. Inform. Theory*, 1988.

92. D. Hausheer and B. Stiller. PeerMart: The technology for a distributed auction-based market for peer-to-peer services. In *Proc. IEEE ICC*, May 2005.

93. D. Hausheer and B. Stiller. PeerMint: Decentralized and secure accounting for peer-to-peer applications. In *Proc. IFIP Networking Conference*, May 2005.

94. J. Heinanen, T. Finland, and R. Guerin. A single rate three color marker. *IETF RFC 2697*, Available: http://www.ietf.org, 1999.

95. J. Heinanen, T. Finland, and R. Guerin. A two rate three color marker. *IETF RFC 2698*, Available: http://www.ietf.org, 1999.

96. H. Higaki and S. Umeshima. Multiple-route ad hoc on-demand distance vector (MRAODV) routing protocol. In *Proc. 18th International Parallel and Distributed Processing Symposium (IPDPS)*, Santa Fe, New Mexico, Apr. 2004.

97. R. Holley and D. Stroock. Simulated annealing via Sobolev inequalities. *Commun. Math. Phys.*, Vol. 115, No. 4:553–569, Sept. 1988.

98. D. Hong and S. Rappaport. Traffic model and performance analysis for cellular mobile radio telephone systems with prioritized and non-prioritized hand-off procedures. *IEEE Trans. Vehicular Technol.*, VT-35:77–92, Aug. 1986.

99. R.A. Horn and C.R. Johnson. *Matrix Analysis*. Cambridge University Press, London, 1987.

100. J.Y. Hui. Network, transport, and switching integration for broadband communications. *IEEE Network Mag.*, Mar. 1988, pp. 40–51.

101. C. Huitma. *Routing in the Internet*. Prentice-Hall, Englewood Cliffs, NJ, 1995.

102. A. Hung and G. Kesidis. Bandwidth scheduling for wide-area ATM networks using virtual finishing times. *IEEE/ACM Trans. Networking*, Vol. 4, No. 1:49–54, Feb. 1996.

103. A. Iamnitchi, M. Ripeanu, and I. Foster. Small-world file-sharing communities. In *Proc. IEEE INFOCOM*, Hong Kong, 2004.

104. K. Ito. *Introduction to Probability Theory*. Cambridge University Press, New York, 1978.

105. V. Jacobson, K. Nichols, and K. Poduri. RED in a different light. Technical report. Cisco Systems, Draft of Sept. 30, 1999.

106. R. Jain. *The Art of Computer Systems Performance Analysis*. Wiley, New York, 1991.

107. P.B. Jeon and G. Kesidis. Avoiding malicious packet dropping in ad hoc networks using multi-path routing. In *Proc. 43rd Allerton Conference on Communications, Control and Computing*, Allerton, IL, Oct. 2005.

108. P.B. Jeon and G. Kesidis. Robust multipath and multipriority routing in MANETs using both energy and delay metrics. In *Proc. Performance Evaluation of Wireless Ad Hoc and Ubiquitous Networks (PE-WASUN)*, Montreal, Oct. 2005.

109. Y. Jin and G. Kesidis. Equilibria of a noncooperative game for heterogeneous users of an ALOHA network. *IEEE Commun. Let.*, Vol. 6, No. 7:282–284, 2002.

110. Y. Jin and G. Kesidis. Dynamics of usage-priced communication networks: The case of a single bottleneck resource. *IEEE/ACM Trans. Networking*, Oct. 2005.

111. S. Jiwasurat, G. Kesidis, and D. Miller. Hierarchical shaped deficit round-robin (HSDRR) scheduling. In *Proc. IEEE GLOBECOM*, St. Louis, Dec. 2005.

112. R. Johari, S. Mannor, and J.N. Tsitsiklis. Efficiency loss in a network resource allocation game: The case of elastic supply. *IEEE Trans. Automatic Control*, Vol. 50, No. 5, 2005.

113. J. Jung, V. Paxson, A.W. Berger, and H. Balakrishnan. Fast portscan detection using sequential hypothesis testing. In *IEEE Symposium on Security and Privacy 2004*, Oakland, CA, May 2004.

114. A. Jøsang, R. Ismail, and C. Boyd. A survey of trust and reputation systems for online service provisioning. *Decision Support Systems*, 2006.

115. S.D. Kamvar, M.T. Schlosser, and H. Garcia-Molina. The Eigentrust algorithm for reputation management in P2P networks. In *Proc. 12th International Conference on World Wide Web (WWW)*, New York, NY, 2003, pp. 640–651.

116. D. Karger, E. Lehman, F.T. Leighton, M. Levine, D. Lewin, and R. Panigrahy. Consistent hashing and random trees: distributed caching protocols for relieving hot spots on the world wide web. In *Proc. ACM Symp. Theory Computing*, May 1997, pp. 654–663.

117. D. Karger and M. Ruhl. Simple efficient load balancing algorithms for peer-to-peer systems. In *Proc. 16th ACM Symposium on Parallelism in Algorithms and Architectures (SPAA)*, 2004.

118. S. Karlin and H.M. Taylor. *A First Course in Stochastic Processes*, 2nd ed. Academic, New York, 1975.

119. S. Karlin and H.M. Taylor. *A Second Course in Stochastic Processes*. Academic, New York, 1981.

120. M.J. Karol, M.G. Hluchyj, and S.P. Morgan. Input versus output queueing on a space-division packet switch. *IEEE Trans. Commun.*, Vol. 35, No. 12:1347–1356, 1987.

121. KaZaALite, http://www.kazaalite.nl.

122. F.P. Kelly. Routing in circuit switched networks: Optimization, shadow prices and decentral-ization. *Adv. Appl. Prob.*, Vol. 1:112–144, 1988.

123. F.P. Kelly. Routing in circuit-switched networks. *Ann. Appl. Prob.*, Vol. 1:317–378, 1991.

124. F.P. Kelly. Charging and rate control for elastic traffic. *Eur. Trans. Telecommun.*, 8:33–37, 1997.

125. A. Keromytis, V. Misra, and D. Rubenstein. SOS: Secure Overlay Services. In *Proc. ACM SIGCOMM*, Pittsburgh, Sept. 2002.

126. G. Kesidis. *ATM Network Performance*, 2nd ed. Kluwer Academic Publishers, Boston, MA, 1999.

127. G. Kesidis, K. Chakraborty and L. Tassiulas. Traffic shaping for a loss system. *IEEE Commun. Let.*, 4, No. 12:417–419, Dec. 2000.

128. G. Kesidis and T. Konstantopoulos. Extremal traffic and worst-case performance for a queue with shaped arrivals. In D.R. McDonald and S.R.E. Turner (Eds.), *Analysis of Communication Networks: Call Centres, Traffic and Performance*, Fields Institute Communications/AMS, 2000.

129. G. Kesidis and J. Walrand. Relative entropy between Markov transition rate matrices. *IEEE Trans. Inform. Theory*, Vol. 39, No. 3:1056, 1057, May 1993.

130. G. Kesidis and E. Wong. Optimal acceptance probability for simulated annealing. *Stochastics and Stochastics Reports*, Vol. 29:221–226, 1990.

131. J. Kleinberg. The small-world phenomenon: an algorithmic perspective. In *Proc. 32nd ACM Symp. on Theory of Computing*, Portland, OR, 2000.

132. M. Kodialam and T. Nandagopal. Characterizing achievable rates in multi-hop wireless networks: The joint routing and scheduling problem. In *Proc. ACM/IEEE MobiCom*, San Diego, Sept. 2003.

133. A.N. Kolmogorov and S.V. Fomin. *Introductory Real Analysis*. Dover, New York, 1970.

134. Y.A. Korilis, T.A. Varvarigou, and S.R. Ahuja. Incentive-compatible pricing strategies in noncooperative networks. In *Proc. IEEE INFOCOM*, 1997.

135. D. Kostic, A. Rodriguez, J. Albrecht, and A. Vadhat. Bullet: High bandwidth data dissemination using an overlay mesh. In *Proc. ACM SOSP*, 2003.

136. P.R. Kumar and P.P. Varaiya. *Stochastic Systems: Estimation, Identification, and Adaptive Control*. Prentice-Hall, Englewood Cliffs, NJ, 1986.

137. S. Kumar, P. Crowley, and J. Turner. Buffer aggregation: Addressing queuing subsystem bottlenecks at high speeds. In *Proc. IEEE Symposium on High Performance Interconnects*, Stanford, Aug. 2005.

138. H. Kunita. *Stochastic Flows and Stochastic Differential Equations*. Cambridge University Press, London, 1990.

139. J.F. Kurose and K.W. Ross. *Computer Networking*, 3rd Edition. Addison Wesley, Reading, MA, 2005.

140. J.-W. Lee, R. Mazumdar, and N. Shroff. Non-convexity issues for internet rate control with multi-class services: Stability and optimality. In *Proc. IEEE INFOCOM*, Hong Kong, 2004.

141. H. Li and M. Singhal. Trust management in distributed systems. *IEEE Computer Mag.*, Vol. 40, No. 2:45–53, Feb. 2007.

142. Q. Li, J. Aslam, and D. Rus. Online power-aware routing in wireless ad-hoc networks. In *Proc. ACM MobiCom*, Rome, Italy, July 2001.

143. G. Liebeherr and M. Nahas. Application-layer multicast with Delaunay triangulations. *IEEE J. Selected Areas Commun. (JSAC)*, Vol. 20, No. 8, Oct. 2002.

144. X. Lin and N.B. Shroff and R. Srikant. A Tutorial on Cross-Layer Optimization in Wireless Networks. *IEEE J. Selected Areas Commun. (JSAC)*, Vol. 24, No. 8, June 2006, pp. 1452- 1463.

145. D.G. Luenberger. *Optimization by Vector Space Methods*. Interscience, New York, 1997.

146. R.T.B. Ma, S.C.M. Lee, J.C.S. Lui, and D.K.Y. Yau. A game theoretic approach to provide incentive and service differentiation in P2P networks. In *Proc. Joint International Conference on Measurement and Modeling of Computer Systems*, New York, NY, 2004, pp. 189–198.

147. R.T.B. Ma, S.C.M. Lee, J.C.S. Lui, and D.K.Y. Yau. An incentive mechanism for P2P networks. In *Proc. 24th International Conference on Distributed Computing Systems (ICDCS)*, Washington, DC, 2004, pp. 516–523.

148. M. Marina and S. Dos. On-demand multipath distance vector routing in ad hoc networks. *IEEE ICNP*, Riverside, CA, Nov. 2001.

149. S. Marti and H. Garcia-Molina. Limited reputation sharing in P2P systems. In *Proc. 5th ACM Conference on Electronic Commerce*, May 2004.

150. W.A. Massey and W. Whitt. A stochastic model to capture space and time dynamics in wireless communications systems. *Proc. Eng. Inform. Sci.*, Vol. 8:541–569, 1994.

151. M. May, J. Bolot, C. Diot, and B. Lyles. Reasons not to deploy RED. In *Proc. 7th International Workshop on Quality of Service (IWQoS)*, London, Apr. 1999.

152. P. Maymounkov and D. Mazieres. Kademlia: A peer-to-peer information system based on the XOR metric. In *Proc. of IPTPS*, Cambridge, MA, Mar. 2002.

153. D. McDysan and D. Paw. *ATM and MPLS: Theory and Applications*. McGraw-Hill, New York, 2002.

154. N. McKeown. The iSLIP scheduling algorithm for input-queued switches. *IEEE/ACM Trans. Networking*, Vol. 7, No. 2:188–201, 1999.

155. S.L. Meyer. *Data Analysis for Scientists and Engineers*. Wiley, New York, 1975.

156. S. Micali and R.L. Rivest. Micropayments revisited. In *Proc. Cryptographer's Track at the RSA Conference on Topics in Cryptology*, Springer LNCS Vol. 2271. Springer, Berlin, 2002, pp. 149–163.

157. J. Mo and J. Walrand. Fair end-to-end window-based congestion control. *IEEE/ACM Trans. Networking*, Vol. 8, No. 5:556–567, 2000.

158. B. Mortazavi and G. Kesidis. Model and simulation study of a peer-to-peer game with a reputation-based incentive mechanism. In *Proc. IEEE Information Theory and Applications (ITA) Workshop*, UC San Diego, Feb. 2006.

159. B. Mortazavi and G. Kesidis. Incentive-compatible cumulative reputation systems for peer-to-peer file-swapping. In *Proc. CISS*, Princeton, NJ, Mar. 2006.

160. M. Naor and U. Wieder. Novel architectures for P2P applications: The continuous-discrete approach. In *Proc. SPAA*, San Diego, June 2003.

161. J.R. Norris. *Markov Chains*. Cambridge University Press, Cambridge, 1997.

162. A. Odlyzko. Internet pricing and history of communications. *Computer Networks*, Aug. 2001, pp. 493–518.

163. A. Okabe, B. Boots, and K. Sugihara. *Spatial tessellations: concepts and applications of Voronoi diagrams*, 2nd ed. Wiley, New York, 2000.

164. A.V. Oppenheim and A.S. Willsky. *Signals and Systems*. Prentice-Hall, Englewood Cliffs, NJ, 1983.

165. T.J. Ott, T.V. Lakshman, and L.H. Wong. SRED: Stabilized RED. In *Proc. IEEE INFOCOM*, 1999.

166. A.K. Parekh and R.G. Gallager. A generalized processor sharing approach to flow control in integrated services networks: The single node case. *IEEE/ACM Trans. Networking*, Vol. 1, No. 3:344–357, June 1993.

167. V.D. Park and S. Corson. A highly adaptive distributed routing algorithm for mobile wireless networks. In *Proc. IEEE INFOCOM*, 1997.

168. K. Pawlikowski, H.-D.J. Jeong, and J.-S. R. Lee. On credibility of simulation studies of telecommunication networks. *IEEE Commun. Mag.*, Jan. 2001.

169. Peer-to-Peer: Monarchy in a decentralized system, http://www.caip.rutgers.edu/~vincentm/p2p.html.

170. G. Peng. CDN: Content distribution network. Technical Report TR-125. Experimental Computer Systems Lab, SUNY Stony Brook, 2006.

171. C. Perkins and P. Bhagwat. Highly dynamic destination-sequenced distance vector routing (dsdv) for mobile computers. In *Proc. ACM SIGCOMM*, Oct. 1994.

172. L.L. Peterson and B.S. Davie. *Computer Networks: A Systems Approach*, 3rd ed. Morgan Kaufman, San Francisco, 2003.

173. E. Polak. *Computational Methods in Optimization*. Academic, New York, 1971.

174. H.V. Poor. *An Introduction to Signal Detection and Estimation*. Springer-Verlag, Berlin, 1994.

175. L. Rabiner and B.-H. Juang. *Fundamentals of Speech Recognition*. Prentice-Hall, Englewood Cliffs, NJ, 1993.

176. S. Ramabhadran and J. Pasquale. Stratified round robin: A low complexity packet scheduler with bandwidth fairness and bounded delay. In *Proc. ACM SIGCOMM*, 2003, pp. 239–249.

177. R. Rao. Purposeful mobility and capacity issues in sensor networks. Ph.D. Thesis, Elec. Engr. Dept, Penn State, May 2007.

178. S. Ratnasamy, P. Francis, M. Handley, R. Karp, and S. Shenker. A scalable content-addressable network. In *Proc. ACM SIGCOMM*, San Diego, Aug. 2001.

179. M.K. Reiter and S.G. Stubblebine. Toward acceptable metrics of authentication. In *Proc. of IEEE Symposium on Security and Privacy*, 1997, pp. 10–20.

180. Y. Rekhter and T. Li. A border gateway protocol 4 (BGP-4). *IETF RFC 1771*, Available: http://www.ietf.org, Mar. 1995.

181. P. Resnick, K. Kuwabara, R. Zeckhauser, and E. Friedman. Reputation systems. *Communications of the ACM*, Vol. 43, No. 12:45–48, 2000.

182. P. Resnick and R. Zeckhauser. Trust among strangers in Internet transactions: Empirical analysis of eBay's reputation system. In *Proc. NBER Workshop on Empirical Studies of Electronic Commerce*, 2000.

183. S.I. Resnick. *Adventures in Stochastic Processes*. Birkhauser, Boston, 1992.

184. J. Rexford, F. Bonomi, A. Greenberg, and A. Wong. Scalable architectures for integrated traffic shaping and link scheduling in high-speed ATM switches. *IEEE J. Selected Areas Commun. (JSAC)*, Vol. 15, No. 5:938–950, June 1997.

185. R.L. Rivest. Peppercoin micropayments. In *Proc. Financial Cryptography*, Springer LNCS Vol. 3110. Springer, Berlin, 2004, pp. 2–8.

186. J. Roberts, U. Mocci, and J. Vitramo (Eds.), *Broadband Network Teletraffic: Final Report of Action COST 242*. Springer, Berlin, 1996.

187. E. Rosen and Y Rekhter. BGP/MPLS IP Virtual Private Networks (VPNs). *IETF RFC 4364*, Available: http://www.ietf.org, Feb. 2006.

188. E.C. Rosen, A. Viswanathan, and R. Callon. Multiprotocol label switching architecture. *IETF RFC 3031*, Available: http://www.ietf.org, Jan. 2001.

189. K.W. Ross. *Multiservice Loss Models for Broadband Telecommunication Networks*. Springer-Verlag, London, 1995.

190. K.W. Ross. Hash routing for collections of shared web caches. *IEEE Network Mag.*, Nov.-Dec. 1997, pp. 37–44.

191. K.W. Ross and D. Rubenstein. Tutorial on P2P systems. Available: http://cis.poly.edu/~ross/papers/P2PtutorialInfocom.pdf, 2004.

192. S. M. Ross. *Introduction to Probability and Statistics for Engineers and Scientists.* Wiley, New York, 1987.

193. S. M. Ross. *Introduction to Probability Models.* Academic, San Diego, CA, 1989.

194. S. M. Ross. *A Course in Simulation.* Macmillan, New York, 1990.

195. G. Rote. Path problems in graphs. *Computing Suppl.*, Vol. 7:155–189, 1990.

196. A. Rowstron and P. Druschel. Pastry: Scalable, distributed object location and routing for large-scale peer-to-peer systems. In *Proc. IFIP/ACM International Conference on Distributed Systems Platforms (Middleware)*, Nov. 2001, pp. 329–350.

197. C.U. Saraydar, N.B. Mandayam, and D.J. Goodman. Power control in a multicell CDMA data system using pricing. In *Proc. IEEE VTC*, 2000, pp. 484–491.

198. S. Saroiu, P.K. Gummadi, and S.D. Gribble. A measurement study of peer-to-peer file sharing systems. Technical Report UW-CSE-01-06-02. University of Washington, CSE Dept, July 2001.

199. S.M. Senouci and G. Pujolle. Energy efficient routing in wireless ad hoc networks. In *Proc. IEEE ICC*, 2004.

200. D. Shah, S. Iyer, B. Prabhakar, and N. McKeown. Maintaining statistics counters in router line cards. *IEEE Micro.*, Vol. 22, No. 1:76–81, 2002.

201. S. Shenker. Fundamental design issues for the future Internet. *IEEE J. Selected Areas Commun. (JSAC)*, Vol. 13:1176–1188, 1995.

202. J. Shu and P. Varaiya. Pricing network services. In *Proc. IEEE INFOCOM*, San Francisco, Apr. 2003.

203. A. Singh, M. Castro, A. Rowstron, and P. Druschel. Defending against eclipse attacks on overlay networks. In *Proc. 11th ACM SIGOPS European Workshop*, Leuven, Belgium, Sept. 2004.

204. A. Singh, T.-W. Ngan, P. Druschel, and D.S. Wallach. Eclipse attacks on overlay networks: Threats and defenses. In *IEEE INFOCOM 2006*, Barcelona, Spain, Apr. 2006.

205. D.R. Smart. *Fixed Point Theorems.* Cambridge University Press, London, 1974.

206. J.L. Sobrinho. Algebra and algorithms for QoS path computation and hop-by-hop routing in the Internet. *IEEE/ACM Trans. Networking*, Vol. 10, No. 4, Aug. 2002.

207. H. Stark and J.W. Woods. *Probability, Random Processes and Estimation Theory for Engineers.* Prentice-Hall, Upper Saddle River, NJ, 1986.

208. J. Stewart. DNS cache poisoning–The next generation. Available: http://www.securityfocus.com/guest/17905, 2003.

209. D. Stiliadis and A. Varma. A general methodology for designing efficient traffic scheduling and shaping algorithms. In *Proc. IEEE INFOCOM*, Kobe, Apr. 1997, pp. 326–335.

210. I. Stoica, D. Adkins, S. Zhuang, S. Shenker, and S. Surana. Internet indirection infrastructure. In *Proc. ACM SIGCOMM*, Aug. 2002.

211. I. Stoica, R. Morris, D. Liben-Nowell, D.R. Karger, M.F. Kaashoek, F. Dabek, and H. Balakrishnan. Chord: A scalable peer-to-peer lookup protocol for internet applications. *IEEE/ACM Trans. Networking*, Vol. 11, No. 1:17–32, 2003.

212. A.-J. Su, D. Choffnes, A. Kuzmanovic, and F. Bustamante. Drafting behind Akamai (Travelocity-based detouring). In *Proc. ACM SIGCOMM*, Pisa, Sept. 2006.

213. D. Subramanian, P. Druschel, and J. Chen. Ants and reinforcement learning: A case study in routing in dynamic networks. In *Proc. IJCAI*, Aug. 1997.

214. S. Suri, G. Varghese, and G. Chandranmenon. Leap Forward VirtualClock: A new fair queueing scheme with guaranteed delays and throughput fairness. In *Proc. IEEE INFOCOM*, Kobe, Apr. 1997, pp. 558–566.

215. S. Suri, G. Varghese, and G. Chandranmenon. Efficient fair queueing using deficit round-robin. *IEEE/ACM Trans. Networking*, Vol. 4, No. 3:375–385, June 1996.

216. B. Turner. Simple lightweight DHT. Available: http://www.xnet.com/pipermail/fork/Week-of-Mon-20050110/033193.html, Jan. 2005.

217. V. Vishnumurthy, S. Chandrakumar, and E. Sirer. KARMA: A secure economic framework for peer-to-peer resource sharing. In *Proc. Workshop on the Economics of Peer-to-Peer Systems*, 2003.

218. M. Vutukuru, M. Walfish, H. Balakrishnan, and S. Shenker. A distributed system for resolving flat names. In *Proc. ACM SIGCOMM*, poster abstracts, Pisa, Sept. 2006.

219. J. Walrand. *An Introduction to Queuing Networks*. Prentice-Hall, Englewood Cliffs, NJ, 1988.

220. J. Walrand and P. Varaiya. *High-Performance Communication Networks*. Morgan Kaufman, San Francisco, CA, 1996.

221. K. Walsh and E.G. Sirer. Fighting peer-to-peer SPAM and decoys with object reputation. In *Proc. of the Third Workshop on the Economics of Peer-to-Peer Systems (p2pecon)*, Philadelphia, PA, 2005.

222. D.J. Watts. *Small Worlds*. Princeton University Press, Princeton, NJ, 1999.

223. N. Weaver. Principles of reactive worm defense. Available: http://www.icsi.berkeley.edu/~nweaver/general_principles.ppt, 2005.

224. P. Whittle. *Systems in Stochastic Equilibrium*. Wiley, Chichester, 1986.

225. D. Williams. *Probability with Martingales*. Cambridge University Press, London, 1991.

226. R.W. Wolff. *Stochastic Modeling and the Theory of Queues*. Prentice-Hall, Englewood Cliffs, NJ, 1989.

227. G.G. Xie and S.S. Lam. Delay guarantee of Virtual Clock server. *IEEE/ACM Trans. Networking*, Vol. 3, No. 6:683–689, Dec. 1995.

228. R. Yates. A framework for uplink power control in cellular radio systems. *IEEE J. Selected Areas Commun. (JSAC)*, Sept. 1995.

229. Z. Ye, S. Krishnamurthy, and S. Thripathi. A frame-work for reliable routing in mobile ad hoc networks. In *Proc. IEEE INFOCOM*, San Francisco, Apr. 2003.

230. K.L. Yeung, K.F. Au-Yeung, and L. Ping. Efficient time-slot assignments for TDM multicast switching systems. In *Proc. IEEE ICC*, 1997.

231. S. Yi, X. Deng, G. Kesidis, and C.R. Das. HaTCh: a two-level caching scheme for estimating the number of active flows. In *Proc. IEEE CDC*, Maui, Dec. 2003.

232. Q. Yin, Y. Jiang, S. Jiang, and P.Y. Kong. Analysis of generalized stochastically bounded bursty traffic for communication networks. In *Proc. IEEE LCN*, 2002.

233. J.-H. Yoo, R.J. La, and A. Makowski. Convergence results for ant routing. In *Proc. CISS*, Mar. 2004.

234. B. Yu, M.P. Singh, and K. Sycara. Developing trust in large-scale peer-to-peer systems. In *Proc. First IEEE Symposium on Multi-Agent Security and Survivability*, 2004.

235. H. Yu, J. Rexford, and E.W. Felten. A distributed reputation approach to cooperative Internet routing protection. In *Proc. First IEEE ICNP Workshop on Secure Network Protocols (NPSec)*, Boston, Nov. 2005.

236. H. Zhang. Service disciplines for guaranteed performance service in packet-switching networks. *Proceedings of the IEEE*, Vol. 83, No. 10, Oct. 1995.

237. H. Zhang, A. Goel, and R. Govindan. Using the small-world model to improve Freenet performance. *Computer Networks J.*, Vol. 46, No. 4:555–574, Nov. 2004.

238. L. Zhang. VirtualClock: A new traffic control algorithm for packet-switched networks. *ACM Trans. Comp. Sys.*, Vol. 9, No. 2:101–124, May 1991.

239. L. Zhang, S. Deering, D. Estrin, and S. Shenker. RSVP: a new resource ReSerVation Protocol. *IEEE Network Mag.*, Vol. 7, No. 5:8–18, Sept. 1993.

240. B.Y. Zhao, L. Huang, J. Stribling, S.C. Rhea, A.D. Joseph, and J.D. Kubiatowicz. Tapestry: A resilient global-scale overlay for service deployment. *IEEE J. Selected Areas Commun. (JSAC)*, Vol. 22, No. 1:41–53, Jan. 2004.